Electronic Evidence

Strategies for Managing Records in Contemporary Organizations

DAVID BEARMAN

Archives & Museum Informatics
Pittsburgh

Published by Archives & Museum Informatics
5501 Walnut Street, Suite 203
Pittsburgh, PA 15232-2311
(412) 683-9775

Library of Congress Cataloging-in-Publication Data

Bearman, David.
    Electronic evidence : Strategies for managing records in
contemporary organizations / David Bearman ; edited and designed by
Victoria Irons Walch.
        p.   cm.
    A collection of articles previously published between 1989 and 1993
in a variety of periodicals and reports.
    Includes bibliographical references and index.
    ISBN 1-885626-08-8
    1. Business records--Data processing--Management. 2. Business
enterprises--Archives--Management. 3. Administrative agencies-
-Records and correspondence--Data processing--Management.
4. Administrative agencies--Archives--Management. 5. Database
management. I. Walch, Victoria Irons, 1950-   . II. Title.
HF5736.B34 1994
651.5'028'5--dc20   94-30864
                                           CIP

Edited and designed by Victoria Irons Walch
Printed in the United States of America

This book is printed on paper that meets the criteria for permanence set
forth in American National Standard ANSI/NISO Z39.48:1993,
Permanence of Paper.

Contents

Preface / vii

Introduction

Constructing a Methodology for Evidence / 1

Section I: The Problem

1   Archival Data Management to Achieve Organizational Accountability for Electronic Records / 11

2   Recordkeeping Systems / 34

Section II: Policy Guidelines

3   Electronic Records Guidelines: A Manual for Policy Development and Implementation / 72

4   The Implications of *Armstrong* v. *Executive Office of the President* for the Archival Management of Electronic Records / 118

Section III: Design and Implementation

5   Archival Principles and the Electronic Office / 146

6   Managing Electronic Mail / 176

Section IV: Standards

7   Information Technology Standards and Archives / 210

8   Documenting Documentation / 222

Section V: Program Management/Frameworks/ Structures

9   Diplomatics, Weberian Brueaucracy, and the Management of Electronic Records in Europe and America / 254

10 New Models for Management of Electronic Records by Archives / 278

Appendix

Functional Requirements for Recordkeeping / 294

Index / 305

Preface

Over the past four years, almost half my professional activity has been directed towards solving problems associated with the management of electronic records in governmental organizations. I have been helped, influenced, and prodded by many colleagues and have benefitted in untold ways from that interaction. The number of my intellectual debts is too great for me to try to explain the circumstances of each, so I hope I will be forgiven for simply mentioning the large number of individuals who have played a role in shaping these ideas. In each case, these individuals contributed something without which the concepts developed here would have been much poorer.

I heartily thank Glenda Acland, Scott Armstrong, Rich Barry, Tora Bikson, Terry Cook, Richard Cox, Charles Dollar, Luciana Duranti, Liisa Fagerlund, Flavia Fonseca, Maria Magdalena Garcia, Sue Gavrel, Christoph Graf, Margaret Hedstrom, Mark Hopkins, Alan Kowolowitz, Clifford Lynch, Richard Lytle, John McDonald, Sue McKemmish, Maria Pia Rinaldi Mariani, Angelika Menne-Haritz, Harold Naugler, Dagmar Parer, Peter Sigmund, Steve Stuckey, Frank Upward, Lisa Weber, Ted Weir, and Ron Weissman for their ideas and the opportunities they provided me to explore mine.

In addition to an intellectual debt, I owe a logistical debt to these individuals because this volume would not have been compiled but for the fact that colleagues, on three continents, provided opportunities for me to publish in a variety of journals, thereby spreading these articles across a range of literature few archivists regularly read. Bringing these articles together for the convenience of the reader presumed the in-convenience of their original placement, so the existence of this collection is very much a result of their generosity in inviting me to work with them, lecture in their countries, and conduct workshops under their auspices.

Finally, I owe a tremendous debt to Victoria Irons Walch who has brought the volume in this form into the world. She edited out my most egregious bad grammar and indexed the work to make it more accessible. In the process whe identified numerous opportunities to clarify my meaning. Without her help, this would be very much less worthwhile. The errors remaining, of course, are my own and are guaranteed to be numerous, not the least because the leitmotif is change; this quest for methods to manage electronic records is not going to end in our lifetimes, which is why I think it fun to be in at the beginning trying out ideas, even if we may later think them foolhardy.

Pittsburgh, January 1994

Introduction

Constructing a Methodology for Evidence

The articles in this volume were written between 1989 and 1993 and published in a wide variety of periodicals and reports.[1] They reflect the development of what I believe is a coherent approach to management of electronic records. However because this volume consists of chapters written while my thinking was evolving, ideas introduced in one chapter may be explored in more depth in another and early articles may have slightly different formulations of concepts that are developed more completely later.

I could have chosen to organize this collection of essays chronologically in order to better convey the evolution of these ideas, but I wanted to emphasize the approach to electronic records rather than my personal intellectual history. I have therefore taken the dual risk of writing a Whig autobiography of ideas and trying to convey a consistent methodology through a series of articles written as that methodology was forming. In arranging the chapters thematically I am hoping that the minor differences between the resulting papers will not interfere with the overall structure of the argument. To this short introduction, I leave the task of connecting the threads of ideas within the book, and between these articles and others which I wrote on this topic during the same years but have not reprinted here.[2]

The title of this collection itself reflects a significant shift in focus from extending traditional practices of archives and records management (of interest, quite reasonably, to archivists or records managers) towards definition of what should be a generic management concern (which is of critical importance to all managers anywhere in the organization). Two years ago, I would have titled it "Electronic Records Management" to remind archivists that records management was at the heart of any approach to electronic records. One year ago, I would have entitled it "Archiving Electronic Records" to use the term archiving in a way that archivists never would but which others do almost exclusively.

In the past year I have become increasingly convinced that the issue is how to ensure that information in computer systems is a record, which is to say that it is evidence of a transaction. I entitled this collection *Electronic Evidence* to emphasize the point that most collections of electronic data, electronic documents, or information are not records because they cannot qualify as evidence. I hope in this way to emphasize that the challenge to archivists, records managers, auditors, legal counsel, freedom of information and privacy personnel, and every program manager in an organization is to ensure that electronic data is captured in a way that makes it an electronic record and to address how this can be done. Over the course of several years, the challenge has become to focus on "recordness," something we were hardly even conscious of during the reign of paper, and to build a methodology for ensuring that this ephemeral attribute of collectivities of data is captured and kept.

THE PROBLEM

The revolution in computing and communications is transforming the way in which we conduct business in our society. This presents archivists with the challenge to explicitly define what requirements must be met by recordkeeping systems so that they can intervene in organizational policy, systems design, and program implementation to ensure the creation of records, preserve their integrity, and provide for access. The most complete articulation of the theoretical framework on which this volume elaborates is contained in Chapter One which explores the accountability crisis confronting many organizations that have adopted electronic information systems in the conduct of day-to-day work. This article was written in the summer of 1992 at the same time as the grant proposal for the University of Pittsburgh study of electronic records management which it describes in detail. The chapter is structured in the same way as this book and that research project: we begin by defining the functional requirements for recordkeeping, examine four tactics for satisfying those requirements, consider variables in the business functions, organizational structures, and technology environment, and then apply risk management principles to determining how much to satisfy the requirements.

The axiom that not all information systems are recordkeeping systems, which is developed in Chapter Two, actually emerged late in the formulation of these ideas, but has become the key to understanding concerns expressed earlier. Creation of records -- taken for granted by archivists in the age of paper documentation because communication in writing required the information content to be fixed on a medium in the form in which it was received -- can no longer be taken for granted. Because conscious intervention is required to shape information systems so that they will create records (rather than just data), organizations are faced with a crisis of accountability brought on by the use of electronic information systems. This article, written in the spring of 1993, references an early draft of the functional requirements for recordkeeping systems developed by the University of Pittsburgh research project on electronic records management, the latest version of which appears as the appendix in this volume.

THE POLICY APPROACH

My ideas about electronic records management were first elaborated in a consulting project for the United Nations Administrative Coordinating Committee on Information Systems Technical Panel on Electronic Records Management (ACCIS TP/REM) in 1988-89. The panel asked me to write the position paper on policy issues in the management of electronic records, a portion of which constitutes Chapter 3. When I had finished writing, I surprised myself by the degree to which policy could address electronic records management requirements that I would at first have considered susceptible only to technical solutions, and then I was intrigued to discover that there were also technical solutions even to the most patently policy- and procedure-related problems. Ultimately this led to the formulation of the hypothesis that there was only one set of functional requirements and that these could be satisfied through one of four tactics: policy, design, implementation, or standards. This idea that different approaches could be employed to satisfy the same underlying requirements has since been adopted as my basic strategy for management of electronic records and is illustrated in the organization of this book.

Other important ideas basic to the framework in this book were also developed in the course of the ACCIS TP/REM study. It was there that I began to focus on business transactions rather than records as the basic unit of archival documentation and on business applications rather than software applications as the source of the evidentiary significance of records on which appraisal and management are properly based. The TP/REM study clarified the practical threats to proper management of electronic records caused by the costs and irreversibility of systems migration. This led to the formulation of the program for the non-custodial archives of the future, published elsewhere under the title "Indefensible Bastions."[3] The ACCIS report also brought to light the role that incorrect mental models of the operations of information systems play in preventing policy from being carried out, and the importance of training if staff are to be held responsible for electronic records creation and retention. Finally, it noted the importance of new genres of communications which will require evolution of broader cultural norms, an idea I have explored in discussions of virtual documents published elsewhere.[4]

That the absence of appropriate policy can effectively undermine accountability for electronic records is illustrated in the case of the electronic mail systems of the White House during the Reagan and Bush Administrations described in Chapter Four. A long series of Federal court rulings, most of which went against the government, underlined the importance of policy in ensuring the creation of evidence. When this paper was written in the summer of 1993 after the final ruling of the U.S. District Court of Appeals, the functional requirements for recordkeeping systems had been articulated by experts convened in the University of Pittsburgh study and by colleagues involved in my Monash University workshops and the concept that archives were in the "evidence business" was part of the framework for managing electronic evidence. It was gratifying to see that the court ruled that to secure evidence it was essential to retain what I had been calling "context and structure data," in addition to content data. Its decision that paper printouts lacking transmission information were not adequate records affirmed the theoretical construct that evidence consists of content, structure, and context data. Unfortunately, the court did not articulate a principle but only provided an example. Since then some commentators and government officials charged with implementing the court ruling have assumed it only applies to information about senders and recipients of electronic mail messages and other "transmission data" rather than understanding it as an illustration of a broader rule about contextual and structural data giving information that would not otherwise be a record its meaning and its adequacy as documentation or evidence.

DESIGN AND IMPLEMENTATION APPROACHES

My fullest elaboration of the concept that records are evidence, and that evidence consists of content, structure, and context data, appears in a talk given at the National Archives of Canada in February 1991, reprinted here as Chapter Five. It reviews the threats to "evidential historicity" posed by a number of common software applications. The role of standards for interoperability and the fundamental problem of preserving software-dependent data are discussed. Some questions which still remain unresolved are raised about the degree of functional similarity that is required for electronic data to function as evidence.

In the spring of 1993, the theoretical components of this approach to electronic records were sufficiently complete that I felt they would allow its application to any business application or technical environment. In Chapter Six the framework is applied to electronic mail, which serves as a vehicle for explaining how the conceptual framework of the Open Systems Environment (OSE) model serves as a scaffolding on which to erect means to intervene in system design and implementation. Concrete suggestions for methods of intervention are discussed and the concept that the "right" approach depends on local technology configuration and competence and local organizational culture, which are discussed more fully in Chapter Ten, are introduced.

THE STANDARDS APPROACH

One constant theme in discussions of electronic records management has been the attraction of technical information systems standards as a means of solving all our problems. While it is tautological true that interoperability would resolve the problems of maintaining records across systems over time, interoperability is still a long way from being achieved. Archivists need an assessment of both the potential of various standards for satisfying recordkeeping functional requirements and the chances that they will be adopted. Chapter Seven, written in response to a request for such an assessment, was delivered at an international conference on archives in Maastricht, Germany, in October 1991. The assessment effort must, however, be ongoing. In addition, archivists need to take the functional requirements for recordkeeping which they have established and identify define how new standards suites could serve to satisfy them.

In addition to information technology standards, archivists need to adopt standards for the documentation of electronic records. Building on observations I have made elsewhere that archival information systems are information systems about information systems, or what information technologists call "metadata systems,"[5] we are led next to ask why and how to capture such metadata. The proposal made in Chapter Eight reflects the conjunction of approaches to electronic records with efforts to define the premises of archival description that began with work on the National Information Systems Task Force and was incorporated into the description framework proposed by the Working Group on Standards for Archival Description.[6] The central concept here is that the information which we must have to describe archival records can be determined in advance because it is based on functional requirements for recordkeeping, the genre of the record, and the evidentiary requirements of the business application. In electronic environments, a specification of this metadata will enable us to design and implement systems to automatically capture metadata documentation when the records are created, and ensure that necessary metadata are incorporated into records when they are migrated, transferred, or accessed.

IMPLICATIONS FOR ELECTRONIC RECORDS PROGRAM STRUCTURE

While Chapters Three through Eight examine the means we have to control electronic records using policy, design, implementation, and standards, they do not help us to choose the optimal approach for satisfying a specific functional requirement in a given institutional context. Chapter Nine reflects on the way in which national and organizational culture might impact on the selection of a tactic. While it does not explicitly develop the implication that each functional requirement could be satisfied in a different way, this is implicit in all discussions of program management frameworks and strategies and was instrumental in the research design of the University of Pittsburgh electronic records study where organizational culture was one of the variables being studied in the choice of tactics to satisfy each separate recordkeeping requirement.

Chapter Ten examines the ways in which archival organizations have adjusted or might transform their approaches to all records in order to deal more effectively with electronic records. Options -- such as proactive systems specification and implementation, non-custodial archives, metadata management for documentation and control, and records scheduling based on organizational function analysis -- are introduced and examples are given of organizations trying these innovative approaches. Dozens of more radical ideas for restructuring or reinventing archives, going far beyond what has been tried, are proposed in an article by Margaret Hedstrom and me that was written in the summer of 1993.[7]

NOTES

[1] Each chapter contains a footnote documenting its publication and prepublication history.

[2] Publications by David Bearman, relating to electronic records in archives during the period 1989-93 which are neither reprinted here nor specifically cited in footnotes 3-7 below, include:

Archival Methods, Archives and Museum Informatics Technical Report #9 (Pittsburgh: Archives and Museum Informatics, 1989).

"The Case for Software as Documentation," IASSIST Quarterly (Spring 1989): 18-23.

"The Impact of Information Format on Management and Policy," in James A. Nelson ed., Gateways to Comprehensive State Information Policy (Lexington, Kentucky: Chief Officers of State Library Agencies, 1990): 22-26.

"Electronic Records Issues," Archives and Museum Informatics 4:1 (1990): 7-9.

"Electronic Office Records," Archives and Museum Informatics 4:1 (1990): 12-15.

"Technology's Impact on the Professions Who Manage it," Current Issues in Government Information Policy Conference Proceedings (Frankfort: Kentucky Information Systems Commission, 1991): 11-23.

"Information Technology Standards and Archives," NAGARA Clearinghouse 7:3 (Summer 1991): 10.

"Developing Guidelines for Electronic Records: Report of a Project to Test the ACCIS TP/REM Electronic Records Guidelines: A Manual for Policy Development and Implementation (ACCIS 89/018(b) 1989-07-17)" in Advisory Committee for the Co-ordination of Information Systems, Management of Electronic Records: Curriculum Materials (New York: United Nations, 1992): 137-147.

"The ICA Principles Regarding Archival Description," Archives and Museum Informatics 6:1 (1992): 20-21.

[3] David Bearman, "An Indefensible Bastion: Archives as a Repository in the Electronic Age," in Archival Management of Electronic Records, David Bearman ed., Archives and Museum Informatics Technical Report #13 (Pittsburgh: Archives & Museum Informatics, 1991).

[4] David Bearman, "Multi-sensory Data and its Management," in *Management of Recorded Information: Converging Technologies*, ed. Cynthia Durance (New York: K.G. Saur, 1990): 111-120.

[5] David Bearman, "The Impact of Information Format on Management and Policy," in *Gateways to Comprehensive State Information Policy*, ed. James A. Nelson (Lexington, Kentucky: Chief Officers of State Library Agencies, 1990): 22-26. David Bearman, "Contexts of Creation and Dissemination as Approaches to Documents that Move and Speak," in *Documents that Move and Speak: Audiovisual Archives in the New Information Age*, Proceedings of a Symposium, National Archives of Canada, 30 April-3 May 1990 (New York: K.G. Saur, 1992): 140-149.

[6] David Bearman, *Towards National Information Systems for Archives and Manuscript Repositories: The NISTF Papers* (Chicago: Society of American Archivists, 1987); David Bearman, "Archival Description Standards: A Framework for Action," *American Archivist* 52 (Fall 1989): 514-519.

[7] David Bearman and Margaret Hedstrom, "Reinventing Archives for Electronic Records: Alternative Service Delivery Options" in *Program Strategies for Electronic Records*, ed. Margaret Hedstrom, Archives and Museum Informatics Technical Report #18 (Pittsburgh: Archives and Museum Informatics, 1993): 82-98.

SECTION I

The Problem

❖

CHAPTER ONE

Archival Data Management to Achieve Organizational Accountability for Electronic Records

❖

CHAPTER TWO

Recordkeeping Systems

CHAPTER ONE

Archival Data Management to Achieve Organizational Accountability for Electronic Records*

Organizations which adopt digital means of communication need to be much more alert to issues of data management throughout the life cycle of records in order to ensure accountability. Requirements for records management and archives need to be made much more explicit than they have traditionally been. Tactics which are available need to be selected based on careful analysis of the organizational culture and technical capabilities. Conscious risk management decisions will need to be made at the highest levels of the organization around numerous decisions affecting records creation, retention, and access. Overall, the electronic office environment will force organizations to view archives in a new light and to change organizational behavior with respect to recordkeeping or lose the ability to reconstruct or defend their past behavior. Archivists will find the demands of data management in electronic records environments force them to reaffirm their most fundamental theoretical tenets, rather than to reject them as they have often feared.

* Originally published in *Archives and Manuscripts* 21:1 (1993): 14-28.

INTRODUCTION

Archives and records management share a simple goal: providing for organizational accountability. However achieving this goal in the era of electronic information systems is far from simple. Accountability depends on being able to demonstrate managed access to information which is important for reasons of ongoing need or future evidence, from the time of its creation. In the public sector accountability must protect privacy at the same time that it ensures the public right to information about the operation of their government. To provide such continued and accountable access, organizations are struggling to redefine archival programs in order to document and preserve the information content, structure, and context of the electronic evidence of activity they undertake as part of their missions.[1]

Articulating and communicating these requirements to program administrators and to data processing or systems managers is a critical archival role. It will only bear fruit when the staff throughout the organization understand the nature of electronic records and the importance of records of business applications in which they participate to accountability. This chapter begins by examining ways of explaining why electronic records present a challenge to organizational accountability and how to articulate archival functional requirements.

Records managers and archivists focus their strategies on application systems, both because business applications generate records and because the specific requirements for retention of evidence arise from the nature of the transactions which characterize different business functions. Once focused on business applications, records managers and archivists can assess the possible tactical approaches to ensuring control over evidence until it is acceptable to discard it. Specific approaches are examined in the third section of this chapter.

Risk management methodologies can help to support their decisions. Risk management approaches place archives and records decisions in a more appropriate context than do cost/benefit approaches. While long-term benefits are largely inestimable, risk assessment is appreciated by experienced managers who use it to estimate the probability of a variety of outcomes.

Because the risks that must be managed by archivists and records managers arise throughout the life cycle of electronic information systems, their control requires continuity of rigorous data management practices. These data management practices are equally applicable to vital records management, privacy, freedom of information, and security. Archivists will find an increasing need to exploit these interests in common with other organizational functions in order to achieve their missions. In addition, they will need to understand the areas of continuity and discontinuity in their own practices that have been introduced by new electronic communications environments.

DEFINING THE PROBLEM

Methods of communication within organizations are being rapidly, and radically, transformed as a consequence of the introduction of electronic, computer-based, communications technologies. It is now becoming evident that these technologies are not just providing a new method for transmission of information but changing the social character of the communication. Instead of compiling an analytic report or sending a reasoned letter to the appropriate corporate authority (and expecting after an interval to receive an equally well researched and reasoned reply), electronic communications encourage an interactive, dialogue-like, interaction. In this dialogue, brief sorties to the database extract further clues and these are passed along in a relatively undigested form. As the character of the interchange is altered, so are the "forms" of the documentary record.[2]

In the world of paper records, we know that particular "forms" are associated with interchanges that have specific functions. For example, archivists and records managers can identify generic forms which will be involved in any governmental service delivery function. These functions will involve transactions in which clients are registered, in which needs are documented, and in which contact histories are kept. Archivists and records managers use their knowledge of the relationships between functions and forms of documentation to "schedule" records or determine how long the information in each needs to be kept. They are able to make these decisions on the basis of the form of the record and the function that created it without looking at concrete instances of these records. Any organization can identify "forms" specific to particular business transactions in which it engages. Data management guidelines will be specific to each form because records need to be kept a given length of time as a consequence of the character of the transaction about which they are evidence, not because of the specific information that may or may not be in them or because of who sent or received them.

The communication environment into which we are now moving is one in which electronic information systems will soon be ubiquitous and communications between persons in and outside of an organization will take place electronically. In addition to altering the "forms" of records, electronic systems erode the basic boundaries used by archives in making their judgments. The location of records storage will increasingly become arbitrary as will the "original order" of the file. With the loss of these landmarks, archivists will be forced to redefine their requirements for managing records. In such an environment archivists and records managers need to have criteria for determining what is a record and tactics for capturing them. Because records are evidence of business transactions, they will always be communicated across a physical or logical communications switch in an electronic system. After all, they can hardly serve as communications unless they are sent. If archivists can define which messages from what transactions are to be captured as records, they can save them.

How well archivists are able to ensure the preservation of evidence will depend on the tactics they employ to enforce good data management practices. However, the fact that different corporate cultures have very different climates for electronic records management and that the variables in corporate culture which influence the success of tactics employing policy, design, implementation procedures, and standards are not yet known. This is still a hit-or-miss proposition.[3]

ARCHIVAL FUNCTIONAL REQUIREMENTS

In 1989 the author was contracted by the United National Administrative Coordinating Committee on Information Systems (ACCIS) to recommend policy guidelines for the management of electronic records.[4] The first step in defining necessary policy guidelines, or necessary systems design, implementation, or standards requirements, is to establish functional requirements for electronic records management. If we could agree on such requirements, we could define policy approaches as well as other approaches to satisfying them.[5]

Nine functional requirements were identified which emerged from three broad areas of concern: (1) the need to identify electronic records within the organization; (2) the need to assign responsibility for administering them; and (3) the need to establish controls that will satisfy accountability and take into consideration the technical nature of electronic records.

The first three functional requirements concern the identification of electronic records, including the identification of electronic records, including defining their essential characteristics and establishing means for retaining them.

(1) Archives must be able to identify electronic records.

We must know what data comprises a record and what is not, and we must know why in terms that can be implemented in, through, by, or around information systems. In the policy guideline we asked "Does policy define the concept of record and non-record electronic information in a way that can be implemented by people and systems?" In discussion of the guidelines and in work which has followed, the author has depended on a definition of records as business transactions. That is records are transactions which have a significance in business terms (rather than in computing terms) because they constitute evidence of a business event, such as making a sale or qualifying a client to receive a benefit. A functional requirement of corporate accountability is: (a) that any such business transaction must create a record, and (b) that archivists must have a business rule for how long and for whom to retain the records and when and for whom to provide for their use.

(2) The organization must decide what to do with its records and why.

As I put it in the UN ACCIS report, archivists must be able to "articulate criteria for retention that will yield acceptable results for electronic records and be consistent with those for eye-readable records even if the results of applying such criteria are different." Archivists and records managers have historically employed implementation-based strategies to ensure application of retention criteria. In effect, we said that organizations will file like materials together because this corresponds to the way they do business, and that as a consequence we can schedule (determine the appropriate disposition for) records without looking at individual items but only at "series." In electronic systems, where physical storage is random and cannot guide us to like records, and logical organization permits many different, overlapping "views" to exist at the same time, the series corresponds to the records of one type of business transaction. For this reason it is clearer that what we are appraising is the need to retain records of a business transaction which is in turn based on a combination of legal requirements, known needs for the records, and calculated risks associated with their destruction. This appraisal can take place before any records are actually created and can be applied without actually looking at any records which result from the process, because the criterion is evidence, not information. Each type of business transaction has an accountability requirement of which the records retention decision is simply a reflection.

(3) Records retention determinations must be executed in a timely fashion.

Again this can be achieved through policy, design, implementation, or standards, and depends only on the unequivocal ability to define when records are no longer needed. While this is usually done with paper records in an extremely simple way, by defining a fixed date for destruction, relative destruction dates and retention for "continuing value" have been much harder to implement in traditional systems than they will be in electronic archives. Because records will be identified as "archival" in the electronic environment from before the moment of their creation the concept of "timely" scheduling becomes superfluous.

The first three requirements spoke to identification of electronic records in the organization. The next three are, broadly speaking, administrative.

(4) No organization can expend more effort or money on managing records and archives than can be justified by the risks it would run or the benefits it would forego if these efforts were not invested.

Criteria must be established to measure program success and to ensure that investments in electronic records management are effective. The fourth section of this chapter identifies numerous generic risks, but organizations need to define their own risks and levels of risk acceptance. Archivists have a role to play in identifying sources of risk and criteria for evaluation based on archival functional requirements.

(5) Appropriate administrative units must be assigned explicit responsibilities in the management of electronic records.

These responsibilities must be defined in a concrete and measurable way and include minimally:

- the articulation of each business application's requirement for evidence,

- the formulation of specifications or system evaluation methods,

- testing the ability of the system to satisfy the requirements,

- educating users in system functions and the risks they avoid,

- establishing data management guidelines and audit plans,

- defining metadata and documentation requirements for data, structure, and context,

- conducting ongoing technology risk assessments,

- developing migration plans that ensure migration of evidence rather than just information, and

- defining access methods for users.

(6) Organizations must decide where, and under whose control, electronic records should reside over time.

Because physical custody of electronic records does not ensure their evidential integrity unless they are defended by other security barriers, the day-to-day data management responsibilities must be assigned to the offices which create and manage the content of the records rather than to an office which has physical control. Intellectual control can be maintained for records which are not in physical (or even legal) custody, but in electronic systems it is difficult to ensure the accuracy of such controls unless they are actively linked to the records.[6] This is frequently where the policies break down.

Archivists are accustomed to demanding physical custody even though they are less well equipped to take on this responsibility than the office in which the records system is currently maintained. In addition, the costs to the organization are likely to be considerably higher because migration of the archival records will need to take place independently from migration of current records.[7]

The seventh through ninth functional requirements address integrity. In each of these areas the organization must act to safeguard the continuity of the evidence it has identified and captured. Failure to establish and maintain systems which appropriately address these requirements abandons the record.

7) The legality of the electronic record must be safeguarded, e.g., it must retain its unequivocal connection to the action of which it is evidence.

The direct analog of this issue, the admissibility of microform in place of original records in courts has long been a feature of archival practice and of the laws of evidence. The criterion which ultimately determines admissibility is continuity of management. If we can demonstrate that normal business practices were implemented and followed, the microform will typically be accepted as best available evidence where no original exists. With respect to electronic records, the concept of managing the data environment to protect the evidential quality of documentation arising from continued and protected custody, becomes critical. Data management practices and procedures, and evidence from audits and observation of their general implementation, will be the best way to preserve the legality of electronic records as evidence.

8) Related data management issues of security, privacy, confidentiality, and, in government settings, freedom of information must be addressed.

Each of these policy concerns requires the same level of data management control as archives and typically needs to be exercised at the same time and in the same ways as for archives. By identifying each of these policy issues up front in systems planning, design, and implementation, similar approaches can be taken to ensure their achievement.

9) The hardware, software, storage media, and documentation techniques must be evaluated to ensure that the records will indeed be preserved and remain usable over time.

Electronic records are always virtual documents, that is they exist under software control and are dependent on some hardware, even if they are (someday) truly "inter-operable" across hardware platforms. Because a generation of hardware and software (the length of time before obsolescence) is less than five years and because storage media generations are equally volatile, the electronic records must be regularly migrated to new hardware, software, and media. How frequently such migrations must occur will depend on how good the decisions about previous migrations have been. How valid the results of any given migration, or of the entire history of movements, will depend on documentation. Documentation also determines whether we can demonstrate the reliability of migrated records as evidence.

Failure to satisfy the functional requirements concerning access renders the entire endeavor purposeless. Here any successful approach must prevent the media and format of records from being barriers to accessing them, and it must establish standards for intellectual control and documentation that rise above the software-dependent norms. For any given records, we must also determine what, if any, functionality of the system must be preserved as evidence, and how to do that.[8] Even if functionality is unnecessary, the program must still dictate how contextual data is to be retained in a usable form so that it will be clear how the record could have been used and would have been seen by those who were conducting the business at the time of its creation.

The organization must also address the basic issues about access that are present for any records, such as who is to be given access and what uses they will be permitted to make of records which they have seen. Archivists must recognize that in electronic environments these issues play themselves out in systems design and implementation, bear on functionality, and must be managed continuously. While in paper environments access is external to the record system, electronic records are accessed through the system. While paper records can hardly be used at all except in their entirety, it is easy to provide partial access to electronic records, indeed preserving the users' view of a database for future research is a matter of masking some data and functionality while exposing other data and manipulation capabilities.

TACTICS

Four tactics (policy, design, implementation, and standards) have been identified as having potential for the accountable management of electronic records. It is essential for us to examine these four approaches to satisfying archival requirements in greater detail in order to develop tactics appropriate to each other.[9]

Policy, both at a general level and in its more detailed form as procedure, provides guidelines for how people should use electronic information systems. By identifying the various needs which the organization has for evidence from electronic information systems, policy can in principle provide instructions to people about how to ensure the creation and retention of such evidence. In most corporate cultures, however, policy will not alone provide adequate assurance that electronic records are created and managed appropriately.

As a result, archivists over the past decade have stressed systems *design* and up front involvement by archivists in the specification of systems as a more certain means of ensuring satisfaction of archival functional requirements.[10] However, design-based approaches have drawbacks: they can be quite expensive, they can defeat the operational functional requirements, and they can depend on archivists being able to specify precisely what systems need to do in order to meet archival needs. In addition, the best designed systems can be defeated by poor training of staff or incomplete or insensitive implementation.

Therefore, *implementation* has also been identified as an approach to satisfying archival requirements in electronic information systems. Providing guidelines for appropriate implementation of systems is not overly complex, but getting the users and the data processing support staff to understand the requirements, without which they will fail to realize the implementation objectives, can be very difficult. Like policy, implementation guidelines may not be applicable in some corporate cultures or with certain business applications. Especially in very routine applications, it may be necessary to depend on external information technology standards to achieve long-term compliance.

Information technology (IT) *standards* have long been attractive to archivists confronted with the problems of electronic records because they appear to be a magic bullet. It is as if we said "If we could make archival functional requirements part of an international IT standard then all systems would automatically meet them." Unfortunately, however, archival functional requirements have not been explicitly articulated and one of the few which has been, e.g., software interoperability, has also been the ultimate goal of IT standards developers for the past decade and is still very far out of reach.

RISK MANAGEMENT

Choosing tactics and defining practical standards for satisfying the functional requirements for electronic archives in the real world involves identifying and judging risks. Organizations have to understand the risks posed by the social requirement of accountability. For public organizations the ultimate risk is the loss of legitimacy and for private organizations it is incurring liabilities beyond the capacity of the organizational purse. Public and private organizations must, therefore, adopt methods for managing the risks created by documentation and its absence just as they adopt strategies for dealing with risks such as changing interest rates, product liability, or employee malfeasance. In fact, the tactics for managing these archival risks can best be tested using methods derived from the experience organizations have in self-insurance, managing financial risks, or managing risks associated with political decisions.

These risks include, but are hardly limited to:

• failure to locate evidence that an organization did something it was supposed to have done under contract or according to regulation,

• inability to find information that is critical for current decision making,

• loss of proof of ownership, obligations owed and due, or liabilities,

• failure to document what the organization knew at the time of an important transaction, and hence whether it behaved according to its own policies or in adherence to law,

• inability to locate in the proper context information which would be incriminating in one context but innocent in another,

• inability to demonstrate a pattern of documentation providing evidence that policies and procedures in effect in the organization were responsibly followed.

These risks are particularly great when employees in the organization do not recognize that records are, or should be, created, as a consequence of transactions. Electronic communications are not uniformly regarded as having the same significance as communications on paper, but are sometimes seen as more analogous to verbal commitments even though the organization will in fact be held liable for them. As a result employees will fail to create records at these junctures or will not require their systems to be designed so as to ensure such record creation. Indeed the concept that what the employee sees on his or her screen may not "actually exist" except on that screen and have no existence as a record is not something that we have successfully communicated even to management. Risk may arise because employees do not see themselves as accountable through records for their actions over time, but a more likely cause is that the concepts of records which employees are trained to use have no analogs in the electronic systems being implemented. If we fail to provide employees with concrete examples of the new risks they are incurring or of new definitions of records, they can hardly be considered individually culpable for overlooking necessary steps in documenting activity. The underlying problem is that employees are not given assistance to modify their own behavior. Organizational requirements for evidence are not explicit or are unknown to those who create and manage records. In the past organizational requirements would probably be satisfied if records were kept as a consequence of forgetfulness. Guidelines for disposition did not need to be well known.

Passive retention will not be adequate in the future however because unless serious attention is paid to data management throughout the life of the record, organizational records will not be created, be retained, or be acceptable as evidence. Now that electronic records show no traces of the changes they have been subjected to unless the system requires such traces to be left, methods for data management throughout the life of a record are critical and cannot be inadequately documented, inadequately followed, or inconsistently applied. Without systematic data management, it cannot be demonstrated that organizational records were not altered over time by purposive intervention or unconscious change introduced during migrations.

In addition to the risk of loss of evidential value, the organization runs a risk of losing even the use value of the information records contain. Often, organizational records in electronic form cannot be related to paper records from the same business transactions which are retained in mixed media archives. Frequently organizational records in electronic form cannot be read, retrieved, decoded, or accessed because they are too fragile, too poorly documented, the software to decode them is unavailable, or the context of their creation and use cannot be reconstructed to give them meaning. Over time the organization may find that its records cannot be invested with the functionality they had in the environment in which they were used and that this functionality is crucial to understanding them. Because records have not been segregated by retention, the organization may find that it can no longer afford to keep all it has nor develop techniques for identifying levels of risk that would permit it to select from among what it has kept. Finally, records which contain information that must be protected for reasons of confidentiality, security, proprietary and other restrictions may not be identified, and as a consequence the organization cannot allow access to any records because their restricted content cannot be separated without the cost of having human beings read through all records with these criteria in mind.

This array of risks can be minimized through planning grounded in risk management. First it requires that senior management define the risks associated with records and make everyone in the organization aware of these risks, of the steps being taken to contain them, and of the penalties which the organization will impose on those who fail to support accountability. Second, management must adopt risk management criteria for program effectiveness and enforce data policy requirements including security, privacy, vital records recovery, freedom of information, and archival preservation. And the organization must implement systems with conscious regard for limits of interoperability, especially with sensitivity to access requirements as the source of media standards.

Management and staff must understand the risks inherent in electronic records. First, electronic records are software- and hardware-dependent to some degree, regardless of standards, because records exist only under software control. What actually existed for the person using or receiving an electronic record is not easy to replicate or document because of the many layers of software through which it is mediated. While in most situations these niceties may not matter a great deal, they do mean that it is exceptionally difficult to retain the actual evidence of a transaction and that the organization runs a significant risk of retaining something which can be argued not to be evidence.

Even if evidence can be kept, the organization runs a substantial risk that continuing access costs are unpredictable even over relatively short periods, to say nothing of the potential cost of "permanent" records. With rapidly changing hardware and software environments, maintaining systems longer than their supported life is dangerous and migrating data and software functions is complex and equally costly. If programmers are going to reconstruct the data to map it to new systems during migration, they need to have the ability to alter the information structure, and often its contents, during the process.

Information content is independent of systems design, but evidence is design dependent. Therefore, even what is maintained may be modified (if inadvertently) by redesign of the system holding it. Such losses of evidential value as a consequence of redesign are extremely difficult to detect. In addition, the actual data content is subject to alteration during the migration because it is not possible to redesign and migrate data in an environment that is sufficiently controlled that we could say without hesitation that no alterations could have been made to the records or that the resulting system operates in all respects like the previous one. Finally, even if the migration maintains absolute fidelity to evidence and functionality, the new system might be perceived by users as different because "records" in electronic information systems are mediated by users' mental models and we understand little about how such models come to be. As such we are unlikely to create the "same" system from a user's point of view when we migrate electronic records.

Despite these risks, the best framework we can provide for access involves: (1) continuing migration as solution to permanence standards; (2) metadata as the mechanism of intellectual control; (3) migration of functionality, contextual documentation and configuration management as strategies for retention of information context; and (4) an Information Resource Directory System (IRDS) as the directory for remote access.

IMPLICATIONS FOR ARCHIVAL PRACTICE

Despite the seemingly alien aspects of electronic records management, there are large areas of continuity with traditional archival practices. To begin with, the fundamental principle of archival practice, its traditional emphasis on "respect des fonds," "provenance," and "original order" reflect evidential value of context of creation and use. In electronic records management these principles are of even greater importance since randomly stored data are otherwise devoid of context and only knowledge of the business application, or provenance, of the system provides guidance for retention.[11]

As with traditional records, the appraisal of electronic records is based on series, rather than items, so that with proper design, electronic records with common content can be identified and controlled. The concept of a series has less of a physical referent with respect to electronic systems, emphasizing instead the relationship between "form" of records and the character of the specific business transaction. As a consequence it is more evident that it is the evidence of a certain transaction which is appraised rather than the records, and hence appraisal can and does take place without records having yet been created.

And while the tendency is admittedly more pronounced with electronic records, there is increasing decentralization of recordkeeping and, therefore, of responsibility for management of organizational memory even in traditional settings and with paper-based systems. Distribution of records creation and management implies that policy adherence depends on understanding of records management requirements by program staff and their ability to use the installed information systems to achieve the objectives of maintaining information quality (integrity, currency, and relevancy) and continuity of access. De facto standards are unlikely to be effective means of ensuring interchangeability of information because system implementations and upgrades will occur at irregular times and in an uncoordinated fashion throughout the institution. Directories bridging distributed files will be essential for stored information to be retrieved.

Of course there are areas of discontinuity as well. The most important and difficult to grasp is that traditional records are created and stabilized on a medium in a single act, thus the record is necessarily evidence of the act. Electronic information systems do not necessarily create or fix evidence of acts, and are designed to be "efficient" by reusing the information content of the system many times, without leaving a trace of its prior state unless systems was designed to document record transactions.

In traditional environments, appraisal is conducted at time of accessioning, and therefore appears to be an assessment of the records themselves. In electronic records management, initial appraisal must take place at the time of system design or before and is therefore more obviously a reflection of the function. Traditional appraisal tends to occur once, based on determination of permanent value, while electronic records management requires focus on continuing value because risk factors change with each system migration.

Because the costs of retaining traditional records are much greater if they are distributed, paper records are typically transferred to central archives. Different cost and risk factors dictate that electronic records be managed within the originating context as long as possible. The difference in outcomes here mask the application of a common criterion, but to most archivists it seems a radical difference.

A similar difference in outcomes reflecting application of a common standard applies to preservation. Traditionally preservation of the medium has been the focus, but in electronic records management, preservation of usable access to information will not be assured by media preservation alone. Hence emphasis is shifted to the information. But in the traditional setting, the preservation of the medium assured continuing access to the information, so there may be no conflict of intention.

Indeed this seems likely when we examine differences directly associated with access. Traditionally users come to records and find information they require because this is the only way it can reasonably be made available to them. In electronic records management the concrete information required can be delivered to remote users by request and in configurations best designed to be usable for their purposes (based on their use of metadata to formulate an inquiry). The costs of making information in electronic form available to the user at his or her site may, in fact, be less than the cost of maintaining a central reference space for such users and the convenience to the users is far greater.

NOTES

[1] David Bearman, "New Models for Management of Electronic Records by Archives," *Cadernos de Biblioteconomia, Arquivística, e Documentação* 2 (1992): 61-70, reprinted in this volume as Chapter 10.

[2] David Bearman and Peter Sigmond, "Explorations of Form of Material Authority Files by Dutch Archivists," *American Archivist* 50 (Spring 1987): 249-253. "Form" is an abstraction of something we recognize culturally but for which we do not have a generally accepted or named concept. Indeed, most people will need to have the concept illustrated (a receipt, a memo, a classified ad, or an application are each a form because we would recognize them even if the words were changed to xxxx's). Yet once they understand the concept it is clear to people both that recognition of a 'form' is a significant part of "literacy" and that electronic information interchange has yet to evolve recognizable 'forms' and that this contributes to the difficulty we have in managing it.

[3] The archives and records management community needs a study of a variety of business application areas, in different firms, with case analysis of the degree of success encountered in implementing solutions to records management problems using combinations of four approaches to satisfying the same set of functional requirements: policy, design, implementation and standards. A large scale interdisciplinary study along these lines was funded by the National Historical Publications and Records Commission to be conducted at the University of Pittsburgh, beginning in 1993.

[4] David Bearman, "Management of Electronic Records: Issues and Guidelines," in United Nations Advisory Committee for Coordination of Information Systems, *Electronic Records Management Guidelines: A Manual for Policy Development and Implementation* (New York: United Nations, 1990), 17-70, 89-107, 135-189.

[5] These functional requirements represented my first private effort to think systematically about this approach to specifying how archives need to work. In the spring of 1993, with funding from the NHPRC, we were able to bring together a group of experts to address these questions collectively. Their definition of functional requirements is reprinted in Chapter 2 of this volume in Figure 2.7. Since then the functional requirements have undergone further refinement and revision, as reflected in the spring 1993 version printed in Appendix A of this volume. While further modifications are likely, the current re-

quirements all have substantial literary warrants and are unlikely to be significantly altered.

6 Links or pointers from one database system to another are increasingly being employed to reduce redundancy and ensure the accuracy of data, but their effect is to change documents and views over time, thereby eliminating the value of a record as evidence. In addition, the assumption in any such live link is that the thing pointed to will still be available, physically and logically, to the pointing system. This assumption becomes increasingly invalid over time, leaving records as mere shells consisting of pointers to non-existence data.

7 David Bearman, "An Indefensible Bastion," in David Bearman, ed., *Management of Electronic Records*, Archives and Museum Informatics Technical Report #13 (Pittsburgh: Archives and Museum Informatics, 1991): 14-24.

8 The functionality of an application system is, of course, directly correlated with the work process it is intended to support. In order to understand what records meant and how they could have been used in the office which created them, it is essential to be able to understand the application environment. As an example, we cannot use a manual record system in which the two series are arranged by date of transfer and by lot number to search for property owned by John Jones. The files we are looking in cannot reasonably be employed in this way unless the user has first gone to the taxation bureau and found, in a series arranged by taxpayer name under John Jones, the lot numbers for the properties on which he paid taxes.

9 David Bearman, "Archival Principles and the Electronic Office," *Information Handling in Offices and Archives*, Proceedings of a Symposium on the Impact of Information Technologies on Information Handling in Offices and Archives, Marburg, Germany, 17-19 October 1991 (New York: K.G. Saur, 1993), 177-193, reprinted in this volume as Chapter 5; also Bearman, "Diplomatics, Weberian Bureaucracy, and the Management of Electronic Records in Europe and America," *American Archivist* 55 (Winter 1992): 168-180.

10 David Bearman, "Information Technology Standards and Archives," *Janus* (1992.2): 161-166, reprinted in this volume as Chapter 7.

11 However, it is clear from our exposure to electronic records that the provenance of records is not equivalent to the "office of origin" but rather the function which gave rise to them, or more specifically the transaction within the function. For recent reflections of this re-

newed emphasis on function in description, appraisal, and archival education, see: Margaret Hedstrom, "Descriptive Practices for Electronic Records: Deciding What is Essential and Imagining what is Possible," paper given at the Association of Canadian Archivists Annual Meeting, Montreal 1992; Angelika Menne-Haritz, "Archival Education: Meeting the Needs of Society in the Twenty-First Century," paper delivered at the 12th International Congress on Archives, Montreal 1992; Helen Willa Samuels, *Varsity Letters* (Metuchen, New Jersey: Scarecrow Press, 1992).

CHAPTER TWO

Recordkeeping Systems[*]

Not all information systems are recordkeeping systems. Recordkeeping systems are the locus of the evidential significance of records, therefore their management is critical to the preservation of evidential meaning. Understanding recordkeeping systems is critical to formulating archival functional requirements for the management of electronic records, defining archival documentation standards, and designing archival control systems. The author argues that recordkeeping systems -- rather than fonds, record groups, or record series -- should be accepted as the fundamental locus of provenance. Recordkeeping systems are preferred to these other concepts because they (1) have concrete boundaries and definable properties; (2) solve the problems identified with the concepts of fonds, record groups, and series in Canadian, U.S., and Australian archival practices; and (3) give archivists new tools with which to play an active role in the electronic age. Also, the focus on functional requirements for recordkeeping systems allies archivists with auditors, administrative security personnel, freedom of information and privacy officers, lawyers, and senior managers -- all of whom have a responsibility for corporate memory and its management. This alliance is both strategically critical and intellectually desirable.

* Originally published in *Archivaria* 36 (Autumn 1993): 16-36. An earlier draft was presented at the Ontario Association of Archivists Conference on Archives and Automation, Toronto, 13 May 1993.

THE PLACE OF RECORDKEEPING SYSTEMS
IN A MODEL OF ARCHIVAL DATA

Recordkeeping systems are a special kind of information system about which archivists should be experts. As the name suggests, recordkeeping systems keep and support retrieval of records while information systems store and provide access to information. Recordkeeping systems are distinguished from information systems within organizations by the role they play in providing organizations with evidence of business transactions (by which is meant actions taken in the course of conducting their business, rather than "commercial" transactions). Non-record information systems, on the other hand, store information in discrete chunks that can be recombined and reused without reference to their documentary context. Archivists ought to have a special expertise in recordkeeping systems because recordkeeping systems are the source of archival records and their context and structure reveal the historical meaning of archives. Nevertheless, the analysis of recordkeeping systems from a theoretical or practical perspective is peculiarly absent from the archival literature.[1]

The sections that follow analyze how information about the content, structure, and context of records is required in order to ensure preservation of evidence.[2] Archivists must understand the nature of recordkeeping systems in order to design and implement records systems that capture, maintain, and access evidence. The evidential purpose of recordkeeping systems provides critical tools for articulation of workable strategies for management of electronic records. I will argue that the design of appropriate documentation methods for archives depends on an appreciation of the centrality of recordkeeping systems to archival theory and practice and on the concept of records as evidence.[3] Our society recognizes some documents as records because they carry out or document transactions. Because records are accepted within this social and legal framework as evidence of an act, they are retained in recordkeeping systems designed to serve the needs of the people and organizations which created or received them.

To understand recordkeeping systems, we must recognize them first as systems and, second, as information systems. Systems consist of interdependent components organized to achieve an end, and information systems are organized collections of hardware, software, supplies, people, policies, and procedures, plus all the maintenance and training which are required to keep these components working together. Recordkeeping systems are organized to accomplish the specific functions of creating, storing, and accessing records for evidential purposes. While they may also be able to retrieve records for informational purposes, they are designed for operational staff, not for archivists or researchers, and thus are optimized to support the business processes and business transactions of the creating organization rather than generic information retrieval.

Although recordkeeping systems are not created for archivists, archivists must appraise recordkeeping systems and make decisions to destroy or keep the records they contain. Traditionally archivists have made these decisions based on the examination of records after the records have fulfilled their role of supporting the operational needs of the organization which created them. The advent of electronic records which are not susceptible to ready examination of the physical documents has led archivists to seek alternative approaches to appraisal. It was soon realized that if archivists could make such decisions on the basis of analysis of the business functions and the need for evidence of these functions, they could avoid trying to assess records themselves. In addition, they could concentrate their efforts on records systems of continuing value, which are relatively few in number, rather than squandering resources equally on appraisal of insignificant records systems.

As a matter of principle, when archivists do decide to retain records, they take special care not to disturb the relations defined by the recordkeeping system. These relations in manual systems are limited to "original order," but in automated environments may involve many types of relationships. They are evidence of how individual records were or could have been used within the record system and thus of what they meant in the context of the business process they document. In manual systems, accessioning records need not disturb this original order. In electronic records systems, however, removing records from the application which supported the relations among records and between the record and the actions which it documents runs serious risks of destroying the structure and context information that preserves the evidential significance of the record.

The relationships among records, business transactions and recordkeeping systems are illustrated in Figure 2.1.

Figure 2.1

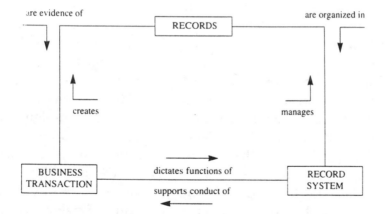

Recordkeeping systems are established to serve institutional or personal purposes and therefore reflect the functions and activities of the creating organization or individual. For more than fifty years, archivists and records managers have assumed the role of experts who can provide assistance to the organization in setting up recordkeeping systems to serve business purposes efficiently and at the same time satisfy archival functional requirements.[4] Recognizing that not all records systems serve organizational purposes equally effectively, archivists and records managers focused on organizing paper records into series, each of which directly supported the execution of specific business transactions. Guidelines for effective file management issued by the U.S. National Archives in 1968 go so far as to suggest that files which require indexing to provide alternative access points are probably not designed to support a specific function effectively, since a single function, conducted in a specified way, will need to access records in only one, or at most a few, different schemes of arrangement.[5]

This may have been true as long as records systems were designed to support isolated business functions but the spread of database management systems (DBMS) has been driven by the information management faith that organizational efficiency can be enhanced by reducing data redundancy through organization-wide data integration. In an integrated DBMS, each area of functional responsibility within the organization is provided views of the database that are limited to the data it requires. The software supports the transactions this functional area conducts, but records of these transactions may not be created or maintained if the system was only designed to serve as an organizational data resource (e.g., be an information system) rather than to preserve evidence of business transactions (e.g., be a records system). The possibility that records could be used by bringing information from various sources together in a logical view at the time of making a decision, while not physically creating a record, is new to electronic methods of manipulating data and presents the first of several serious challenges to corporate memory and operational viability brought about by electronic recordkeeping.

Archivists recognize that organizational functions (or "competencies" as the Europeans call them) are the roots of business processes, which in turn dictate the way in which transactions are conducted.[6] The way the process is conducted is reflected in the organization of records to support a function. In paper systems, the physical records (each document or file) correspond to logical business records (a transaction or case). Therefore, the physical organization of the records in the system, within series, relates records to each other and to the way in which work is done in the organization.[7] In automated systems, logical records (representing business transactions) do not necessarily conform to physical records (which are structured to maximize database efficiency); business records may not only involve combining data from more than one logical or physical record (as they typically do in relational database management systems), but may involve processing this data in ways that are only documented external to the data itself. Information systems might support the ongoing business of an organization on one level, even though they do not create records essential for accountability.

A second reflection of the nature of activity or transactions is what I once called the "form of material" and which has more recently come to be known as the "documentary form."[8] Documentary forms provide a structure for the information within the individual record. They dictate what data will be present for specific types of transactions and facilitate its recognition and use by signaling to readers -- by means of typography, data structures, and electronic links -- where particular information will be located. In the paper world, organizations used particular documentary forms for specific business transactions, but in automated environments the aim is to free the data from the form in which it was created for use in other ways. At the same time, automated environments have spawned new, virtual, documentary forms such as dynamic documents, multimedia documents, and individuated documents with properties that the organization and the broader culture are only beginning to understand.[9] The novelty of electronic documentary forms means that we cannot make assumptions -- common in our dealings with paper records whose forms we understand -- about the relationship between form and content, between form and how the recordkeeping system functioned, or between forms and the processes that created them, just as other periods of radical change in documentary forms and methods of business communication have disrupted the relationship between the expression of structure in documents and their interpretation by recipients.[10]

The relationships among records, business transactions, functions, documentary forms, and record series are depicted in Figure 2.2.

Figure 2.2

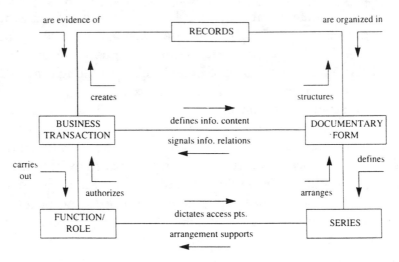

People (as individuals and in their positions as employees) create documents of various types as a consequence of their positions, offices, or roles in life. People also create non-record documents. Information created by people only becomes a record when, and if, it participates in a transaction. Purely private information, not shown to others, is not a record. In modern organizations, if records are created, business practice requires them to be "filed" where in principle they are available to others. Archivists and records managers instruct filing clerks to create job, project, case, or subject files around functions of the organizational unit and to file individual records into these structures. In bureaucratic organizations, specific forms of records (often literally numbered and pre-printed forms or "form-letters") are linked to particular business transactions conducted by organizational units. Procedures may dictate that a given type of file will always contain certain of these categories of records. Only specific information is present in each form of record, although the case as a whole contains all the information required for any aspect of the mission of the organization. The same principles apply to records created by individuals in the modern world; different forms such as diaries, correspondence, and subject files of personal "business" will make up the series of records in the home of a private person. When we speak properly of the records of a family, we mean by this that the record system was used by more than one individual, often siblings or multiple generations, of the same family. Otherwise the "family" papers are really an artificial collection, as we call groupings of manuscripts or records made by the collectors rather than the creators.

While the relationship between recordkeeping systems and functions is, therefore, always straightforward, the relationship between a record system and organizational units is not. This has been the cause of many of the problems of locating provenance in organizations in the past. Even paper recordkeeping systems are not necessarily owned, built, or maintained by the organizational unit that creates the records they contain, although they will be used by that organization. Traditional central registry offices and the contemporary data processing departments which have succeeded them were assigned the function of maintaining records. The records they maintain are created and used by numerous different organizational units. Thus records must be linked not only to the organizations which created them, but also to those that maintained them, used them, and owned them. Each of these organizations may know the same records system by a variety of different names. The views of information held by the organization that are available to a given office of origin are limited by both the record system and the office's access to it, usually to those views for which it has a business need. Further, it must be remembered that especially for electronic records systems, recordkeeping systems may encompass records physically located in more than one place. Indeed such distributed logical records systems will become increasingly common during the 1990s, with the acceptance of client-server architectures. Logical records systems are even more radically the norm in object-oriented environments in which the record alone will carry the methods by which it is searched, disseminated, and disposed, and the procedures governing the recordkeeping system are distributed to the level of the individual records and do not exist in a higher aggregation.

Figure 2.3 represents the elements discussed so far and their relations.

Although these relations among elements are the same in manual as in electronic records environments, the character of recordkeeping systems is being radically transformed by automation, as is the character of series, forms, and records themselves. Changes that are significant to archivists include the software dependency of recordkeeping systems, the existence of recordkeeping systems which serve many different and physically remote offices (each office having its own views of the system and also its own functions), and business processes which do not create records although they use information from dynamic information systems.

Before examining the implications of these changes both for archival automation and for management by archivists of electronic records of organizations, it is useful to establish the relationship between the concept of a record system and the fundamental archival principles.

Figure 2.3

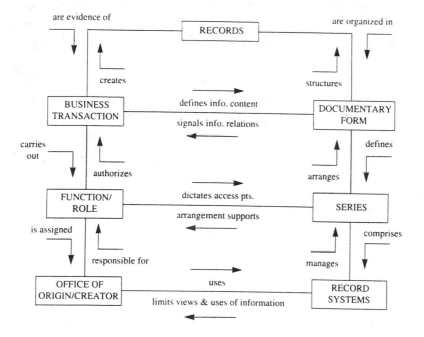

ARCHIVAL DOCUMENTATION AND RECORDKEEPING SYSTEMS

Provenance, inarguably the most important concept in archival theory, dictates that records are to be understood with reference to their origins in activity.[11] As a shorthand, archivists often equate the provenance of records to the organization in which records were created or received, i.e., the "office of origin." However, as the preceding data model makes clear, the provenance of archives is better understood by reference to the function of which they are evidence and the record system in which they were created, stored, preserved, and accessed by the organization. Elsewhere, I have written on why archivists must recognize function, and not organizational setting, as the locus of provenancial meaning.[12] Suffice it to say here that what systems analysts would call the business function being conducted, not the "office of origin," determines the form and content of records and dictates the procedures for their creation and dissemination. As a consequence, when functions are transferred from one office to another, the records that document the function typically are stable and recordkeeping systems are usually transferred lock, stock, and barrel with the transfer of responsibility. On the other hand, if a new function is assigned to an office it will usually require new procedures accompanied by new documentary forms, new series of files, and often entirely new, separate, recordkeeping systems.

Archives appraise and accession recordkeeping systems, not individual records, because recordkeeping systems do not just passively reflect how the creating organization used information, they actively determine it. As such, recordkeeping systems are an organic whole. Some recordkeeping systems -- like central registries or decentralized filing systems operating with a shared classification structure (thereby resulting in "virtual" central registries) -- may be managed at the corporate level during their active life. Other recordkeeping systems -- such as subject files, chronological transaction files, or incoming and outgoing correspondence -- may be managed at a work unit, or even a work-group level, with or without reference to a larger corporate records system. In North American organizations it is even common for some records to be managed by individuals, either because in the prevailing corporate culture larger scale systems do not exist or because the individuals want to retain control over the information they contain.[13] If information or documents pass across the boundaries between individuals, work groups, formal organizational units, or independent organizations, recordkeeping systems should create records. However, the definition of a record-creating boundary is not absolute or fixed and depends on the nature of the transaction, aspects of the organizational culture, and boundary perceptions in process definitions.[14]

Ability to access and use recordkeeping systems, rather than employment within the office of origin, determines the role records play in specific business processes during their active life. Relationships and structures established in recordkeeping systems determine the connections that can be made between records they contain both during and after their active life. Although archivists know that recordkeeping systems provide evidence of the role records played in the organization, they have not developed tools or techniques for documenting how recordkeeping systems relate to organized activities through established procedures. In traditional paperbased systems, neither archivists nor the operating entity can typically document who accessed recordkeeping systems or how records they retrieved were used. Although when a record is thus used, it is participating in a new business transaction and should, in principle, become a record of that transaction.[15] In electronic information systems, tools for representing such relationships as permissions, views, and actual uses of records exist, and data administrators and configuration managers can document the participation of records in concrete transactions over time.

Archivists have not made use of these tools in automated archival control systems. Indeed, the history of archival automation has not been a story of great successes. The relatively early adoption of a data content and interchange standard did not lead to the development of methods to bring archival documentation from active office settings directly into archival finding tools, but to a species of rigid text editors designed to create databases of MARC AMC records.[16] In so far as archival automation exists, it builds databases that replicate the data that was previously found in paper finding tools and indexes, although it may provide more access points. Data gets into these systems by means of archivists preparing finding aids and it generally is used by archivists acting as reference inter-mediaries.[17] Automation, as implemented in archives today, is not integrated recordkeeping systems documentation, contri-butes little if anything to archival productivity, and does not insinuate the archival function into the operating environment of the parent organizations.

Some archivists have been working to analyze archival systems in a way that would generate requirements for archival documentation standards which would move auto-mated archival information systems beyond their role as fast paper.[18] In a recent effort to define the information architec-ture of archives in order to provide a framework for more in-tegrated archival automation software, it was consistently found that the data archivists need to describe the context and structure of records originates in documentation of organiza-tional missions and recordkeeping systems.[19] It was also found that current data models and flow diagrams for archival information systems overlook the nexus of records creation and recordkeeping in the record system and that the archival function was being implemented as if it could be logically seg-regated from the recordkeeping systems of the business.

This segregation is impossible except at the expense of total redundancy, because archival information systems have always been information systems about recordkeeping sys-tems, or what data administrators call "metadata systems." Al-though data administrators developed automated systems called data dictionaries and Information Resource Directory Systems to document and manage electronic recordkeeping systems, archivists have not adopted them but have instead tried to employ traditional methods for describing electronic archival holdings.[20] Unfortunately, the prose narrative and the simple data structures archivists use in traditional finding aids cannot rigorously describe the myriad links of records with each other or transactions which are supported in automated systems. In addition, because they are constructed after the fact from evidence still visible after the records come into the archives, they also do not document the evolution of relations which takes place over the life of a system. When automated, these simplistic representations of information systems fail to help researchers reconstruct archival evidence or permit archivists to achieve operational efficiencies.

By failing to employ techniques of documentation available from the domain of systems design and management, archivists have overlooked a pre-existing source of documentation which would, if properly regulated, mitigate the need for archivists to engage in the *post hoc* documentation of accessioned systems.[21] More importantly, archivists have missed the opportunity to maintain systems that serve as the repository of organizational memory of functions, structures, and events, although such databases are much needed by contemporary organizations and the data is necessarily present in an adequate archival information system.[22]

I know of no archival institutions that serve as repositories of the life-cycle software configuration management documentation essential for establishing evidential context and structure in an adequate archival information system. This is especially unfortunate as it appears that the data management requirements, and hence the metadata documentation requirements, of archives are identical to those of vital records management, privacy administration, freedom of information, and administrative security. If archivists did their jobs documenting recordkeeping systems, they could exploit the often greater political and financial clout of constituencies for these other interests. Such an integrative function speaks directly to strategic opportunities for contemporary archives.

Archivists must find ways to make the data they manage or create regarding organizational functions and structures sufficiently important to the organization that others will keep it up to date and use it as an official referent. If archivists do not become the authoritative source of information about what recordkeeping systems exist and how they are implemented, they cannot identify the records which should be preserved archivally. Ultimately archivists will need to design ways to acquire descriptions of individual records, files, and record-keeping systems directly from the self-documenting features of electronic records systems, because they will otherwise never have the resources to obtain this level of detailed documentation.

Documentation of recordkeeping systems in metadata systems that contribute to fundamental organizational data management will dictate a very different agenda for standards for archival description. Hints of this agenda were present in the report of the Working Group on Standards for Archival Description which defined archival description as:

> "the process of *capturing*, collating, analyzing, and organizing any information that serves to identify, manage, locate, and interpret the holdings of archival institutions and explain the contexts and *record systems from which those holdings were selected*." [emphasis added][23]

Careful readers saw a radical shift from "making" description to capturing it, and from describing records to documenting contexts and record systems. An extension of this shift of focus led to two critiques of the proposed International Standard Archival Description (ISAD).[24] The critique is equally applicable to the recently developed Canadian *Rules for Archival Description* framework which is built around the concept of fonds, the U.S. reliance on record groups, and the Australian primacy of series.[25] I believe what each framework really needs is the concept of a recordkeeping system.[26] Readers will note that in the model in Figure 2.3, fonds and record groups are unnecessary theoretical constructs that do not consistently correspond to any combination of other concepts. Series only provide context when they are not part of a multiple-series record system.

Archivists, like Ptolemaic astronomers, are struggling with "very subtle" notions to make reality fit theory. When applied, the theory of fonds leads to inherent contradictions. This is because fonds are defined simultaneously as having what Terry Eastwood calls an external and internal dimension[27] or what Terry Cook describes as the product of a "defined creator" and a "linked record-keeping system."[28] The effort to define fonds as being a theoretical construct that is simultaneously organizational in context and the relations among records needs to be abandoned in favor of what Angelika Menne-Haritz calls functional provenance.[29] Recordkeeping systems have the virtue of the locus of functional provenance and, at the same time, being real things with concrete boundaries in time and space which do not require philosophy to locate. Their characteristics are precisely the variables that are involved in defining documentary evidence: content, structure, and context.

Recordkeeping systems defy the traditional approaches we have taken to documentation, and even resist the more innovative efforts to forge descriptive systems around the concept of series linked to organizational units, which was pioneered by Peter Scott in Australia and explored in North America by Max Evans.[30] Recordkeeping systems have complex structures that give meaning to records. Although some manual records systems may consist of a single series, most involve multiple series, with links between them that facilitate the ongoing work of the organization. Changes in either documentary form or arrangement that signal a change in record series are physically revealed in manual recordkeeping systems, but are not self-evident in electronic systems, where both format and order are logical constructs. In electronic recordkeeping systems, the documentation that describes what we have come to regard as series (either a "view" or separate physical file with defined links) may be part of the logic of the software, the content of tables which the software reads, a function of the architecture of the system, or external to the electronic form record system.

Of course, in both manual and electronic systems, the documentation itself is a record series that is part of the record system. However, electronic records systems retained without appropriate documentation will hold no evidence. In order to retain evidence, archivists need to assure that series of records within a record system are retained as they were employed together by the creators and users of the record system. In the process, the separate description of each series, which sufficed for manual systems, becomes inadequate. Recordkeeping systems must be documented using data administration techniques for metadata representation, because relations between series are complex data structures with links into elements of the business environment in which they operate. This will become more obvious as MIS offices try to implement "enterprise computing," process control, corporate decision support systems, and object-oriented systems.

Metadata documenting a record system needs to link organizational structure and function, business and archival processes, software procedures, and documentary forms. As such, it needs to be represented in a relational data model supporting processing along connections between the files. In defining what data is needed to describe the record system entity in such a model, it is clear that this data is different from data describing an organization, a records creator, or an accession -- although record system documentation is linked to documentation of these entities in the metadata system.[31]

Figure 2.4 illustrates the data about records systems that we might need in a metadata system. As laid out in the illustration, it appears to be a flat record of the sort we might "write" in an archival finding aid, but readers should note that the field names indicate that numerous record types are present and linked, and that other attributes of the entities referenced by the first word in the field label would be present in a fully coherent meta-documentation system. The data values in the working metadata system would not contain the sorts of words used in this example for the purpose of helping archivists to imagine the meaning of these fields, but rather

Figure 2.4

Metadata files partially describing recordkeeping systems with descriptive text of the sort found in archival finding aids.

System Name: Environmental Disaster Record System

System Owner Name: Health & Public Safety Division

System Owner Business Function: Service delivery

System Authorized Record Creator Names: State Department of Environmental Affairs, Health & Public Safety Division, City Police Department, State Department of Highways, State Department of Education, City Welfare Services Division

System Implementation Date: April 1972

System Abandonment Date: Active

System...

User Name:

User **Views:** Accident Report; Service Cost Analysis; Application for Assistance; Application Approval Hearing Evidence; Grant Award; Disbursement Authorization; Case File Summation; Geographic Locations Report

User Permission View Files: Accident report file, claim file, hearing file, client file, incident file, agency file

User Permission Update Functions: Relief recipient data

User...

Hardware Configuration CPU:

Hardware Configuration **Storage Devices:**

Hardware Configuration...

Data Configuration...

Data Elements...

Data Output Products: Report 534; Report 9876; Report 46; GIS forms 2, 9-14, 63, 66-87; Stat Report forms 1-231

Data Input Products: Screens 1-56

Data...

Figure 2.4, cont.

Software Configuration...
Documentation Products: Disaster Relief Coordination System Procedures Manual 101; Disaster Response System Software Documentation; System Permission Configuration Audit Trail   **Documentation Data Test Set:** File 1344   **Documentation Data Audit Set:** File 87654   **Documentation Data Configuration History:** File 76

would consist of pointers to other records and data represented in a fashion that enables it to be processed consistently. In this illustration, the data resembles our current archival finding aids more than that found in Information Resource Directory Systems, but is included to introduce archivists to the range of content that is necessary to describe a record system, rather than to suggest an actual data structure for an archival metadatabase on record system entities. Even so, it is noteworthy that these fields of data about recordkeeping systems are absent from *RAD, MAD,* and *APPM.*

As can be seen from the above list of files and fields, which represents a small portion of what would be required to document a recordkeeping system, it is not possible to implement a metadata system in a "flat" format. Such a descriptive approach would not link the views that a given department had with the content of the data in those views and the state of the software configuration at any time. It would be unable, for example, to determine how the input from the State Department of Environmental Affairs would be acted upon by the system and thus whether the input files, the case record as retained in the database, or the output in response to particular user queries made as part of certain service delivery processes, would be the evidence required to document the function.

While archivists will not need to make or maintain all this metadata about electronic information systems by themselves, they will not be able to define what metadata would be required to document recordkeeping systems nor how it would need to be represented without understanding the functional requirements for archival recordkeeping systems. These functional requirements dictate what documentation we actually require to preserve the evidential value of records.

FUNCTIONAL REQUIREMENTS OF RECORDKEEPING SYSTEMS

In contemporary organizations, electronic records systems create, store, disseminate, and retrieve records. Software applications developed specifically for organizations and generic commercial applications are operating on a wide variety of hardware to support these systems. Archivists would like to assure that electronic recordkeeping systems developed or acquired to support other functions of the organization are implemented and managed in such a way as to assure that records are captured and preserved. But electronic records systems differ from their manual counterparts in several ways that are of considerable significance to archivists, including that they are typically designed and operated by people other than either archivists or the records creators. In addition, they are typically dependent for functioning on the hardware and software in which they were implemented. The professionals who manage electronic information systems demand that archivists articulate their functional requirements so that decisions can be made whether, to what extent, and how they should be satisfied.

The failure of archivists to understand records systems in their practice with paper records has left them without analytical tools with which to approach electronic records. Instead of defining the functional requirements for archivally sound records systems, archivists have been trying to preserve "machine-readable records" or output products from systems.

Instead of defining how systems would self-document the content, structure, and context of records, archivists have tried to document their provenance, their dependencies, their relationships, etc., in descriptive activity. Without understanding the record system in relation to processes and activities of the organization, however, it is not possible to identify what data in the system constitutes evidence of an activity and which activities and competencies spawned or used the record. From output products it is not possible to reconstruct the record as evidence and looking at output products has obscured the need for archivists to develop methods that will permit long-term retention of and access to systems. Moreover, the least effective way to document systems is after they have been retired; on-going documentation, maintained from design specifications onwards, is a much more reliable and effective means of systems control.

Because records systems are a logical construct rather than a physical one, they may span many "volumes" in computer disks and many offices in location, but a single documentation or description will define the selection of records to the system, their arrangement within it, and the methods of access to it. Such documentation enables systems staff to operate the system, to integrate it with other systems, and to modify its functionality and ultimately "migrate" the data it contains to a new hardware and software environment. Unfortunately archivists are not conversant with such documentation or with the formal properties of recordkeeping systems. Documentation of recordkeeping systems is not easily isolated from documentation of the software application as a whole because most software applications have historically stored data in their own record system.[32]

Regardless of the implementation environment, the archival management of electronic records is an inseparable component of ongoing data management in electronic recordkeeping systems. It should be approached first with a clear definition of what we want "archivally responsible" systems to do. Once we enumerate these functional requirements, we should ask when (in the life of the system) and how (by what means) we could intervene to satisfy the requirements. Then we should test these intervention strategies in installed recordkeeping systems in the real world in order to refine heuristics that can be used by others.

In a study based on these premises currently underway at the University of Pittsburgh,[33] we hypothesize that the functional requirements apply to any recordkeeping system. They are not unique to electronic recordkeeping systems, although the means for satisfying a requirement will be dependent on the way the system is implemented. The methods available to satisfy functional requirements include policy, procedures, system design, and standards.[34] In electronic systems these are often referred to collectively as data management practices. We expect that success in using data management practices to satisfy archival functional requirements will be a factor of the interaction of the choice of strategies with the features of the business application, the software application, and the corporate culture. Different business applications will have differing levels of risk associated with non-satisfaction of each requirement. Different software applications will have different barriers to use of design, implementation, and standards-based approaches to requirements and will be correlated with implementations at different levels in the architecture. Different organizational cultures will be correlated with different approaches to satisfying each requirement. A representation of this research project, showing the variables, their anticipated interactions, and the hypotheses of the researchers, is shown Figure 2.5.[35]

These functional requirements were initially identified from a review of the literature on electronic records management, archives, and organizational information systems management. A draft statement of the functional requirements for archiving[36] was then submitted to critique by a group of experts in the field. After two days of deliberations, a revised

Figure 2.5
University of Pittsburgh Electronic Records Study

Variables

Archival Functional Requirements x	Tactics	Business Funct's /Applications	Software Applications	Business Sector	Organizational Culture
	(given in proposal)	(to be defined with literature and analysis)	(to be defined w/ survey/analysis)	(given in proposal)	(to be defined with literature and experts)
Compliant	Policy	Examples may include:	Examples may include:	Government	Examples may include:
Accountable	Design			Commercial	
Responsible		Financial	Transaction		Open/Closed
Implemented	Implementation	Management	Oriented	Non-Profit/	
Reliable				University	Hierarchical/Flat
	Standards	Service	Document		
Capture		Delivery	Oriented		Full
Comprehensive					Bureaucracy/
Complete		Fulfillment	Data Oriented		Market
Indentifiable					Bureaucracy/
Authentic		Production	Intelligent/		Workflow
			Analytic		Bureaucracy/
Maintain		Research &			Personnel
Sound		Development	Object Oriented		Bureaucracy
Auditable					
Exportable		Communication	Remote Sensing		Central/
Removable					Decentralized
		Education &	Procedural		
Access		Training			Micro-managed/
Available					Autonomous
Usable		Personnel			
Understandable		Management			
Redactable					
		Policy Formulation & Regulation			

Hypotheses:

1a) The functional requirements for archival management of electronic records are the same as for traditional records.

1b) Many functional requirements will not be satisfied by traditional records system.

2a) It will be possible to satisfy each of these functional requirements following any of the four tactics.

2b) Many requirements will be more fully satisfied for electronic record than they could be for paper records.

3a) Different business applications will share different sets of functional requirement, and

3b) Differing degrees of risk are associated with non-satisfaction of requirements in different business applications.

4a) Different software applications will not dictate different fuctional requirements, but

4b) Different packages within application categories will satisfy the fuctional requirements to different degrees.

4c) Software dependent data objects are not records and as evidence will generally be saved in an independent format.

5a) Functional requirements will be the same for each business sector, and

5b) Different sectors will not determine choice of tactics as much as different corporate cultures.

6a) The best way to satisfy functional requirements will depend heavily on corporate culture.

6b) The techological capabilities of the archives and its agents will be less critical in satisfying archival requirements that will be the acceptance of archival responsibility by managers throughout the organization.

statement of functional requirements for recordkeeping was prepared, as illustrated in Figure 2.6.

Figure 2.6
Functional Requirements for Recordkeeping[37]

COMPLIANT ORGANIZATIONS		
ACCOUNTABLE SYSTEMS		
responsible	implemented	reliable
FUNCTIONAL RECORDS		
CAPTURE	MAINTAIN	ACCESS
comprehensive	sound	available
complete	auditable	usable
identifiable	exportable	understandable
authentic	removable	redactable

To understand how these functional requirements relate to the concept of recordkeeping systems, it is important to free ourselves from a physical model of recordkeeping systems tied to a specific implementation. We need to adopt a conceptual framework in which a system is understood to be the totality of people, policies, hardware, software, and practices surrounding the creation or acquisition and the use of information within any organization. The business application for which these particular functional requirements are being specified is archiving. All other business applications of the organization, such as correspondence management or order fulfillment, are presumed to have their own functional requirements in addition to archiving requirements.

The requirements are purposefully stated as outcomes rather than as methods. As mentioned earlier, each requirement could be satisfied through either policy, systems design, systems implementation, or standards -- or through a combination of these tactics. Indeed, it is assumed that no organization would seek to satisfy all of these requirements using a single strategy. In this, the functional requirements depart significantly from the approaches that have been used by archives to achieve these ends in manual recordkeeping systems, which have often assumed that all of the (unarticulated) functional requirements could be satisfied at once, in the same way, and in the same place in the overall system design.

This has significant implications for the architecture that we envision to satisfy the requirements. Insofar as systems design, implementation, and standards (rather than policy) are employed to satisfy these requirements, the functionality required for archiving may be located within the Application Software, in a service located in the Application Program Interface, in any of the services of the Application Platform (such as the operating system, user interface, network services, etc.), in the External Environment Interface, in the External Environment itself (for example, in the communications systems or the telecommunications environment).[38] Each individual functional requirement may be satisfied by solutions implemented within one or more software layers, and no two functional requirements need be satisfied in the same way. By taking the view that each transaction generates a record -- rather than the perspective of the document, which views documents as participating in many transactions -- we save ourselves the very complex modeling requirements posited by Richard Barry's work with state transition diagrams.[39]

Except that it is only possible to satisfy functional requirements relating to storage, preservation, and access of evidence insofar as those relating to its creation have been satisfied, there is no presumption that any system would, could, or would want to satisfy all these requirements fully. It is known that these functional requirements are not completely satisfied within existing paper-based information systems on which we have long relied. For example, few paper-based systems maintain evidence of who used the records in the course of what decision-making (although some registry functions retain this data with files). Virtually no paper-based system can document whether the individuals or offices named in a distribution list for a document actually received it (or were ever sent it). In electronic recordkeeping systems it may be easier in some cases, and more difficult in others, to satisfy these functional requirements. Always, the decision regarding the degree to which any functional requirement will be satisfied is a business decision grounded in risk assessment. Whether risk management methodology is formally applied or not, costs and benefits, specific liabilities, and organizational needs and priorities will always be taken into consideration. Decisions not to satisfy functional requirements are just that; they do not invalidate the requirement.

It is the intention of the University of Pittsburgh research project, for which this articulation of functional requirements was undertaken, to examine business functions, software applications, and organizational culture variables relating to the satisfaction of these functional requirements, in order to develop heuristics that can guide practice. Figure 2.7 presents these requirements as articulated in spring 1993. [*Editor's note:* The appendix in this volume contains the latest version of these requirements, dated spring 1994.] They suggest some of the power of the concept of recordkeeping systems as the locus of provenance to define effective strategies for electronic records management.

Figure 2.7
Functional Requirements for Recordkeeping Systems
(interim version, Spring 1993)

I. Compliant

Recordkeeping systems comply with the legal and administrative requirements for recordkeeping within the jurisdictions in which they operate, including specific requirements not referenced below.

II. Accountable

Responsible: The organization must have policies, assigned responsibilities,and formal methodologies for management of its recordkeeping systems.

Implemented: Records must have been created and maintained in the normal course of business and documented procedures which were followed should conform to common practices in the industry.

Credible: The system must control quality characteristics of information being input and process information in a fashion that is consistent and accurate.

III. Functional

Recordkeeping systems must capture, maintain and access evidence over time. If they do, records will be:

Complete: Records accurately capture all information recorded or generated by their creators. Records incorporate or link to a representation of the software functionality that created them, other versions or views, a data model of relations between elements of information within a record, eye-readable conventions such as placement or font, and other structural information that adds to their meaning. Records incorporate or link to information about the context of their creation.

Identifiable: A distinctive and bounded record exists for every business transaction.

Authentic: The system must validate records creators and/or authorizers.

Communicated: The systems must capture a record of all communication in the conduct of business between two people, between a person and a store of information available to others or between a source of information and a person.

Sound: Record integrity is protected from accidental or purposive damage or destruction and from any modification after they have been received by anyone other than the creator.

Figure 2.7, cont.

Auditable: Record documentation traces the processes in which records participated, including indexing, classification, filing, viewing, copying, distribution, disposition, use and destruction throughout the record life. Management controls preserve auditability of interactions external to the system (such as during media migration or transfer).

Understandable: Records documentation should permit stored business records to logically reconstructed. Information content, plus any structure and context must be preserved in meaningful and documented relations. For records with functionality, business application procedures must be documented so that they can be correctly associated with the status of the system at the time of record creation and later.

Removable: It must be possible with appropriate authority to remove records from the system leaving only audit trails to document their prior existence.

Exportable: Record content, structural representation and representation of context must be exportable, in standard protocols if such protocols exist.

Available: The system must document all logical archival records it contains, indicate the terms under which they are available for research, and retrieve them for authorized users.

Renderable: The system must render records by display or otherwise as they appeared to creators with views in effect at time any record was used or retain structural data necessary to determine such views.

Redactable: The system must support delivery of redacted, summarized, or censored copies and keep records of the version released.

SOME STRATEGIC IMPLICATIONS OF FOCUSING ON RECORDS SYSTEMS

The concept of recordkeeping systems as the locus of provenance provides tools for understanding archiving requirements which are missing if we retain traditional definitions of provenance and equate it to records creators or to fonds. The recognition that records systems have concrete properties directly related to their ability to capture, maintain, and access records is the first step in directing archival intervention so that evidence can be saved. When archivists understand the concept of recordkeeping systems, they are freed from imagining that such intervention only takes the form of a unified policy, an isolated "archival" application, or a universal archival standard. By taking a systems approach, it becomes evident that the satisfaction of each separate archival requirement can be approached separately. Thinking in systems terms permits us to imagine architectures for satisfying these requirements. These architectures would satisfy the overall requirement by satisfying particular requirements at various different places, and in different ways, within the system of people, procedures, hardware, software, and data.

Recordkeeping systems-based strategies may have fundamental implications for archival program structures.[40] Focusing on functional requirements allows us to emphasize outcomes of archival actions rather than outputs. It also suggests a framework for regulation in which the archival function of the organization can require other units to address these functional requirements for those recordkeeping systems identified as linked to mission important functions, but not dictate specific solutions or records that must be saved. The program units of the organization must then consider the risks and the opportunities, and develop plans for data management that address each functional requirement to the degree required by the business function, and in a way suggested by existing technology applications and the corporate culture.

Archival data management would complement data management requirements of other corporate control functions and of operational managers, and lead to construction of archival information systems that are operationally useful information systems about recordkeeping systems or metadata systems. Because the information these systems contain about recordkeeping systems is inherently part of the documentation of these systems themselves, archivists would less have to "describe" records systems than to "gather descriptions" of them. Archivists will find natural allies in their documentation efforts because the same documentation of recordkeeping systems required to support archival needs supports FOI, security, vital record, and privacy requirements.[41]

With control coming early in the life of the system, responsibility being accepted by line management and senior management, and documentation collated in metadata systems, archivists would have less reason to accession records from recordkeeping systems. The existing recordkeeping systems would enable archivists to exploit search mechanisms already constructed by program offices to retrieve records. Patrons could thereby be assured of evidentially reliable records through mechanisms which themselves are evidential, and archivists would eliminate the need to create external search systems which introduce artifacts into the search process and could retrieve information that is not a record. The methods employed within recordkeeping systems can be augmented by information obtained by full-text analysis, statistical analysis, or artificial intelligence from records maintained by the record system. Such methods could also be employed for retrieval in situations where the patron of the archives is interested in information which may be contained in recordkeeping systems rather than in records themselves. Archivists would been seen as professionals who assist in mining the records of the organization for evidence and information rather than custodians who oversee the destruction and storage of old documents.

Recordkeeping systems-oriented thinking not only gives archivists a tool that supports documentation, appraisal, preservation, and retrieval, it defines for them a unique role among information professionals as defenders of records rather than processors of information. It defines special skills which archivists can learn in their educational programs and apply in their professional lives and which are not the province of the other information professions. And it leverages the most important traditional archival concepts into tools for the information age, making it clear that the recordkeeping system is the locus of provenance.

NOTES

[1] The concept of record systems, and especially of filing systems, was present in the U.S. archival literature through the 1950s but has disappeared since. The only direct treatment of recordkeeping systems that I have discovered was published in the *American Archivist* in 1950 (vol. 13, pp. 259-267). The author, Helen Chatfield of the U.S. Bureau of the Budget, discussed "The Development of Record Systems" with attention to the history of chronological, subject, and alphabetic classification schemes in government offices and the role of self-indexing or separate indexes in each configuration.

[2] *Editor's note:* This chapter extends the analysis in an earlier article, David Bearman, "Information Technology Standards and Archives," *Janus* 2 (1992): 161-166, which is reprinted in this volume as Chapter Seven.

[3] This will likely involve considerable rethinking of archives in the U.S. and Canada. I found the index entry "systems" utterly absent from indexes to the *American Archivist* since its inception. *Archivaria* presents the same picture. It is noteworthy that the Australian literature up to and including the last edition of *Keeping Archives* is replete with references to recordkeeping systems, but following Peter Scott it nonetheless focuses on the series as the fundamental archival unit of control and description linked to records about organizations and their functions rather than to documentation of recordkeeping systems. I imagine recognizing the role of recordkeeping systems will be easier for archivists in Australia who already acknowledge the recordkeeping system as an identifiable element in control but have not brought it into a rigorous model of appraisal or documentation.

[4] An example of the kind of analysis of recordkeeping systems which was once basic to archival practice is found in Howard Crocker and Kenneth L. Brock, "Building a Records Filing System for New York State Schools," *American Archivist* 19 (1956): 249-260.

[5] U.S. National Archives and Records Service, *Guidelines For Effective Files Management* (Washington, D.C.: General Services Administration, 1968).

[6] Luciana Duranti, "Diplomatics: New Uses for an Old Science," *Archivaria* (1988-1992), Part I, 28:7-27; Part II, 29:4-17; Part III, 30:4-20; Part IV, 31:10-25; Part V, 32:6-24; Part VI, 33:6-24.

[7] T.R. Schellenberg, *Modern Archives: Principles and Techniques* (Chicago, University of Chicago Press, 1956), 77, quotes Australian archival management guidelines for registry systems which stated that they should: "be planned in relation to the functions and activities of the department" and "as far as possible reflect the organization of the department."

[8] I used the term in my draft of the NISTF Data Dictionary, but my definition of it appears under the heading "form" alone in Nancy Salhi, ed., *MARC for Archives and Manuscripts: The AMC Format* (Chicago: Society of American Archivists, 1985). For a discussion, see David Bearman and Peter Sigmond, "Explorations of Form of Material Authority Files by Dutch Archivists," *American Archivist* 50 (Spring 1987): 249-253; and David Bearman, " 'Who About What' or 'From Whence, Why and How': Intellectual Access Approaches to Archives and their Implications for National Information Systems," in *Archives, Automation and Access*, Proceedings of a Conference held at the University of Victoria, British Columbia, 1-2 March 1985, ed. Peter Baskerville and Chad Gaffield (Victoria, British Columbia: University of Victoria, 1986).

[9] Ronald Weissman "Virtual Documents on an Electronic Desktop: Hypermedia, Emerging Computer Environments and the Future of Information Management" in Cynthia Durance ed., *Management of Recorded Information: Converging Disciplines* (New York: K.G Saur, 1990): 37-59; also David Bearman, "Multisensory Data and Its Management" in the same volume, 111-119.

[10] See, for example, Barbara Craig, "The Introduction of Copying Devices in the British Civil Service, 1877-1899" in *The Archival Imagination: Essays in Honour of Hugh A. Taylor*, ed. Barbara Craig (Ottawa: Association of Canadian Archivists, 1992), 105-133. Also Frank Burke, "Chaos Through Communications: Archivists, Records Managers and the Communication Phenomenon," in the same volume, 154-177.

[11] "Provenance" is defined in *A Glossary for Archivists, Manuscript Curators and Records Managers*, Lewis J. Bellardo and Lynn Lady Bellardo, comps. (Chicago: Society of American Archivists, 1992) as "The organization or individual that created, accumulated and/or maintained and used records" without any reference to recordkeeping systems. Eastwood argues for both the external (organizational) and internal (systematic) referent for provenance but asserts their equality as elements of the fonds. Terry Eastwood, "General Introduction," *The Archival Fonds: From Theory to Practice*

(Ottawa: Bureau of Canadian Archivists, Planning Committee on Descriptive Standards, 1992): 1-14.

[12] David Bearman and Richard Lytle, "The Power of the Principle of Provenance," *Archivaria* 21 (Winter 1985-86): 14-27.

[13] David Bearman, "Diplomatics, Weberian Bureaucracy, and the Management of Electronic Records in Europe and America," *American Archivist* 55 (Winter 1992): 168-180, reprinted in this volume as Chapter 9.

[14] Jon Harrington, *Organizational Structure and Information Technology* (New York: Prentice Hall, 1991) discusses the concept of "perceptual" boundaries in organizations and how these can be changed (or not) by implementing electronic information systems. When the perceptual boundary is not changed but the pattern of work is, the system will often fail. Note that the concept of organizational and perceptual boundaries employed by Harrington conforms to that which we are introducing here, e.g., business rules establish how a recordkeeping system functions.

[15] David Bearman in UN ACCIS, *Electronic Records Management Guidelines: A Manual for Policy Development and Implementation* (New York: United Nations, 1990): 17-70, 89-107, part of Section II of the ACCIS Report is reprinted in this volume as Chapter 3.

[16] See the *Directory of Software for Archives and Museums*, 1990-91 edition and 1992-93 edition (Pittsburgh: Archives and Museum Informatics, 1990 and 1992) as evidence for paucity of archival software, In 1979-80 when he was involved in drafting a standard for archival data interchange the author convinced his colleagues that one of the principal benefits of such a standard would be to increase the availability of archival description software; he was wrong.

[17] North Carolina State Archives MARS system is an exception but its very status as the first, and still only widely available online public access catalog for archives proves the point. See David Bearman, "MARS: The Archives and Manuscript Reference System," *Archives and Museum Informatics* 4:4 (1990): 10-11.

[18] See the reports of the Working Group on Standards for Archival Description, *American Archivist* 52 (Fall 1989) and 53 (Winter 1990).

[19] Archival Information Systems Architecture Working Group, working papers, unpublished (Salt Lake City: Utah State Historical Society, 1990-93).

[20] David Wallace, "Metadata and the Archival Management of Electronic Records: A Review," *Archivaria* 36 (Autumn 1993): 87-110.

[21] David Bearman, "Documenting Documentation," *Archivaria* 34 (Summer 1992): 33-49, reprinted in this volume as Chapter 8.

[22] The AT&T Bell Laboratories archives got itself on the main menu of every employee of the company by establishing a service which reported daily on the important activities in the corporation including major product announcements, policies and reorganizations. This function, initiated by archivist Marcia Goldstein and implemented under then librarian David Penniman is one of the most successful manifestations of a suggestion made by Richard Lytle an this author in op.cit. #13, although theirs was an independent invention.

[23] Reports of the Working Group on Standards for Archival Description, *American Archivist* 52 (Fall 1989) and 53 (Winter 1990) [emphasis added, although present in accompanying explanations].

[24] David Bearman, "Documenting Documentation," reprinted in this volume as Chapter 8; and Bearman, "ICA Principles Regarding Archival Description," *Archives and Museum Informatics* 6:1 (1992): 20-21

[25] Bureau of Canadian Archivists, Planning Committee on Descriptive Standards, *Rules for Archival Description*, looseleaf, still being issued; Steven Hensen, *Archives Personal Papers and Manuscript Collections*, 2nd ed. (Chicago: Society of American Archivists, 1990); *Keeping Archives*, 2nd ed., ed. Judith Ellis (Melbourne: D.W. Thorpe, 1993).

[26] Interestingly Bruce Dearstyne observes of Holmes' five levels of description that "modern archives are inclined to add a sixth level, usually below the subgroup, of 'information system.' The term [is] primarily associated with electronic records and databases." Bruce W. Dearstyne, *The Archival Enterprise: Modern Archival Principles, Practices and Management Techniques* (Chicago: American Library Association, 1993), 132. Unfortunately, when I inquired, Dearstyne was unable to suggest any examples of a sixth level of description in theoretical papers or actual information systems.

[27] Terry Eastwood, *The Archival Fonds*.

[28] Terry Cook, "The Concept of the Archival Fonds: Theory, Description and Provenance in the Post-Custodial Era" in *The Archival Fonds: From Theory to Practice*, ed. Terry Eastwood (Ottawa: Bureau of

Canadian Archivists, Planning Committee on Descriptive Standards, 1992), 34-85.

[29] Angelika Menne-Haritz, "Introduction" in *Information Handling in Offices and Archives*, ed. Angelika Menne-Haritz (New York: K.G. Saur, 1993), 9-25.

[30] In this I believe Max Evans ("Authority Control: An Alternative to the Record Group Concept," *American Archivist* 49 (Summer 1986): 249-261) may be more at fault than Peter Scott from whom he borrowed (though he probably had not read the five-part series in *Archives and Manuscripts*, vols. 7-9, published between April 1979 and September 1981, in which the full explanation of Scott's position was laid out). Evans essentially proposed a mechanical data representation solution for linking series to organization, elaborating on Bearman and Lytle, while Scott's model had a place for recordkeeping systems even if he did not employ a formal methodology for describing them.

[31] The author has been engaged in an effort with the Metropolitan Toronto Archives to define an archival control system that incorporates both *RAD* and the representation of recordkeeping systems in order to enable the jurisdiction to utilize metadata created with records during their active life and integrate it into the records management and archival life cycle control process.

[32] In the future, architectures which utilize the "client-server" model of computing will use specialized applications running on servers which have the sole purpose of filing and retrieving data for other applications (running on "client" machines) which will process, analyze or disseminate it. When this concept is widely implemented it will become easier to define record system properties, but it will still be necessary to understand how applications were enabled to use the record system. Similarly when object-oriented systems come into general use, it will be easier to assure that data objects obey archival retention rules and access rules if archivists learn to articulate explicit requirements that can be translated into object-oriented methods and classes.

[33] Richard J. Cox, University of Pittsburgh, Electronic Records Management Study, "Research Prospectus: Variables in the Satisfaction of Archival Requirements for Electronic Records Management" (Pittsburgh, University of Pittsburgh, 1993), typescript. Available from Amy Winegarden, Electronic Records Project Secretary, School

of Library and Information Science, University of Pittsburgh, Pittsburgh PA 15260.

[34] See David Bearman, "Archival Principles and the Electronic Office," in *Information Handling in Offices and Archives*, ed. Angelika Menne-Haritz (New York: K.G. Saur, 1993), 177-193, reprinted in this volume as Chapter 5.

[35] David Bearman, University of Pittsburgh, Electronic Records Management Study, "Project Methodology Overview" (Pittsburgh, University of Pittsburgh, 1993), typescript. Available from Amy Winegarden, Electronic Records Project Secretary, School of Library and Information Science, University of Pittsburgh, Pittsburgh PA 15260.

[36] Archivists have generally resisted the use of the term archives in the form of an active verb "archiving." I am consciously adopting this terminology both because our customers use it, and we must communicate with them, and because the implication of these requirements is that they will be met through active involvement with systems at the level of policy, design, implementation, or standards and archiving is an active verb.

[37] "Functional Requirements for Recordkeeping Systems," David Bearman, Version 1.0, 23 May 1993, reprinted in this volume as Appendix B. This draft was prepared following the meeting of an experts advisory panel on 20-21 May and incorporates their recommendations. It was widely circulated for professional critique during the summer of 1993.

[38] National Institute of Standards and Technology (NIST), *Application Portability Profile (APP): The U.S. Government's Open Systems Environment Profile*, OSE/1 Version 1.0, NIST Special Publication 500-187 (Washington, D.C.: NIST, 1991).

[39] Richard Barry, "Electronic document and records management systems: towards a methodology for requirements definition," typescript draft of a paper for OIS93 examines the concept of a record from the point of view of the document. This reveals that a document may participate in numerous transactions during a life-cycle which is not a linear sequence but a peripatetic path. Representing these states of the document requires state-transition diagramming. While ultimately this is equivalent to the result of viewing records from the point of view of transactions, the author believes the latter is significantly less complex to model and implement.

[40] The author has recently published a series of writings on the possibility of new program structures and organizational models for electronic records programs. See David Bearman, "New Models for Management of Electronic Records by Archives," *Cadernos de Biblioteconomia, Arquivística, e Documentação* 2 (1992): 61-70, reprinted in this volume as Chapter 10; "An Indefensible Bastion: Archives as a Repository in the Electronic Age," in *Archival Management of Electronic Records*, ed. David Bearman, Archives and Museum Informatics Technical Report #13 (Pittsburgh: Archives and Museum Informatics, 1991); and the introductory essay in David Bearman and Margaret Hedstrom, *Program Strategies for Electronic Records*, Archives and Museum Informatics Technical Report #18 (Pittsburgh: Archives and Museum Informatics, 1993).

[41] David Bearman, "Archival Data Management to Achieve Organizational Accountability for Electronic Records," *Archives and Manuscripts* 21 (May 1993): 14-28, reprinted in this volume as Chapter 1.

SECTION II

Policy Guidelines

❖

CHAPTER THREE

Electronic Records Guidelines:
A Manual for Policy Development
and Implementation

❖

CHAPTER FOUR

The Implications of
Armstrong v. *the Executive Office of the President*
for the Archival Management
of Electronic Records

CHAPTER THREE

Electronic Records Guidelines: A Manual for Policy Development and Implementation[*]

Policies for management of electronic records must be tailored to management requirements of each organization and must define electronic records in a way that can be implemented by people and machines. Record retention decisions are risk management decisions. Immediate responsibility for appropriate retention and ongoing accessibility of electronic records must be clearly assigned to line management. Information managers -- including archivists, records managers, telecommunications and data processing staffs -- all need to contribute through systems design and implementation, technology assessment, and ongoing technology monitoring. A sound program will be based on a systems life-cycle approach that logically integrates records without respect to media. Information Resource Directory Systems can help bridge disciplines and organization units. Line units should retain physical control over electronic records and should be required to ensure retention, preservation of functionality, security, and confidentiality. These policy objectives can be achieved by focusing on application systems as the loci of records policy implementation and practicing documentation as a means of control. Increased awareness of technical obstacles to adequate management of electronic records must be achieved throughout the organization.

[*] Originally published in slightly longer form as Sections A, B, and C of Chapter II in Advisory Committee for the Co-ordination of Information Systems, *Management of Electronic Records: Issues and Guidelines* (New York: United Nations, 1990): 17-34.

INTRODUCTION

Managing large, complex organizations and ensuring that they are accountable for their actions requires that administrators have access to records documenting official activity. Increasingly, a substantial proportion of these records are created, maintained, and disseminated by electronic information systems.[1] Naturally, administrators want to ensure the same level of access to records in electronic form that they have historically had to paper records.

Electronic information systems have made the complex, modern international organization possible.[2] Beginning with the introduction of telegraphy in the middle and telephony at the end of the nineteenth century, these technologies have transformed the office by defining the means by which decisions are made and communicated. Since approximately 1960, the computer has been introduced into organizational activity with similar revolutionary effect. The wide variety of silicon chips are driving this computing and telecommunications technology into all recesses of contemporary office functions.

The automation of human activity, especially those activities defined by or dependent upon recording, retrieving and communicating information, is everywhere driven by the rising cost of relying upon people and the falling cost of electronic information systems. Even in parts of the world where the reduction of manpower is not a requirement, the introduction of computerized information systems is accelerating and is likely to extend automation into organizational programs that have previously been impervious to it because of their complexity and sophistication. Substantial investments will continue to be made in information systems to support all aspects of operations and program administration. Archivists and records managers must, therefore, accept the inevitability of these operational decisions. At the same time they must learn to shape them through policy, because although ongoing operations may well be managed less expensively and more efficiently with electronic information systems, the costs of archival and records management of machine-readable data will be much greater than those associated with traditional records.[3]

Reliance upon electronic information systems is not without substantial risk. Computer and telecommunications technologies are created and sold in a highly competitive marketplace into which new products and services are being introduced regularly and from which older products and services are being displaced. Competition has increased the importance of standards to users, but managers who are trying to establish policies for information resources management are still faced with markets they cannot control, or predict with any reasonable degree of certainty.[4] As a consequence, managing information created in electronic systems after the active life of those systems will continue to require careful planning, prescient technology assessment, and ongoing data manipulation.

New functional capabilities are being added to information systems on a regular basis as the costs of memory plunges. New capabilities can be added without driving up costs of the whole system. Each generation of new capabilities is seen as a minimum foundation requirement by users, who demand systems with these powerful features. Hardware is becoming obsolete after no more than five years; some feel that software obsolescence takes only three or even fewer years. Migration from one system to another is becoming a full-time activity for data processing and telecommunications units. The most serious challenge to continuing access is, and will continue to be, technological obsolescence.

Changes to storage formats and layouts employed in electronic information systems pose more severe challenges to continued access than does the (admittedly short) life of the still dominant magnetic media. Since the earliest introduction of magnetic tape storage as a medium for digital data, dozens of incompatible formats have been developed and discarded. The most ubiquitous medium of the 1960s, punched cards, has virtually disappeared, along with the de facto 8-inch PC floppy disk standard of the late-1970s. Increasing density of magnetic storage, the absence of standard layouts or structures for most optical media and the tyranny of the consumer market in areas of sound and image recording formats and media ensure that records managers will have to continue to incur costs of recopying electronic records once an organization adopts non-human readable forms of records as long as access to the records is desired. Unless methods can be found to provide the functions embodied in the original software-dependent systems to generic processing environments, records managers may also find themselves forced to maintain operating computing museums![5]

Even such "museum" environments could not replicate the systems of the past. As most astute managers now realize, computing has become an invisible glue in all systems of communication and control. Smart switches, remote and memory communications devices, and all forms of information collection equipment depend on instructions recorded in silicon chips. In the large interconnected telecommunications networks we rely on daily, messages are written from one buffer to another, "addresses" are decoded and read, and their instructions acted upon. One effect of the convergence of these technologies is that a very large part of the information created by any organization today exists, at least for any instant, in electronic form (as either analog or digitally encoded signals), even if it resides only in paper storage. Even very simple devices, like the electronic typewriter, have small buffer memories to store character correction information from one carriage return to the next; facsimile transmitters which we are coming to employ even for internal communications, have substantially larger buffers to store the bit-mapped image of a page.

Because change is one of the few constants in the equation that management faces as it seeks a means of controlling the effects of electronic technologies, any approach to managing electronic information will need to be sufficiently flexible to accommodate substantial change. No viable approach can be based on rejecting change, even if it does require that the social consequences of some technologies be channelled. Nor can a management approach itself be just another technology. Finally, the method must make sense within the overall mandate and mission objectives of the organization. Thus, by definition, a strategy for this kind of control will be based in policy, not in expedient or technological solutions.

POLICY ISSUES

Criteria for Policies

Guidelines for policy must meet a number of tests. They should be generalizable to the range of agencies and problems being addressed. They should pose clear alternatives with sufficient basis to support judgment. And they should be implementable, flexible, and cost-effective.

The test of any policy is whether it can be put into day-to-day practice or operationalized in the organization. Therefore, this chapter does not propose approaches that depend on waiting for some not yet realizable technological means, though numerous promising technologies are mentioned. It also discards solutions that depend on people to have knowledge, sophistication, and analytical skills that they are unlikely to possess. The recommendations made relate to the process of policy formulation and do not depend on any particular organizational structure. Proposed solutions are likewise as free of implications for internal organizational arrangements as possible and should be read as speaking about business functions not about specific units assigned responsibility for those functions.

Policies should derive from goals. These guidelines acknowledge the legitimacy of a wide range of possible ends, and therefore they address policy issues from the broad principles which inform them and identify options so that management can define policies and procedures to meet its objectives. They do not, therefore, require any particular policy choices, though some specific tactics for implementing policies are recommended.

Defining Records and Non-Records

ISSUE: Policy must define the concepts of record and non-record electronic information in a way that can be implemented by people and systems.

Electronic information consists of pulses or signals representing text, data, image, or sound. Electronic information may be transmitted and stored in digital (discontinuous) or analog (continuous) signals. Whether digitally encoded or represented by analog signals, these modalities (text, sound, and image) are indistinguishable except to software and hardware constructed to decode them for the human senses. Electronic information may exist only for an instant as it passes across a switch during transmission, or it may be recorded on relatively permanent magnetic or optical storage media. It may be disseminated in finished products such as Compact Disc Read Only Memories (CD-ROMs), floppy diskettes, or videodiscs, or accessed by users from a remote source using telecommunications. The products themselves may be finished and edited, such as an electronic journal or a television broadcast; volatile, like document drafts and online databases; or continuous, as are those generated by sensing and monitoring equipment or videotape.

Policy must distinguish between record and "non-record" information. The purpose of such a policy is to ensure that anything which might be important to retain will not be destroyed, while permitting the greatest quantity of information of no value for continued retention to be declared non-record.

One such broad definition holds that information sent or received in the conduct of an official activity is considered a record. By this definition, to be used in the conduct of an official activity, information must be communicated to a person or database as part of such an activity. Information which remains in the head, the home, or the pocket of one individual and is not available to any other is not considered an institutional record. By extension, information that remains in the personal computer of one employee, but is not communicated to another or others, is not a record.

Another common definition holds that information created in the course of official business is a record. By this definition, information received from outside an organization would not be a record but that created on the job but not communicated to others would constitute a record.

When program managers ask for policy guidance to define an electronic record, they are seeking to distinguish between information in electronic form that is official documentation of organizational activity and electronic information which is non-record material by virtue of being transient, personal, or external to the organization. Management needs to articulate policy criteria that can be operationalized and which are sufficiently clear cut for staff (and information systems) to implement them easily. These criteria should apply equally to documents and to data.

Assigning Responsibility

ISSUE: Policy must identify which organizational entities should have what specific responsibilities for management of electronic records.

Electronic information has largely escaped records management control despite the fact that it can, in principle, be documented. The proximate cause is the absence of organizational policy directed at capturing electronic records, but this is only a reflection of more complex physiological, organizational, and sociological barriers.

Electronic information has no meaning to the human senses without first being transformed by a technological intermediary into a modality which is humanly sensible. Whether electronic information exists in digital encoding or as analog signal, it must be translated to be readable/viewable, hearable, or touchable. Because it exists without our knowing it directly or being able to extract its meaning without an intermediary device, the designers of an electronic information system are held responsible for the kinds of records it creates. Also, because electronic records are at some point managed by an electronic information system, and because they are inseparable from that system except by means of facilities integral to the system itself, records managers must be involved in the design of those systems to ensure that records passing through them serve organizational needs for accountability. Records managers and archivists must therefore develop close working relationships with, and play part of the role of, systems designers.

Historically, electronic records have been transmitted through systems which generated hard-copy products. Because records were by-products of the communications process, the transmission system of the information was ignored by records managers and archivists because its only function was to accurately represent its contents at a distance. This was reasonable because even though they held information in electronic form for a time in buffers prior to batch dispatch or after receipt, transmission systems did not process it. Now, however, many of these same systems are capable of altering and analyzing information; digital copying machines do not necessarily produce "replicas"; facsimile transmitters may enhance the images they scan; computers may "read" incoming telecommunications to forward or even answer them; and database management systems automatically index, update, back-up and even delete records based on the contents of the record or the total state of the database.[6] These trends to ever more intelligent transmission networks are accelerating. As a result, records managers and archivists need to cultivate close relations with telecommunications systems managers.

In electronic information systems, where records are "views" of a larger data pool -- defined by permissions granted by the system -- and functions of the system are likewise restricted to those with permission, defining a record system has direct programmatic consequences. The involvement of archivists and records managers in design decisions concerning the structure and content of electronic information within an organization -- including responsibility for the means of accessing information in these systems and the format and medium of information storage -- presents an organizational challenge. Program staff must understand that records managers and archivists can exercise this responsibility without being involved in defining the values of data in the system or the processing functions the system provides to users other than the records management staff. Records managers and archivists must be involved with program managers in their roles as records system designers.

Information resources managers and data processing and telecommunications systems staffs must not feel that archivists and records managers are challenging their authority over the operation of the system or its integration with other electronic systems. All other participants in the design process must feel that records managers and archivists are bringing useful skills and institutional policy objectives to the table. These conditions will not be met unless management clearly defines the roles of each group and establishes the areas of shared responsibilities.

Adjusting to Cultural Change

ISSUE: Policy must accommodate shifting behaviors and attitudes, as well as changing technologies.

The social and cultural impacts of electronic communications are not yet fully apparent. Electronic information management technologies are undergoing rapid change. Somehow policies must be tied to continuities that can be relied upon to remain relatively fixed or employees will not be able to execute the policies without continual re-education.

For example, there are substantial sociological barriers to capturing electronic mail communications. Like other forms of interpersonal communications at a distance, electronic inter-course follows complex social rules. Telephonic communication is considered private and is not captured verbatim even when the subject of the conversation is a public policy matter; individuals in modern societies universally regard recording of telephonic communications as a breach of privacy equivalent to recording interpersonal face-to-face conversations. Some written forms of electronic communication, such as intra-office uses of electronic mail, are currently undergoing cultural definition and could come to be perceived as private in the absence of institutionally defined etiquettes and records policies. Indeed, because electronic communications are technically easy to capture at the point at which they pass across a communications switch, the issue at the heart of electronic records management is policy with respect to the *capture* of electronic records and the mechanisms by which these policies will be enforced.

Similarly, new electronic information technologies are introduced daily. If the policies we adopt are specific to particular technologies, they will become obsolete rapidly and will leave confusion in their wake. Managers must tie their policies to characteristics that lie beneath the implementation of the information system, characteristics that define the function the technology plays for the organization. In this way the policy will be tied to a business purpose and not to a transient implementation, and employees will be able to see the rationale and carry it out across technologies and time.

Assuring Legality

ISSUE: Policy must require taking actions that will safeguard the legality of the electronic record.

Records are being created in electronic form. Are they legal evidence? Would the format in which they are retained contribute to or diminish their legal value? Would any methods of managing these records during their active and archival life threaten or enhance their legal status? These questions arise because even though electronic records are generated by operational organizational information systems and are used in the conduct of organizational business, they are perceived to be less real, more ephemeral, than hard copy. There is very little statutory or case law anywhere in the world that clearly defines their status.[7]

However, despite the lack of precedent for the introduction of electronic records as legal evidence (except for analog audio-visual recordings), there are prima facie reasons to accept such records under the same terms as other formats of evidence, subject to authentication.[8] The problem presented by the caveat "subject to authentication" is familiar to those involved in the admissibility of microforms where admissibility has come to depend upon the record being generated in the normal course of business.[9] The basis for these rulings, which is likely to find expression with respect to electronic records as well, is that if the normal procedures are followed, the likelihood of planting disinformation on an ongoing basis for some yet-to-be discerned future purpose is low.

Because there is no "original" record in electronic information systems (it is impossible to distinguish physically between the "real" record and a modified electronic copy), policy will have to dictate designing systems for electronic records that can be shown to be secure from tampering and maintain audit trails for authentication, rather than relying upon physical inspection of outputs. The legality of electronic records will depend on evidence that creating records electronically was normal operating procedure and that appropriate care was exercised during the life of the record to ensure continuity and inviolability of the records system.

Scheduling

ISSUE: Policy must ensure timely disposition of records (retention of records for only as long as required by law, organization objectives, and scholarly needs).

Traditionally, records managers and archivists have established "schedules" calling for the retention of inactive records for stated periods, after which disposal or transfer to archival custody is authorized. Such schedules can be implemented because records in the same "series" share the retention periods and are filed together. Thus physical location supports the physical disposition. Equally importantly, the scheduling of records can take place after the records are created through visual examination and evaluation of their significance.

Because active storage space (online memory) is expensive, electronic records are less likely to be waiting for records management review and scheduling if they are not scheduled at their creation. At the same time, because electronic records can be conveniently acted upon under the control of the software that created them -- as a "set" without physically bringing them together -- if they can be scheduled at creation, it will be simple to carry out the proper disposition at the right time.

Therefore, policy must establish, and systems must implement, means of scheduling electronic records at (or even before) their creation.

Appraising

ISSUE: Policy must dictate criteria or bases for retention that will yield acceptable results for electronic records and yet be consistent with criteria (if not the results of applying them) for eye-readable records.

Policy needs to address whether there should be a difference between what was kept in paper form and what is retained electronically. Arguments have been made that because electronic information can be easily manipulated and analyzed, disaggregated information should be kept electronically that would have been discarded in paper formats.[10] Arguments have also been made that the nature of the costs of electronic retention should force us to reconsider whether we have been retaining too much information in the past because the costs of retention in paper formats are less apparent. Who should bear the costs of accessing data in electronic form in the future?[11]

Integrating Access

ISSUE: Policy must require actions that will prevent the format of records from being a serious barrier to access.

Organizational operational requirements insist that electronic and hard copy records must be integrated, physically or intellectually. While it is possible to transform paper records into electronic information by scanning (and may be possible to transform some paper records into full-text searchable electronic information by subsequent Optical Character Recognition or OCR) and it is possible to transform electronic information to hard copy (paper or microform), neither practice can be recommended without reservation at this time, for both economic and technological reasons. Conversion of all paper records to digital-coded form is not cost-effective at prices which in the U.S. today are over $1 per page. Conversion to digital bit-maps forces us to decide on acceptable resolutions at a time when image quality compromises are still economically and technologically necessary. At the same time, most electronic data is much more usable as electronic information than it would be in paper, so conversion from electronic to paper formats is also generally inadvisable.[12] Two interim solutions seem viable:

(1) Paper records can be bit-mapped when called for and be transmitted to users in this form with the electronic copy either being discarded or held for future reference. This adds no effort to the reference process, delivers the user an electronic (but not text-searchable) copy, and can select for storage only the 5% or so of documents that are likely to be reused.

(2) Electronic records can be output to Computer-Output-Microfilm (COM), and then input back into electronic systems by Computer-Input-Microfilm (CIM) which includes Optical Character Recognition (OCR) when needed and when elec-

tronic manipulation of ASCII is valuable.[13] The electronic file can then be discarded.

In any event, as long as we have mixed systems of paper and electronic records, records managers and archivists -- together with information managers and program offices -- need to find means of integrating hard copy and electronic records from different systems within the same organization. As long as physical integration is inadvisable, intellectual approaches must be developed that can make the linkage. This has implications both for the control of electronic information and for the description and control of conventional records. Attributes of hard copy that are difficult and expensive to capture in manual systems, such as item-level data about date, place of origin, author, and natural language content indexing, are trivial problems for electronic records archives. Attributes of hard copy that are easier to capture -- such as provenance, organization and arrangement, and record type or form-of-material -- are often difficult to document, or even meaningless in electronic information systems. Policy must guide managers to use the needs of future users as criteria in providing integrated intellectual access to mixed systems as long as integrated physical and intellectual access is impractical.

Documenting

ISSUE: Policy must prescribe intellectual control and documentation standards for electronic records.

Consistent methods of describing records from their creation to their destruction will save energy and improve access. Because records are under control of different offices and professions during their lifetime, policy must dictate what standards should be followed. The methods traditionally employed by archivists and records managers to describe records systems are not much different in intent from those used by data administrators and data processing configuration management, but they produce a result that is considerably less usable than that of a fully implemented information resources directory system. Approaches to filing in program offices meet some, but not all, of the requirements for future access by others. Policy should take into account national and international standards for the collection-level description of archival materials that have been developed over the past few years and consider the organizational requirements for data element and report-level information. At the same time, policy must encourage records managers and archivists to explore the possibilities of employing automatic document marking based on figural aspects of documents, self-documenting systems, artificial intelligence, and other means of substituting machine documentation for human description.

Storing

ISSUE: Policy must state who should have physical custody of archival electronic records.

Records managers have traditionally transferred records to archives long after the records become inactive. Unlike hard copy records which are essentially unaffected by sitting dormant (as long as they are stored under constant environmental conditions that are reasonably easy to achieve), electronic records require much more attention for three reasons: the media on which they are stored is less stable; the format of the medium is subject to rapid obsolescence; and the information itself is under control of software that is usually short-lived and owned by an organization other than the licensee.

Records centers and archives were established for the physical control of hard copy records because it is more cost-effective to store such materials centrally and in low cost facilities than to have them in office environments. Efficient retrieval argues against decentralization. Similar cost/benefit analysis for electronic records and archives suggests that they should remain in, or be transferred to, the physical custody of information systems departments which already maintain the equipment required for their continuing management and must in any case migrate active records systems across new technologies and configurations. If these implications are accepted, the responsibilities of records managers and archivists will shift from physical custody to administrative and intellectual control.

Because this represents a fundamental redefinition of the operational role of records managers and archivists, it is worth examining how we are forced to make this fundamental tactical choice not to physically transfer archival electronic records from the offices that maintain the active systems to an archive. First, we confront the fact that if the records were to be transferred, they would need to be copied on an ongoing basis out of record systems appraised for archival retention or acquired when those systems became obsolete. In the first case, accessioning scheduled records as they are created has significant implications for the role of archives and records centers as offline storage to active systems, because, unless means are found to keep software-independent data which retains the necessary evidential values (and at present such means are lacking),[14] the archives would have to possess the capability of migrating data and systems to subsequent generations of software. In the second case, the archives would need to be in a position to provide equivalent functional capabilities to those of the active records system and import data from those obsolete systems to such an environment. In either case, such complete systems redundancy would be an unjustifiably costly proposition.

As a result, policy needs to consider decentralized electronic records storage, with responsibility for regular migration of systems being assigned to the department that maintains active information systems. The burden of continuously migrating archival information systems will then become part of the requirement to upgrade active information systems, which is a necessary business expense for which the expertise and technologies will be provided. Archives will not run the risk of having records "left behind" by several generations of technology changes.

Preserving Media

ISSUE: Policy must establish standards for care and storage of electronic records and address the basis upon which storage media decisions are to be made.

When electronic information systems were only data transmission facilities -- such as the telegraph -- that did not alter or process the information they transmitted, records managers and archivists treated their hard copy output (if any) as records. Responsibility for turning printed records over to archives could be successfully assigned to those who created the records. In theory, all text and data in electronic form could be printed out and scheduled in its printed form. In practice, all the reasons why electronic data processing systems came to replace paper-based systems prevent us from simply printing out their contents: the volume of paper would be preposterous, the information would not be organized in all the ways that users wished to access it, the processes executed by the system would each have to be captured as well, etc. Yet the information is at great risk in electronic form because of the fragility of the medium on which it is recorded, the rapid obsolescence of the technologies it depends upon to be read, and the connection between the information content and the way the system in which it was implemented delivered that content.

Data archivists have developed standards of storage and procedures for "exercising" magnetic tapes to ensure that electronic records will be readable if stored without activity for a considerable time. Standards for handling other media are being developed by testing and standards bureaus. Data archivists, along with information systems administrators, pay careful attention to migration of media to ensure that information being kept in an organization can be read by devices maintained by its data processing facility. In this respect it should be noted that traditional archivists have often retained electronic media -- such as sound recording cylinders or reel-to-reel magnetic sound recordings -- that they do not have the facilities to "read" and should reconsider such practices.

Probably the most pressing issue involving transfer from active records systems is not addressed by media preservation standards or media migration procedures because it has no analogy in conventional records. Electronic records must be retired from active systems by the system itself, under software control. They can only be communicated elsewhere through the telecommunications facilities (software and hardware) of the system in which they are operating. The hardware environment in which they run will determine the media upon which they can be recorded. The hardware and software environment of the archival facility will determine what data layout formats can be supported.

Preserving Functionality

ISSUE: Policy must define to what extent original functionality is to be replicated or documented when migration of data and systems is necessary to ensure continuing access .

Regardless of who houses electronic archives, the burden of justifying a budget for archival retention of electronic records will fall on archivists and records managers. These costs, already considerable, are likely to increase despite the rapid decline in the costs of information system hardware. The source of these costs will be the need to continuously migrate records across media and records systems to ensure that they can be used in a constantly changing technological environment. Because archives cannot afford to become museums of obsolescent hardware or software, they will need to move the data to newer devices. Because the evidential value of information resides in the way it was used in the organization, not in its information content alone, archivists will be forced to re-create software capabilities as well. When archivists can rely upon standard media, standard operating systems, standard methods of recording data in storage devices, and standards at every other level of the Open System Interconnection Reference Model, systems migration-related expenses will be substantially less. At present they cannot, and the continuing migration of records and systems will be expensive. Archival management of electronic records promises to be an increasing programmatic investment even if the costs of all other aspects of information management continue to decline. This forces records managers and archivists to make the case for an institutional requirement for electronic records management or face a diminishing capability to cope with a growing challenge.

Ensuring Security

ISSUE: Policy must ensure the security of electronic information and preserve the rights of individuals and the confidentiality required of the organization.

The security of electronic information systems is a serious concern to management for a number of reasons that are not applicable to paper records. Like paper records, one must secure against unauthorized viewing of information of a confidential nature, but in electronic systems the opportunities to alter data without leaving a trail and to make massive deletions of information with little effort mandate a higher profile for security concerns. In addition to security concerns driven by the opportunity for mischief and criminality, management needs to be aware of security concerns of the normal operating environment in which data can be easily lost through accident, non-specific acts of sabotage such as computer viruses, and acts of nature. In addition, the very nature of the integrated information system raises the issues of permission management that only infrequently accompany paper records that are normally stored in distinct areas for different purposes.

Providing for Use

ISSUE: Policy must dictate how the organization and others entitled to access will be enabled to use electronic records.

Traditionally, archives have been accessible only to those authorized and willing to go to them. Search methods have emphasized recall over precision, requiring users to read through volumes to obtain information pertinent to a query. Electronic records -- selected with considerable precision -- can be sent to users in whole, or in part for those who lack authority to see the whole. Archival electronic record systems can be made to maintain interest profiles and alert users to the acquisition of new electronic records of potential interest. Knowledge of electronic records can be integrated into active work environments so as to retrieve relevant archival documents automatically. Electronic records could be automatically translated into other languages, be spoken or reproduced in braille by machines for the blind, or be combined so that appropriate texts, sounds and images are delivered in response to queries from program officers or school children, whether in the next office or a remote area of the world. One of the most significant policy challenges of electronic records will not be to plan for their acquisition and maintenance, but to adjust to the potential of their use. If electronic records are to be preserved (and that preservation demands their early identification, appraisal and transfer), then archives and records must be integrated into the active, operational information system.

Electronic records are most useful in electronic form and in the software environment in which they were created. Many questions cannot be answered unless both these requirements are met. Therefore, archives should provide users access to records systems, not simply deliver records. If the records systems have been lost or discarded and the data is in software-independent format, it will be most useful to provide the data in a medium and format in which the user can manipulate it on a local system. These and other issues about the nature of reference services in electronic archives must be addressed as policy issues.[15]

Controlling Costs

> **ISSUE:** Policy must address how the organization will avoid unnecessary costs and target essential expenditures in the management of electronic records.

The unit costs of preserving electronic information are only somewhat higher than those for preserving information on paper, but the costs of identifying and subsequently culling appropriate records and the expenses involved in preserving their functional characteristics and thereby their evidential value are substantially greater. The potential costs of bad planning and failure to control electronic records throughout their system life-cycle are substantially higher than those involved in temporary loss of control over paper records. Management inattention in the sphere of electronic records will prove extremely costly and is likely to result in complete loss of significant documentation. On the other hand, careful technology forecasts and adherence to standards can be combined with internal vigilance and good systems design procedures to limit costs and target expenditures in areas that will generate the best possible return.

RECORDS MANAGEMENT FRAMEWORKS

Goals: Organizational Accountability

Records and archives management are housekeeping functions of an organization. The necessity for them reflects the very basic truth that organizations must keep certain records in order to account -- to themselves and to society -- for their actions. The job of records managers and archivists is to ensure that all the records necessary to document the actions of the organization -- but only those records -- are retained as long as they continue to have value.

By returning to the fundamental goal of accountability, we can find reason to adopt a particular definition of records and non-records that will serve better in the electronic world than that which has been used in paper-based systems. Traditionally records have been defined as information, usually in any format, created (and sometimes including received) by an organization and its employees in the conduct of business. This definition usually contained two clauses intended to capture the entire universe of information and one operational clause that distinguished records as part of that universe.

The first clause included all forms of information, either by using the phrase "in any format" or by enumerating and then providing a way out, such as "or any other medium." The second clause sought to incorporate information made (or received) anywhere and by anyone in any capacity, so as to ensure that business conducted from the home or on the road would create records. The definition itself revolves around the activities of the organization; it emphasizes that records flow from official actions and are evidence of such actions.[16] The United Nations, for instance, defines records as "documentary materials, regardless of physical type, received or originated by the United Nations, or by Members of its staff . . .." The U.S. federal government definition of a record as an "item that documents the actions of an agency in the conduct of its business," is broader but may be less useful to the average employee.[17]

One problem with these definitions is that they depend in the first instance on our being able to see the items at hand and recognize how they came about and what official import they had. In practice, records managers and archivists are not in a position to see electronic records as they are created and transmitted because the documents themselves exist only under software control. Determining the source and function of an item an item or document, even when we do have the data of which it is comprised, is impossible except within the context of the system out of which it arose.

In fact, content-based definitions have proved impractical with paper records as well, so records managers and archivists have adopted a more operational definition that serves equally well: records are recorded transactions. Recorded transactions are information communicated to other people in the course of business via a store of information available to them. While this definition is more explicit than the one archivists have traditionally used with paper records, it is consistent with the concept that a record is created by an official action of receiving or sending information. Both paper-based records management and electronic records management must distinguish between the hour-to-hour or day-to-day changes in a draft of an official document and records sent or received by the organization. In both situations making an entry in a bookkeeping journal, a case file, a database, or even a "memo to the file" is creating a record even though the information is not "sent," because others are intended to receive this communication at a later date. Each system must distinguish official from purely private information; thus jotting a note about an expenditure or change of address on a loose slip of paper or in an electronic memo pad to remind ourselves to make such an entry at a later time is not a record-transaction, and, hence, not a record.

Throughout this chapter, recorded transactions, called record-transactions, will be taken as a basic building block of an electronic records management policy. Applying the definition of record-transactions in electronic information systems environments will often prove more complicated than it has been for paper-based contexts because we cannot see electronic data, because it is stored randomly, and because electronic systems were installed precisely because of the ease of updating and recalculating within them.

Strategies: Applications Systems

Archivists and records managers confront vast quantities of records created in their organizations. For practical reasons alone they must usually manage these records in some aggregate manner or be overwhelmed by their volume. But there are also sound intellectual reasons for managing records collectively which relate to the nature of organized work and the structures of communications within organizations. Both work and communications are conducted by individuals, but they take place within well understood -- if not always well defined -- systems. Systems for work and communication lead to regularized, predictable, and accountable outcomes. The informational systems that support communication and work in an organization may be thought of as either infrastructural systems or application systems. Electronic information systems can also be categorized in this fashion.

Infrastructural electronic information systems have presented problems to records managers and archivists for 150 years, but these problems have only been recognized as belonging to a class of electronic information issues since the widespread introduction of the computer and associated microprocessors into office environments in the past decade. Telegraphy is the oldest infrastructural electronic information system, but the telegraphic record is delivered to the user as a printed output, even when the information it contains is first telephoned. As a result, records managers and archivists have been able to treat telegraphic traffic as a form of correspondence within conventional record systems rather than confronting the issues it raises as an electronic information system. About 100 years ago, the telephone system, another infrastructural electronic information system, introduced analog transmission of sound, but for historical and sociological reasons this form of electronic information has been (reluctantly?) accepted by records managers and archivists as non-record material. It is important to note, however, that for most of the past 100 years this form of electronic information could have been recorded on disk and tape recorders and could have been appraised by archivists and records managers along with other documentation. Infrastructural systems for transmission of images, employing telegraphy technologies, have been used heavily for newspaper photography and military purposes for almost 100 years. Thus infrastructures supporting electronic transmission of text, sound, and image are hardly new. Indeed, as radio, the telephone, and television illustrate, infrastructural electronic information generation and reception facilities are among the most conspicuous features of our current civilization.

Electronic information application systems are not very new either. Routine sensing and control devices, often using paper tape for data storage, were introduced fifty years ago for numerous applications, but because their information product was considered non-record material, many records managers and archivists simply ignored these devices. Since the introduction of mainframe computing in routine organizational information processing applications in the 1950s, records managers have been unable to ignore applications generating electronic information. In most large organizations, applications such as inventory, personnel, and accounting, are now automated. More recently, non-routine, decentralized, and programatically important aspects of organizational activity are being assisted by automation. The introduction of these systems, with their inherent ability to capture electronic information locally and retain it in an electronic form, is transforming contemporary organizations.

Organizational application systems are not the same thing as applications software. General capabilities such as word processing, spreadsheets, electronic mail, project management, and statistical analysis are often referred to as applications software, but in the context of an organization these facilities are infrastructural tools, not applications. The existence of word processing and an electronic mail utility within an organization no more defines the kinds of records that will be created and sent than does the installation of typewriters and postal meters. Organizational applications of electronic mail may include its use for the dissemination of directives, policies, and procedures and its use for making personal lunch dates. Word processing can be used to keep private notes of meetings or to write organizational reports. Spreadsheets reflecting departmental or sub-unit budgets kept by line managers for day-to-day control purposes do not substitute for the accounting system. However, spreadsheets developed for the purposes of submitting proposals or rescheduling debt for the organization may be of long-term value for accountability and of historical interest. Records management policies have always taken the organizational application system as their focus and will need to continue to do so in the electronic information systems environment.

A basic tenet of the remainder of this chapter is that the object of records management and archival control is organizational applications systems, the nature of activity in the organization that remains the focus of records management attention. In the electronic environment, it is often easy to lose sight of this critical focus both because of the terminological confusion arising from the concept of a software application and because the tactics for implementing records management control are necessarily dependent on exploiting aspects of the way infrastructural systems work.

Tactics: Systems Management

The primary conceptual framework of paper records management and archives is the life cycle of records. Paper records were obviously created, filed and sent, consulted, annotated and refiled, scheduled, and removed from active files according to schedule, disposed of by destruction or retention in an archives or records facility, maintained by that facility, described and accessed. Each stage in the life cycle of the records was marked by an activity in which people with different job responsibilities participated, and each resulted in a new status for the records which was evident from physical examination.

At first it seems that the concept of the life cycle of records must be discarded in the electronic environment. The record itself has lost physicality, in being stripped of the corporeal manifestation of a record. Records managers and archivists have also lost their most fixed bearing. In place of a simple progression from creation to destruction, the electronic record partakes in a multitude of independent acts of information acquisition, manipulation, and production, each of which creates new records for some user, potentially without changing the original or generating any (retained) copy. None of the familiar life cycle landmarks is unaltered by the advent of electronic records, and many stages appear to have conflated. For example, the creation of a document using word processing, whether or not it is a record, involves copying it from RAM and filing it on a disk. It may also involve sending it to a printer or a remote disk. Thus the steps of creating, filing, and sending a document are collapsed into one. Consulting a document (and even refiling it after use) does not necessarily involve moving it, but it does involve making a temporary copy in RAM; copies can also be made and filed elsewhere without the document moving. Annotations to the document, and updates, are both actually made in a separate physical place from the rest of the document; "deletion" does not actually erase the text that is deleted, but only changes the links between segments of the text. Disposition is likely to involve a change of status, not place, and description and access is largely determined prior to the creation of the record by the design of the system in which it was created.

Indeed, as we examine the electronic records landscape, it becomes increasingly evident that the life cycle of the records (application) system, not the record, must be the new focus of attention. And, on reflection, we can see that it was, or should have been, the focus of attention in paper systems as well, but the physicality of the individual paper item once again led us astray. In practice, making item-level disposition decisions for all records (e.g., deciding first whether any given item of documentation is a record and then whether it should be retained as evidence) has always been impractical. Organizations cannot have a 1:50, or 1:20, ratio of records managers and archivists to staff able to create records. Therefore, records managers and archivists have always relied upon user discretion and aggregate decisions in making retention and disposition decisions. They may decide, for example, to keep all the records filed in the policy files and the case files and discard client correspondence after five years. These decisions employ the intervening records system (in this case a file clerk) to aggregate records of common character and make retention decisions affordable. In some international organizations, especially in Europe, item-level control over records received and sent from an organization is exercised by a central registry or records and communications section.[18] Even with substantial manpower commitments, such offices do not provide item-level control over all internal memoranda and exchanges, the internal reports, project case files, financial transactions data, or information generated or used in internal decision making.

Instead, records managers and archivists have perfected means of collectively appraising all records generated by a specific application and then controlling records within applications at levels determined by the character of the application. In paper record environments, these methods involved defining segregated files (records series) for each discrete type of records generated by the application, establishing filing procedures to ensure that records were filed in the appropriate file and in a sequence required by the office of origin, and determining disposition for the entire series in a single appraisal, either before or after actual records were filed. Records managers and archivists have had much greater difficulty making bulk appraisals of record types generic to all activities such as the correspondence, memoranda, and internal draft distributions. In controlling such materials, they have relied most successfully on organizational source/destination of these documents to make determinations about whether and how they should be filed and upon where they are filed to make determinations concerning their retention. Thus, we must acknowledge that while records managers and archivists make appraisal decisions at the item-level as rarely as possible, and often only in the case of special categories of records, such as vital records, they are dependent on personnel of line offices (or in central registry offices) who make filing decisions and who decide what application any given information was part of, for the validity of appraisal decisions made at the series level.[19]

Electronic information systems present records managers and archivists trying to extend these tactics to electronic records with some significant challenges. The first is to sculpt the application software so that the user interface presents itself as a number of distinct organizational applications, rather than simply as a set of tools. For example, when the user saves a word processing document, the application provides a dialog screen that enables the user to assign it to the appropriate organizational file (which requires, of course, a word processing software application with the necessary escape to a programming language and a programmer to write the necessary organizational interface). Similar special interfaces would be constructed to subdivide generalized software applications that serve as organizational utilities such as electronic mail, spreadsheets, or statistical analysis packages.

The second challenge is to sculpt the record-transaction itself. This also will by necessity involve records managers and archivists in the design of the application system before their implementation. The objective of their involvement here is to harness software capabilities to generate (and segregate) records required for organizational accountability. Unlike the paper environment, electronic records may need to be "created" in order to be retained because many records that would have existed in manual systems contain substantially redundant information and would normally be "designed out" of automated applications. For example, electronic building permits and electronic certificates of occupancy would be defined in a modern database management system as "views" of a database, not as separate records. If the information in one was scheduled for archival retention and the other was considered a routine working document, an electronic information system would need to "create" the permanent record and discard the temporary record.

The focus on systems management as the primary strategy to effect records and archival control rather can be seen throughout this chapter. For example, in discussing the problems of legality of electronic documents, the emphasis of tactics is on the authenticity of the record which can only be ensured through management of the system continuity and internal procedures, much as it has been with microform. In the discussion of preservation and storage concerns, and the longevity of electronic media and formats, the emphasis is on the life of systems that will continue to provide access to data and on preservation of system functionality, rather than on the physical conservation of the medium, because in a world of rapid hardware and software obsolescence, a perfectly preserved disk can contain data which cannot be read by existing equipment. In the discussion of integration of hybrid systems, it is acknowledged that mixed paper and electronic systems are not an anomaly of our historic moment, but a reflection of the fact that today's technologies permit records created in both paper and electronic forms to be electronic in many systems at a number of points in their life cycle and hard copy at other stages. Thus all tactics for management of electronic records must, in the end, be tactics for systems management.

Objectives: Information Content and Context

Records managers and archivists seek to ensure the retention of information required for organizational operation and accountability. The information may be contained in documents and databases or it may be contained in the way those documents and databases were used. In this sense, records managers and archivists have always recognized the validity of Marshall McLuhan's famous dictum that "the medium is the message."

One way that records managers and archivists preserve the informational content of context is to establish files and filing procedures that reflect the communications systems of the organization by leaving a trail. In the paper-based organizational and technological context, a transaction is conveyed only to those offices which need to know its contents, and it can be assumed to become part of their activity by the fact of its transmittal. If stored within their files, it will be organized with respect to the role it played in their activity, so that correspondence will be organized in a chronological or subject file reflecting the needs of the office, and documents about individuals and events will be organized into case files. In such an organizational and technological milieu, the file is a records system that adequately reflects activity.

Preserving the context of use of records in an organization is more difficult if the records management system is centralized in a registry office, but the difficulty of tracking use is offset by the convenience of reduced redundancy. Indeed, since the advent of convenient means of copying documents, beginning with carbon paper, we have witnessed the demise of the recipient's incoming file as a non-redundant source of information, because the record creator could file the copies of one original document in a number of separate files. With the introduction of photocopying machines, numerous copies could be readily made after the creation of the original, making it possible for the recipient to generate additional copies for his files or those of others in the organization. Files soon became crowded with many items of marginal interest, sent "For Information." It was no longer possible to ascertain from the files whether items they contained had been seen by the recipient or used in an important decision process. The introduction of automation in the creation of documents added two more dimensions to the problem: now we no longer have an "original," so it is even less evident what "copies" might be discarded without loss of accountability or information content,[20] and, because we can view documents remotely without transferring them to our own files, the "copy" used in any given decision-making process need never have been physically "copied" to the recipient's file. The fact that machine-readable files lend themselves to ready manipulation and on-the-spot analysis, is, of course, one of the primary reasons that spreadsheets (and word processors) have taken over the office. It also means that important decisions can be made based on analysis of information from a variety of electronic files without altering the saved versions of those files or creating a saved version of the new manipulations.

Files have also become less useful as means of documenting accountability as decision making has shifted from the hierarchical organization, with its relatively permanent organizational units which create and file records, to the realm of ad hoc working groups and task forces and inter-organizational entities. These types of organizational constructs tend not to maintain offices or keep records of their own, but live instead on borrowed staff time and facilities. Their records, therefore, are usually dispersed through the organization, reflecting the roles played by individuals. As we come to rely more and more on decision making in group settings, the role played by visual aids (overhead transparencies and business graphics) and by what people say in those situations is critical to reconstructing how and why a decision was reached. The approach archivists have relied upon for the past hundred years assumes that decisions are made and promulgated through the kinds of textual documents in our files. The disjuncture between reality and the theory has been appreciated by others, but the technological facility for merging text, image, and sound in digital stores will dramatically affect our recordkeeping systems. We will need to consider the potential for the visual and oral message to be archival.

The coup de grace to traditional file-based rather than systems-based records management has been delivered by the database management system, which by definition manages information in more than one file. None of the files alone contains the information that might have been in a "record," because a record is defined by a function supported by the system that enables users to find information in a variety of files and view it in a variety of formats. Databases whose files are all physically on one device have been perplexing enough to records managers; now we need to develop strategies that will also work for databases and database management systems that span many physical devices, either because a networked architecture is employed (in which physically separate computers, strung together by a dedicated cable or bandwidth on a cable, act as a unit), or because a variety of devices interact according to strict information protocols using telecommunications.

In any database, individual "record segments," may change independently of each other, but in traditional systems one could in principle reconstruct the state of the database from a full transaction log. In distributed databases, which may employ different kinds of audit trail facilities and backup strategies, and fall administratively under different records management and archival jurisdictions, it is not reasonable to imagine reconstruction of the state of the database as a documentation tactic. The individual files, even with time stamped transactions, will not support reconstruction at a reasonable cost, and reconstruction would need also to reflect the software facilities and data access permissions and views available to any given user in order to provide evidence for purposes of accountability. If a record is the information used from a given source at a given time (a record-transaction), in a database environment it may only exist as that particular constellation of information for one user. At the price of substantial redundancy, record-transaction capture -- in which all information seen by an individual as part of an activity must be copied as it was viewed -- appears to be the only acceptable method of unobtrusive records retention.

Throughout this chapter the emphasis is on organizational accountability as the ultimate goal of records management and archives. As a result, the objective of documenting how information was used in an organization will be considered of equal importance to the objective of documenting the information content of organizational communications.

Methods: Documentation

Archives and records management are information management activities which carry out their functions by acquiring or creating documentation concerning records and record systems and acting upon the basis of that documentation to destroy or retain records and to provide access. The central premise is that the fundamental method of records management and archives is documentation. The specific methods of documentation that archivists and records managers have employed must, therefore, be understood if we are to develop viable approaches to the electronic information environment.

Unlike most other information service providers, records managers and archivists do not describe or classify items. Records managers almost never document holdings at the item level, except in registry offices which serve an active information retrieval function more than a life-cycle management role. Archivists reject classification as an approach to managing records at the document level because classification is linked in paper-based practices to physical reorganization of records and archivists feel strongly that the original order of records should be preserved as evidence of the way in which they were created and used. Archivists may occasionally prepare indexes to the records themselves or to finding aids.

Yet users have an interest in getting access to specific documents. The way that records managers and archivists traditionally provide for such access is to exploit the "original order," which is to say the filing order, of the records. Sometimes, if they are fortunate, archivists and records managers may be able to point users to a series of records that is itself an item-level index to another records series. In either case, item-level access to records is obtained by actions of the record creators (and the staff their offices).

In the electronic environment, archivists and records managers must depend even more upon the creators of records and records systems for documentation. While they have displayed some enthusiasm for full-text retrieval of electronic records, the primary method for identifying information in records systems retained for continuing value will be exploiting information created by others. Some of the tactics discussed in this chapter relate to, and depend on, capturing information about information systems in what data processing personnel call "metadata systems." Metadata systems document much more than the information content of records systems. They document the input and output products, the relations between files, the nature of software facilities, and the functions supported by the systems. Traditional records management and archival practice has also collected much of this information in building collective-level, contextual, records system descriptions (usually at the file level) to provide access by provenance. Approaches at the systems level, including system design data administration and configuration management, are necessary if records managers and archivists are to adequately document the informational environments of contemporary organizations. These approaches, using the tools of information resource management, will also enable archivists and records managers to provide information of value to their organizations, not just references to records that might be of value.

Throughout this chapter, systems documentation using the approaches of data administration and the tools embodied in metadata systems (called Information Resource Directory Systems or Data Dictionary/Data Directory Systems) is advanced as a primary tactic for control of information about records. The reason for this focus is found in the emphasis placed on applications as the focus, and systems management as the tactic, of records management and archives in an electronic environment.

Investments: Staff

Because the management of the records of an organization is an activity in which all staff are engaged, one of the central issues in implementing any policy is how the organization can mobilize its personnel and use their skills. Throughout this chapter, skills and knowledge essential to controlling electronic information are identified and described which are rarely found on present archives and records management staffs.[21] It is an essential conclusion, therefore, that records management is not the sole responsibility of the records management staff, and that the introduction of electronic records will demand a distribution of responsibilities (one which, in the view of the author, is long overdue in the paper records world as well).

In addition, the demands of electronic records will require that archivists and records managers acquire new skills and competencies. For instance, to present useful and credible systems requirements, the records managers and archivists sent to participate in the design process must be conversant with the capabilities and limitations of database management and telecommunications systems. They should be able to articulate logical designs and suggest physical implementations for them. Indeed, they should become partners with the systems development and systems implementation teams. This expertise could be acquired by substantially retraining present records managers and archivists, hiring new staff with these skills, or assigning staff with these skills who are presently attached to units responsible for systems development to archives and records management responsibilities. Because team work is essential to achieve the ends of records administration through systems management, the last option of bringing staff with different skills together in one administrative unit will probably prove the best means of combining the skills needed and can serve as a vehicle for a subsequent union of the responsibilities. In any event, major investments in staff training must accompany the introduction of electronic systems and some of this training should be directed at teaching staff throughout the organization about their responsibilities for management of electronic records. Some should also be targeted for retraining professional records managers and archivists to deal with the new environment as a long-term investment.

No amount of staff training, however, will substitute for the absence of a sense of responsibility for records on the part of line managers throughout the organization. In the paper record environment, line managers took a relaxed view of their responsibilities and were largely permitted to do so by the organization except when accountability was an essential element of their jobs, as in financial and personnel offices where data integrity, security, access, and retention were audited and were clearly recognized as professional and organizational obligations. In the electronic environment, the same passive disinterest will result in the organization losing its memory, which cannot be condoned. Management expectations will need to be dramatically altered so that line managers understand clearly that they are accountable for the record of actions taken by their units. Of course the organization will need to provide not only policies that are clear but also guidance in how to apply them and tools with which to implement the policies. Ultimately, however, the fate of electronic records will depend on the degree to which line managers perceive records management as their responsibility rather than the future responsibility of a records management and archives staff.

Promoting an Electronic Records Culture

While records managers and archivists can occasionally be heard wishing that the electronic information revolution bypassed their institutions, they need to recognize that many of its problems result from the immaturity of the implementations and the lack of experience of our culture in treating the new cultural forms that the technology is making possible. Attempting to stand in the path of implementation desired by program managers to improve their productivity is a futile position. Just as records managers failed in restricting distributions of documents by trying to control copying machines, they will fail in restricting access to automation if they attempt to limit the number and capability of computers, limit the iteration of document drafts, or establish corporately determined draft stages in the electronic mail process or centrally control topics for bulletin boards and teleconferences. Records managers and archivists who attempt to limit electronic mail to make it look like Telex, or to limit spreadsheets so definition of cells cannot be shared between offices, will, very simply, lose both the battle and the war. The option of standing firm is not even suggested here, because it is not a real option.

On the other hand, archivists and records managers can help to shape the electronic culture within their organizations. They can play a role in defining its explicit rules and implicit etiquette, and they can be perceived as promoters of cautious utilization of the best in information technology.[22] For example, by teaching users about the problems they might have as a consequence of lost records and lost access opportunities, records managers and archivists can help themselves.

Policy aimed at developing a management culture open to new technologies and yet sensitive to their risks, is a consistent theme of this chapter.

GUIDELINES FOR IMPLEMENTATION

A practical methodology for establishing an electronic records management program has four stages, each of which returns to policy refinement before going on to the next. The four stages are: (1) establishing goals and objectives of an electronic records management program; (2) defining the scope of the program; (3) identifying strategies and tactics to be employed; and (4) securing necessary staff support and other resources.[23]

Goals and Objectives

The first step of any policy development process is to define, as clearly as possible, the goals and objectives of the organization. Records managers and archivists may begin by searching through existing organization policy and mission statements -- as well as through any discussions that have led to the attempt to formulate an electronic records management policy -- for statements of purposes. They should convene an internal working group consisting of staff from data process- ing, telecommunications, and other information management areas to draft a preliminary statement of policy. The draft should address all the issues identified in the policy section of this chapter. By selecting sample electronic records systems, the working group can assess the adequacy of existing policies within the organization and establish a baseline against which to test their proposed policy recommendations. In the process, the working group can identify areas of organizational culture that may prove most resistant to various policies -- and thereby find ways of implementing the resultant policy that stand the greatest chance of succeeding.

If necessary for reasons of the corporate culture, the initial statement can be broad so as not to require redefinition. The ultimate policy statement, on the other hand, should be ex- plicit, written, and as detailed as possible and should try to set limits based on costs and benefits. As new issues arise in the formulation of policies, the statement of goals and objectives should be reviewed. If it does not adequately reflect the deci- sions being made as concrete policies, the objectives or the policies should be revised. Objectives will vary somewhat from one part of the organization to the next. They must take into account individual missions and resources.

Scope

The scope of an electronic records program has several aspects: the types of electronic information systems to be cov- ered, the organizational functions to be included, and the de- gree of authority to be vested. The best way to clarify these is- sues is for the policy working group to undertake an analysis of the existing and planned electronic information systems in the organization. The analysis should be informed by pro- curement records for equipment and supplies, records of telecommunications charges, and documentation from the information management function. In addition, it should include surveying the staff (in part to alert them to the policy review and in part to acquire information about the applications view of systems under the control of an individual or small group of individuals). With a profile of the present situation in hand, archivists and records managers should examine budgets, plans, and public statements of senior organization officials for evidence of future systems plans.

These profiles should be gathered together and recommendations should be forwarded concerning which systems ought to be included within the scope of the program (if not all) and what criteria should be employed. The scope statement should address the desired assignment of responsibilities for creation and identification, appraisal, control and use, and disposition to each system. Particular attention should be paid to whether additional resources will be required in the short term and over the next five years, and the purposes to which these resources would be put. External sources of information used by organization staff should be examined and determinations made whether to include them, and if so, in what way.

Strategies and Tactics

Once objectives and scope have been defined, management should review a number of strategic and tactical alternatives that might well lead to substantial revision of both. For example, if an objective is to ensure that archival records retention decisions reflect a ten-year cost-of-retention, then models will need to be developed that can be used to estimate these costs. If an objective is to provide access to electronic information through media or access methods requested by users, then it will be necessary to determine which media the function would be prepared to provide and what types of security would need to be established to permit access to duplicate databases as well as the cost implications of such a policy.

Of course, strategies will not be sufficient to enable staff to implement policy. Management needs to provide some guidance, in the form of administrative requirements, to shape action. This can be achieved if all statements of policies have clearly defined responsibilities and if a number of implementation methods are suggested as examples of the way organization staff might satisfy the policy.

In implementing the electronic records policies, the institution needs to be realistic about the degree to which it will be able to save data and documents from past and present electronic information systems. Only the most important of such systems should be evaluated unless adequate resources exist to appraise all such systems and to implement proactive tactics, including educational programs and system design involvement simultaneously.

Securing Support

The most important aspect of adopting a policy with respect to records management and archiving of electronic records is to ensure that the policy is understood throughout the organization. Records management and archives will need to act through records creators and managers of the computer and telecommunications infrastructures since they can no longer act as a line function due to the character of electronic information itself.

Dissemination of the policy is the first step in its implementation, but simply promulgating the rules will not lead to their successful implementation. Archivists and records managers will have to meet with staff throughout the organization to express their enthusiasm for electronic information systems, explain the problems these systems pose for organizational accountability, and help to develop a culture of electronic information comparable in effect to that in the paper world. This will include definition of types of documents, database access and use rules, and electronic information dissemination etiquette. It will be important in these sessions for both staff and management to understand that -- even if the records manager or archivist were in full control -- the implementation of electronic information systems is likely to so transform the "culture" of the office. It will be difficult to predict what records might exist and only ongoing dialog with users will determine what is valuable to keep.

The next step in implementing the policy will be working out concrete agreements with other information managers in the organization to ensure that they understand their roles in helping to identify and document, maintain, and provide access to electronic records.

Finally, it will be necessary to return to senior management with a plan that includes the costs and staffing implications of moving forward following the accepted strategies and tactics to achieve the articulated goals and objectives. It would be useful to have examples of existing information systems which satisfy the requirements of the electronic records management policy. These examples will demonstrate that it is possible for program office line management to take responsibility for electronic records and to implement adequate procedures to safeguard records. If no fully adequate examples exist from traditional applications environments -- such as financial or personnel systems -- the best approaches available should be used for illustration and their shortcomings identified. Senior management should be encouraged to praise the managers of these exemplary systems, if possible in public in conjunction with the introduction of the new policies.[24]

NOTES

[1] Committee on the Records of Government (sponsored by the American Council of Learned Societies, the Social Science Research Council and the Council on Library Resources), *Report* (Washington, D.C.: Council on Library Resources, 1985). Oklahoma State Archives, *Report to the Archives and Records Commission on Machine-Readable Computer Records in Electronic Format* (Norman: Oklahoma Department of Libraries, 1986) reports "a significant portion" of records are electronic.

[2] Alfred Chandler, *Strategy and Structure* (Cambridge: Massachusetts Institute of Technology Press, 1972).

[3] Paule Rene-Bazin, "New Archival Materials Principles: Creation and Acquisition," unpublished paper, 11th International Congress on Archives (Paris 1988).

[4] National Archives of Canada, *Data and Document Interchange Standards and the National Archives*, Project No.1-6465 (Ottawa, June 1987); Charles M. Dollar and Thomas E. Weir, Jr., "Archives Administration, Records Management and Computer Data Exchange Standards: an Intersection of Practice, unpublished draft, National Archives and Records Administration, 1988 (later published in Steven Spivak and Keith Winsell, eds., *A Sourcebook of Standards Information* (Boston: G.K. Hall, 1991): 191-211).

[5] Too many discussions of this issue still treat the problems of continued access to machine-readable information as a traditional medium/signal preservation issue, as does Feodor M. Vaganov, "Conservation of New Archival Materials," unpublished paper, second session, 11th International Congress on Archives, Paris 1988. Useful warnings are being issued by some, like Margaret Hedstrom, "Optical Disks: Are Archivists Repeating Mistakes of the Past?," *Archival Informatics Newsletter* 2:3 (1988): 52-53.

[6] Ithiel DeSola Poole, *Technologies of Freedom* (Cambridge: Harvard University Press, 1983).

[7] U.S. National Science Foundation, Electronic Records Committee, *Electronic Records: Legal and Policy Considerations, Report of the Electronic Records Committee* (Washington, D.C.: National Science Foundation, April 1987).

[8] Douglas P. Allen, "Optical Disk and the Law -- Texas Style," *Inform* (April 1988): 43-44.

[9] Richard Barry, Chairman of ACCIS TP/REM, informs me that "The United Nations has accepted microform as evidence in the case of the Palestine Land Registers (made by the British in 1948) and the closed portions of the United Nations War Crimes Commission Files."

[10] Charles M. Dollar, "Appraising Machine Readable Records," in *A Modern Archives Reader*, Maygene Daniels and Timothy Walch eds. (Washington, D.C.: National Archives and Records Administration, 1984): 71-79; Harold Naugler, *The Archival Appraisal of Machine-Readable Records: A RAMP Study with Guidelines* (Paris: Unesco, 1984).

[11] David Bearman "Editorial Commentary," *Archival Informatics Newsletter* 1:4 (Winter 1987): 71-72.

[12] Too little research has been conducted into data-strips and other such compact methods of storage of electronic data on paper that permit rapid recovery of electronic files, but it seems likely that the specialized nature of the readers for bulk reading of such media would render them less than competitive.

[13] C. Lee Jones, "Microform vs. Optical Disc," *Archival Informatics Newsletter* 2:1 (Spring 1988): 16-17.

[14] Thomas Elton Brown and William A. Reader, "The Archival Management of Machine-Readable Records from Database Management Systems: A Technical Leaflet," *Archival Informatics Newsletter* 1:1 (Spring 1987): 9-12.

[15] Thomas E. Brown, "Standards for Machine-Readable Records Reference Service," *Archival Informatics Newsletter* 2:2 (Summer 1988): 34-35.

[16] ST/AI/326/28 December 1984. More narrowly, a record according to Florida statute is a "written memorial made by a public officer . . . . one required by law to be kept, or necessary to be kept in the discharge of duty imposed by law, or directed by law to serve as a memorial and evidence of something written, said or done." (Florida State Legislature, 1985).

[17] Planning Research Corporation, Inc., *Army Implementation of DOD & Federal Standards: Annex C - Records Management* (6 May 1988).

[18] Brian Denton and Charles Dollar, "Draft Report on TP/REM Interview with Staff of the International Atomic Energy Agency" (23-24 February 1989).

[19] In one sense, the approach proposed for management of electronic records by the National Archives of Canada in Management of Information in Integrated Office Support Systems, (Canada, National Archives of Canada, "Management of Information in Integrated Office Support Systems [IOSS]: Preliminary Functional Requirements," Third Draft (24 May 1988) is to extend these same responsibilities for item-level identification to the creators of records within the application for electronic document filing.

[20] Oklahoma State Archives, *Report to the Archives and Records Commission*, 1986. The legal definition of an original in Oklahoma is: "If data are stored in a computer or similar device, any printout shown to reflect the data accurately, is an 'original'."

[21] Patricia Aronsson and Thomas E. Brown, "Government Archivists and Government Automation," *Government Publications Review* 13 (1986):561-570.

[22] Norman Z. Shapiro and Robert H. Anderson, *Toward an Ethics and Etiquette for Electronic Mail*, Rand Report R-3283-NSF/RC (Santa Monica: Rand Corporation, July 1985).

[23] David Bearman, "Developing Guidelines for Electronic Records: Report of a Project to Test the ACCIS TP/REM *Electronic Records Guidelines: A Manual for Policy Development and Implementation*," in Advisory Committee for the Co-ordination of Information Systems, *Management of Electronic Records: Curriculum Materials* (New York: United Nations, 1992): 137-147.

[24] The full TP/REM report includes, on pp. 35-65, the actual recommended policies and practices for implementation.

117

CHAPTER FOUR

The Implications of *Armstrong* v. *the Executive Office of the President* for the Archival Management of Electronic Records*

This article reviews the arguments presented by both sides in the lawsuit *Armstrong* v. *Executive Office of the President* which concerned the electronic mail created by the Reagan and Bush White House on the IBM Profs system. It examines the emerging consensus among archivists worldwide on approaches to managing electronic records and considers the ways in which the position taken by the government failed to reflect best practices. Specifically, it examines recent discussions of functional requirements for recordkeeping systems and raises some implications of a functional perspective for archival programs and strategies. It concludes by arguing that archivists will need to play a more active role in the society at large in order to ensure that the broader culture understands and acts on the threats to accountability presented by computer-based electronic communications.

* Originally published in *American Archivist* 56 (Fall 1993): 674-689.

INTRODUCTION

On 19 January 1989, the final day of the Reagan administration, after repeated efforts to secure their retention by other
means, Scott Armstrong (then Executive Director of the National Security Archive) and others filed a Freedom of Information Act (FOIA) request and turned to the Federal Court
system to ensure that the contents of the White House electronic mail and records system would be subject to archival
review before disposition. They sought an injunction pro-
hibiting the destruction of backup tapes from the IBM Profs
system which served the agencies of the Executive Office of
the President (EOP), including the National Security Council
(NSC). This is the same system that earlier achieved substantial notoriety because it revealed that Lt. Colonel Oliver North
and his superiors had engaged in a scheme to sell arms to Iran
and use the profits to aid the Nicaraguan Contras after North
had destroyed the paper trails that might have implicated the
National Security Council staff in the effort.

The suit that Armstrong, et al., filed claims that some information on the Profs system qualifies either as agency
records under the FOIA and Federal Records Act (FRA) or as
Presidential records under the Presidential Records Act.[1] They
asserted that the Executive Office of the President failed to
formulate guidelines consistent with law and regulation for
the management of its electronic mail and to implement these
in White House agencies. And they contended that the
Archivist of the United States neglected to carry out his statutory responsibilities with respect to the electronic record on
the Profs system. The suit asked for relief in the form of implemented guidelines for future electronic mail and for appraisal of the records that were on the Profs system at the time
of filing.

On the afternoon of 19 January 1989, Judge Parker of the
D.C. District Court issued a temporary restraining order en-
joining the government from disposing of the Profs tapes and

the government agreed to maintain the information that was at that time in the Profs system until final resolution of the suit. The defendants (the government) then filed a motion to dismiss the case or issue a summary judgment. That case was heard by Charles R. Richey who denied the motion for dismissal or summary judgment on 15 September 1989.[2] The government appealed the Richey decision to the U.S. Court of Appeals arguing, among other things, that the plaintiffs did not have standing to sue under the Presidential Records Act because the act did not permit judicial review. The appeals court of Judges Wald, Ginsburg, and Randolf ruled that while the claims made by the plaintiffs were within the purview of the records management provisions of the FRA and PRA, the actions of the president under the PRA were not subject to judicial review[3] and returned the case to Judge Richey. After considerable maneuvering and many delays in the discovery process, Judge Richey handed down a decision on the substantive issues on 7 January 1993, which declared the procedures established by the White House "arbitrary and capricious" and completely rejected the claims made by the government that untold harm would result from accepting the claims of the plaintiffs.[4] At the same time, Richey, who felt he was constrained by the earlier appeals court ruling, declined to review decisions by the president as to what records on the system might be covered under the Presidential Records Act, effectively leaving open a back door to declare any records presidential and then dispose of them without further oversight or archival appraisal.

The Richey decision was also appealed by the government but the unanimous ruling of the appeals panel upheld the decision against the government on 13 August 1993.[5] In a cross-appeal, the plaintiffs asked that actions of the president in determining which records were not federal records be made subject to review and the court reversed the Richey decision in this respect, dealing a second defeat to the government.

While this case may not yet be resolved in a legal sense, the issues it raises, both about the specific defenses made by the government regarding the Profs electronic mail system in the White House and about requirements for archival management of electronic records, have been fully laid out in the case to date and are not going to change. I do not intend to contribute to the discussion of the legal issues which may still need to be resolved by the courts. Nor, except in passing to clarify other points, will I comment on issues raised by the case with respect to the doctrine of separation of powers, which are quite obviously unique to the particular setting and irrelevant to electronic records management in general. Instead I would like to focus archival attention on the claims made by the government and rejected by the appeals court which reflect prevalent misunderstandings of the implications of electronic records and on the larger professional challenges presented by electronic records management for archivists. Finally, I will comment on the need this case exposes for archivists to be come involved in policy debate to clarify their role in society.

THE FACTS

In *Armstrong* v. *the EOP* (also referred to in this chapter by its colloquial name, the Profs Case) both parties agree that the Profs system was used in the White House for communication among the president and his closest advisors at the National Security Council from April 1985 and in the rest of the Executive Office of the President after November 1986. Both agree that at the end of the administration government officials intended to erase all remaining data on the system. Both acknowledge that the White House created both presidential records and federal records and that each of these categories of records is governed by separate acts. Both parties also agree that the NSC and some other components of the Executive Office of the president are federal agencies and as such are subject to the FRA which requires that the head of each federal agency "shall make and preserve records containing adequate and proper documentation of the organization, functions, policies, decisions, procedures and essential transactions of the agency" where the terms "records" includes "all books, papers, maps, photographs, machine readable materials, or other documentary materials regardless of physical form or characteristics, made or received by an agency of the United States Government...."[6]

The plaintiffs and the government disagreed about when records are covered by the PRA and when by the FRA. Under the PRA, presidential records are defined as "documentary materials, or any reasonably segregable portion thereof, created or received by the president, his immediate staff or a unit or individual of the Executive Office of the President whose function is to advise and assist the president, in the course of conducting activities which relate to or have an effect upon the carrying out of the constitutional, statutory, or other official or ceremonial duties of the president."[7] Also, the parties agreed that some records might be personal records not covered by the PRA; the intent of Congress being that "all records which are neither agency records subject to FOIA nor personal records would fall within the ambit of Presidential record."[8]

The PRA provides that all materials produced or received by the president or his staff "shall," to the extent practicable, "be categorized as presidential records or personal records upon their creation or receipt and be filed separately."[9] During his term of office a President may "dispose of those of his Presidential records that no longer have administrative, historical, informational, or evidentiary value."[10] The government argued that this right was absolute and not subject to review, but the plaintiffs successfully argued that the authority to dispose of presidential records was granted only if the president first obtains the written views of the Archivist of the United States and the archivist states that he does not intend to notify Congress of the proposed disposal. The PRA states that the archivist "shall request advice of congressional committees as regarding disposals when he considers records proposed for destruction may be of special interest to the Congress" or that consultation with Congress would be "in the public interest."

Reversing a ruling of the lower court, the appeals court ruled that although it had previously concluded that decisions to dispose of presidential records were not subject to judicial review, it did not follow that the president could declare anything to be presidential. "Contrary to the district court, we conclude that the PRA allows limited review to assure that guidelines defining presidential records do not improperly sweep in non-presidential records. Accordingly we remand to the district court to determine whether the relevant NSC and OSTP directives categorize non-presidential records as subject to the PRA."

The government argued that any records created by anyone who serves in an advisory capacity to the president at any time are thus presidential records while the plaintiffs successfully argued a narrow interpretation which in effect allows only the specific records created solely for briefing the president to be considered presidential and then only if they are not previously or subsequently distributed as federal records. The expression used by the court was that federal records "trump" presidential records.

The parties agreed that the Archivist did not give prior authority to the disposal of the electronic records of the Profs system and the government admitted that the archivist was advised by the plaintiffs of the proposed destruction of these records before it was scheduled to take place and did not elect to act. Even though Congress was not given an explicit means of vetoing a presidential destruction request, the legislation provided that such a request needed to be received sixty days prior to the proposed disposal date. The clear intention was that Congress could use political means of pressuring the president if it disagreed with a particular disposal request.

Finally the PRA requires that the Archivist of the United States "shall assume responsibility for the custody, control and preservation of, and access to, the Presidential records" on conclusion of the president's term of office and that disposal of such records thereafter will require sixty days published public notice.[11] As the Archivist did not take custody of the records, except following the court injunction and then only as a means of securing them physically, this point was not disputed.

ARCHIVAL ISSUES RAISED BY THE CASE

The case *Armstrong* v. *the Executive Office of the President* is obviously of great importance because of the nature of the defendant and the records at issue. However, many of the judgments made by the court have significance for the archival management of electronic records outside of the U.S. federal government because they are not grounded simply in narrow interpretations of regulations and law but on a relatively sophisticated understanding of how electronic communications have come to be used in modern organizations and on the nature of the software employed in electronic communications systems. Specifically, the court dismissed four arguments made by the government which are typically made in other organizations unable or unwilling to manage electronic records.

First, it rejected the government argument that electronic copies are convenience copies if the primary organizational records are maintained in paper format. The court sided with the plaintiffs who argued that if anything is to be considered a convenience copy in an electronic communication environment it would have to be paper copies because more can be done with the electronic record, not all records are copied to paper, and more information is present about the structure and context of the record in its electronic form.

Second, following standard corporate practices and other court rulings, the court rejected the government claim that calendars and some notes were private and personal information, not government records. The plaintiffs noted that electronic calendars of important White House officials were made available to many people throughout the organization and were essential to the conduct of day-to-day business by many people other than the principals. They pointed to patterns of use, and to the intentions of the implementers of electronic communication systems, to demonstrate that these systems have become integral to the operations of organizations, including the White House.

Third, a major issue in the dispute was whether the White House agencies, prior to or following the filing of the case, gave adequate instructions to their staffs to prevent the unauthorized destruction of electronic mail. While this issue was muddied because the parties never agreed on the basic facts of whether the agencies gave the advice they said they gave, much less whether than advice was legally correct, administratively implemented, or adequate, the court decision in this arena was far reaching. "The government's basic position is flawed because hard-copy print-outs that the agencies preserve may omit fundamental pieces of information which are an integral part of the original electronic records, such as the identity of the sender and/or recipient and the time of receipt."

The FRA states that the Archivist "shall provide guidance and assistance to Federal agencies", "promulgate standards, procedures, and guidelines.[12] The court decision in effect upholds the standards and guidelines with respect to electronic records that were in place: these state that when both paper and electronic records exist, both must be separately scheduled because they have different value. The court found that employees had not been given written instructions to print electronic mail notes, calendars, and documents to paper, that insofar as they had "implicitly" been given such instructions by virtual of instructing them how to keep paper records, the instructions were flawed because they suggested that records need only to be printed to paper. The flaw here was two-fold. First, the instructions suggested that records need only be copies when the information they contain does not exist in any other record, when of course the same information may exist in many records while the fact that they contain the same information does not in any way make them copies. Second, the printing of electronic mail messages would have resulted in the loss of structural and contextual information required to understand their significance including the names of recipients and senders, the date and time of receipt, the link to prior messages, full distribution lists, and so on.

Thus the basis for the court ruling is identical to the reasoning employed by archivists worldwide (outside the U.S. federal government) in the past few years: structural and contextual data in addition to the content of messages are crucial to "recordness," and "archiving" without capturing such critical evidence is equivalent to destroying the record.[13]

"Even assuming, without of course deciding [the issue of copies] that one set of parallel documents retained in a different records system and a different medium than another set may be classified as a 'cop(y)' under the FRA and thus subject to unobstructed destruction, the electronic records would still not qualify as 'full reproduction(s) or transcription(s); imitation(s) of a prototype . . .duplicate(s),' [*Websters New Universal Unabridged Dictionary* (2nd ed., 1979)] of the paper print-outs. This is because important information present in the e-mail system, such as who sent a document, who received it, and when that person received it, will not always appear on the computer screen and so will not be preserved on the paper print-out."

Finally, the court found that electronic mail was used for substantive business communications but that neither the White House nor the Archives treated Profs as a record-keeping system. The intention of Profs, according to IBM which was quoted in court briefs, was "reduce your dependence on mail, telephone, and other conventional systems" so users can "perform daily office jobs" such as sending and receiving messages, keeping calendars, scheduling meetings and storing documents. Affidavits filed in the case make it clear that Profs served all these roles in the White House and that it was increasingly heavily used. The court noted that "the 1,300 federal employees with access to the EOP and NSC electronic mail systems can, and apparently do, utilize them to relay lengthy substantive -- even classified -- "notes" that, in content, are often indistinguishable from letters and memoranda."

Additionally, testimony makes it clear that users of the system considered it "unusual" for information in Profs to be thought of as a "record." In the White House, as in many other organizations with integrated office automation systems, employees were expected to delete most of the information in the electronic system on a regular basis for the convenience and ease of the data center. They were not given any written instructions on how, when, and by what criteria to do this nor were the deletions considered actions of disposal with respect to recordkeeping requirements. Until May 1993 when the EOP decided to implement a front-end program, the Profs system was not set up to permit differentiation between types of records at the time of creation. Even then it only allowed the individual who created the record to code whether it was "personal" or "record" (as required in this case by the law). It did not established any review procedure for deletion of non-personal materials (although such a procedure was also required and specified by law). In addition, the designation given to a record was subject only to the record creator's judgment, in this case informed by a faulty briefing on the law, and not to archival review.

Unfortunately, the passive role played by the U.S. National Archives in this situation was not atypical of the role played by archivists elsewhere. In the selection and implementation of the White House Profs system, archivists were not included among those defining the initial procurement and their requirements were not taken into account. In response to the court, a front-end enabling users to classify the archival value of their own records was belatedly constructed but no criteria were defined for determining record status and no automatic criteria, such as capturing any information sent to other individuals, were implemented. Archivists were not involved in the review of materials selected for deletion or in the definition of filing structures.

The Archivist of the United States in this case, as is true of archivists in most such cases, did not take custody of electronic records of the office (even though the law states that when the administration ends the archivist "shall assume responsibility for the custody, control, and preservation of and access to" all records), in part because the archives lacked experience and competence to process such material. The Archivist of the United States was found negligent for not reporting the imminent destruction of the records when he found out about it, not demanding better records management practices for electronic mail at the White House, and not promulgating guidelines with sufficient specificity to be followed by agencies. Like his counterparts in archives elsewhere, the archivist had not done so because he lacked an intellectual framework in which to ground such guidelines.

FUNCTIONAL REQUIREMENTS FOR RECORDKEEPING SYSTEMS

A framework of guidelines for archival management of corporate electronic records was in the earliest stages of being articulated in 1989 but has since been very much more fully elaborated and now can serve as a basis for practical action to assure that electronic information systems create and maintain records. The Profs Case even contributed to framing some of the issues in the emerging archival professional consensus but the case made by the U.S. government appears to have been frozen at the very time that the archival community worldwide was making tremendous strides towards resolving the issues raised by electronic records management. As a consequence, the position taken by the government in the Profs

Case is not informed by the best thinking that has taken place since 1989.

In January 1990, a group of experts (including several members of the NARA staff) attended a meeting held under the aegis of the Benton Foundation which sought to establish a professional consensus regarding how best to approach the archival management of electronic records. The meeting, which was called specifically to see if the profession could develop consensus around issues raised by the Profs Case, focused on systems design and implementation strategies in addition to policy.[14] At the time, the conclusions reached at the meeting were reported only in *Archives and Museum Informatics*, a technical newsletter addressed to a relatively small segment of the archival profession. At their request, the names of some NARA and OMB participants in the discussion were not reported. But the degree of consensus and the extent of the framework adopted by that group was tremendous and, even though it was not reflected in subsequent legal briefs by the U.S. government in the Profs Case, the position advanced at that meeting became a common foundation for the work conducted by many of the participants (including Charles Dollar of the NARA Research and Evaluation Staff) in the years that followed. It is useful to review the conclusions of that conference in the context of the appeals court decision in the case of *Armstrong v. the Executive Office of the President* because the thinking of that group and of the court coincide.

The group agreed that the ultimate solutions to electronic records management problems would only come when archivists were involved in defining the requirements for new systems acquisition and applications implementation. This became the basis for numerous efforts since then to define functional requirements for electronic records systems. The meeting also agreed on ten steps to implementing acceptable (if not ideal) records management control within existing systems:

(1) Reinforce to users that electronic data may be records.

In the Profs Case the government minimized the record-ness of these systems referring to them as telephone surrogates and convenience copies. The language used by the White House even when it was defending its practices, did not place emphasis on the fact that electronic documents are presumptively records but rather acted as if being a record was an exception, if not even an exceptional case. If, as the government asserted, it instructed employees to copy to paper those electronic documents that "rise to the level of a record" it was simultaneously conveying to them their superiors did not feel that these systems created records.

(2) Identify the organizational requirements for access.

Records required by more than one individual are communicated transactions. Other people than the author must therefore have access to them. Determining why, and for how long, the organization needs to have a record is a critical task in information management. In the Profs Case the government claimed that calendars made for distribution to many parties were, nevertheless, private personal records not subject to FOIA. The court rejected the concept that a record that was disseminated as a basis for action by others within an organization could be considered personal.

(3) Establish that documentation is a basic management responsibility.

Without formal accountability in mid-level management for documentation of all programs there will not be such documentation. In the system established at the White House there was no responsibility beyond the individual record creator, and no reporting of creation of records and destruction patterns by the system. Even though this guidance acknowledges that archivists cannot assure that electronic records management guidelines will be followed on their own, it assumes they will be present and involved; in the White House Profs Case the archivist disclaimed any responsibility and the Court found that the guidelines adopted by the White House did not even contain the correct interpretations of the definition of records, of responsibilities of individuals, nor of the degree of agency authority over records.

(4) Require program managers to establish guidelines for use of systems that are dictated by organizational policy interests; do not permit guidelines to be driven by the data center or systems administrators based solely on system administration efficiencies, such as reducing storage loads.

The guidelines established by the White House were driven by convenience of data center managers or by the administrative interests of individual agencies rather than by the broader interests of the federal government as a whole. Interestingly, because users of the Profs system did not care about records policies at all (and because no method was introduced into system design to assure that these policies would be acted on) the system as it was backed up under injunction on the final day of the Reagan Administration was replete with electronic mail dating from the inception of the system despite the instructions from data center managers to delete records.

(5) Begin establishing guidelines with systems that may otherwise not produce paper trails, like electronic mail.

Needless to say the White House did not follow this advice.

(6) Construct shared files and common file structures and naming conventions to support retention decisions and access.

No guidelines are provided to users of the White House system about how they could implement a central electronic filing system instead of storing idiosyncratic directories in a physical file that happened to reside in one place. Even distributed network PCs can achieve a virtual central file by rigorous adherence to such conventions.[15]

(7) Implement backup procedures dictated by the requirements of the application area.

In the White House, knowing where advice comes from, who gave it, who signed off on it, and when it was communicated are all critical application requirements, but the procedures implemented to save electronic mail, even if they had been used, were particularly deficient in not being able to capture structural links and contextual data necessary to reconstruct these fundamental evidential properties.

(8) Define the data to be captured including stamps of creation and use which need to be defined and implemented through the system.

The court decision focused on documentation of the creation of records and found it necessary to retain structural and contextual information along with the content of the record. Although the court did not address documentation of the use of records, provisions are made for tracking access to files in paper record systems in the EOP. The use of electronic documents, however, was not audited by the systems set up in the White House.

(9) Avoid the guidance to "print records out to paper" unless all the data in the system can be routinely printed out and will be filed.

While the experts assembled in 1990 could not completely agree on never printing records out to paper or microform, they agreed completely that it would only be acceptable if all the associated data about the record, including data known only to the system such as permissions, was assembled in a meaningful relationship to the content and also printed out. The White House made no provision for this requirement.

(10) Adopt only administrative solutions that pass the tests of operational utility and legal acceptability. Archival concerns per se are tertiary.

The decision in the Profs Case settles whether the approach used was legally acceptable, but it failed equally the test of operational utility. Some individuals never deleted a record during their tenure while others routinely deleted everything. No systems were in place to conveniently retrieve a specific record unless the name given it by the record creator was known. No guidance was given to employees on how to organize files and no facilities were provided to do so conveniently. Finally, the authority given to individuals to make decisions about what constitutes a record and to remove those which they did not want to have serving as evidence violates the basic principles of bureaucratic accountability, as well as the principles of government accountability to its citizenry.

Since January 1990 substantial work has been done to extend the analysis of the functional requirements of record-keeping systems and define strategies for assuring that information systems create, maintain, and provide access to records, not just to data. The first major study bringing together a strategy for archival management of electronic records was a policy guideline drafted for the United Nations Administrative Coordinating Committee for Information Systems (ACCIS) and subsequently adopted and published by them. In the body of that document, this author proposed a working definition of electronic records that was suitable for articulating systems requirements.[16] According to this definition, since widely adopted elsewhere, records are information that participate in "transactions." The guidelines further focused attention on the documentary requirements of business applications rather than of software applications, files, or particular transactions, a source of some confusion in the Profs Case where answers are often being sought in terms such as "what should we do with electronic mail" rather than in terms of the business applications and transactions which alone define the appropriate retention period for records.

The ACCIS report also stated the requirement to be able to segregate records and non-records at the time of creation and to protect their "recordness," including contextuality and structure, over time. These requirements, which were then addressed in so far as they could be satisfied through policy approaches taken alone, have since been incorporated into subsequent statements of functional requirements for electronic recordkeeping.

During 1989, the National Archives of Canada was working through the Office Systems Working Group of the Treasury Board in an effort to define the functional requirements of a corporate office application that satisfied records management requirements.[17] Reports from that project, including the software application specification called FOREMOST and the studies of office systems implementations conducted under the IMOSA project, informed archivists worldwide. Emphasis in these studies was placed on the identification of records, the filing rules that determined how records would be maintained over time, and the requirement that archives must be preserved so as to be "available, usable and understandable."[18] The National Archives of Canada IMOSA project has also defined "Functional Requirements for a Corporate Information Management Application" (November 1992) and conducted surveys of vendors to establish what high level requirements of corporate information management applications are currently satisfied by the marketplace.[19]

In 1991, the international consensus about approaches to electronic records management was advanced by meetings of experts in Macerata, Italy, Perth, Australia, and Marburg, Germany (whose proceedings are published) and have been reinforced by workshops led by the author and others in 1992 and 1993.[20] More recently, as a result of the National Archives of Canada, the Australian Archives, and a conference sponsored by the National Historical Publications and Records Commission conference on research issues in electronic records, archivists in English-speaking countries are moving towards a consensus from archivists, records managers, auditors, Freedom of Information and Privacy Act administrators, and security personnel on the data which is required to assure that a record constitutes evidence.[21]

A major study currently underway at the University of Pittsburgh has codified an initial draft set of requirements which has had input from a broad segment of the knowledgeable community.[22] Additional elements of a full functional requirement are being sought and the criteria incorporated into the draft are being tested in a variety of locations. These functional requirements, the reasons for their definition and promulgation, and the ways archivists can use them, are discussed elsewhere in the literature, but the important core of the requirement is the way in which it reiterates in the capture, the maintenance, and then access to records the importance of content, structure, and context. The essential theme running through the requirements is that not all information is a record. Records are tied to transactions by contextual and structural links that are not necessarily part of their content and may even (like the post-dated check and the distribution list which contains names which never were sent copies) belie their content. The fundamental archival concern is to assure that records are evidence, and are retained with their evidential properties intact, and are available as evidence when they are needed in the future.

DO WE LACK AUTHORITY OR WILL?

The government, in *Armstrong* v. *the EOP*, claimed that the actions of the president with respect to his records were not subject to judicial review. Further, it claimed that, if they were, his actions in issuing guidelines to White House staff about retaining records would place him in full compliance with the law since it falls to the president as executive and as agency head to determine what is and is not a record. The same claim is essentially made by any manager who asserts that he can determine what is a record. In the face of such claims, given the realities of electronic communications which are so easily compromised, do archivists require a kind of authority they have previously lacked? Or do they only need to act in a different manner and at a different time than with paper records in order to fulfill their mission?

The Archivist of the United States was held to be in contempt of court (although this order was subsequently dismissed on appeal for technical reasons) for failure to act to protect electronic records as soon as he knew they were going to be deleted. The archivist was further cited for failure to develop and promulgate standards for government-wide management of electronic office systems. Obviously the court did not believe that the archivist lacked authority, but was applying a standard to the timing of actions with respect to electronic records that would have been quite unusual to demand for paper records.

The need to expand the actions of archives, if not their actual legislative authority and possibly even their mission statements, was recognized by the conferees at the 1990 Pittsburgh summer institute sponsored by the National Association of Government Archives and Records Administrators (NAGARA).[23] State archivists gathered at this meeting issued a final series of papers from that meeting in which they envisioned archivists as taking an active role in intruding themselves into the development and requirements of systems and into their operation within agencies. A similar position was taken in the UN report in which the policy requirements identified included policies that specified the involvement of archivists in systems development and implementation. It argued that unless the archivists could influence the design of systems they would not be able to exercise the kind of control over records based on activities in which those records participated that is required to assure the satisfaction of the documentary requirement of an application.[24]

A proactive stance based on achieving data administration control over active records was recommended to the Archivist of the United States by the National Institute of Standards and Technology in 1989.[25] NIST argued that the archivist needed to define government-wide standards for data dictionaries and establish a unified information directory system for the government in order to adequately control the electronic records of the office systems. A role of NARA in building a metadatabase, called the Federal Information Locator system, was proposed when this concept was first enacted as law in the Paperwork Reduction Act and urged on NARA by this author in 1981.[26] Unfortunately, in their response to NIST it is evident that NARA staff still do not understand how to implement metadata guidelines to document documentation.[27]

By 1990, archivists in the New York State Archives and the National Archives of Canada (institutions which led the way in establishing programs for the management of machine-readable records), concluded that unless the archives enter into agreements with agencies about the desired result (e.g., adequate documentation) of records management programs, they will need to be involved in the design of every electronic system, or in the specification of requirements that will govern acquisition of every system, in their governments. John McDonald and his colleagues in Canada were already working on specifications for office records systems (the FOREMOST specification) and Margaret Hedstrom and her colleagues in New York were exploring system-level appraisal of multi-agency and multi-jurisdictional electronic information systems.[28]

At the 1990 NAGARA conference, five of six speakers in two sessions devoted to these topics reached agreement that what was required on the part of archivists was a willingness to depart from the way in which they have managed the paper record.[29] This departure would include involvement directly or indirectly in the definition of information systems requirements based on the documentary requirements of applications. It would probably also include willingness to consider not taking physical custody of electronic records in favor of exercising control over them.

If it was the case (and it may be in some instances) that government archives programs lacked the statutory authority to intervene in the definition of up front systems requirements based on archival policy requirements or that they lacked the authority to exercise control without custody, then archivists should be out lobbying legislatures to establish these authorities and they should employ in their arguments for such powers the illustration of cases such as the Profs Case that demonstrate this need. The legislatures and the governing boards and authorities under which non-public archives are administered need to understand that the problems confronting archivists in the management of electronic records are not going to be solved by employing the techniques that were used to control paper records. New techniques may or may not require new authorities, but if they do, archivists should be prepared to argue for them.

Recently the recognition that electronic records management may require new activity on the part of archives has led to a discussion of program strategies for archives, especially for electronic records. One implication of these discussions is the possibility they present of a radical redefinition of the archival profession and a reintegration of records management and archives. Ties between them were severed in many programs over a decade ago but must be recombined if electronic archival records are to be imagined.[30]

PUBLIC UNDERSTANDING OF RECORDS POLICY ISSUES

Regardless of the outcome of *Armstrong* v. *the EOP*, the broader society in which we live needs to reach an understanding about the nature and importance of records and the issues affecting the retention of electronic evidence if archivists are to have any future in the twenty-first century. This law suit may or may not be resolved by the recent Appeals Court ruling which could be further appealed until mid-November 1993 and which will in any event not be the last legal tangle in this complicated case. The Freedom of Information Act request which lies at the heart of the case has not yet been acted on and it is likely that the government will not release any records under that request for many years. But electronic communication systems will play an increasingly important role in the formulation and execution of public policy. The recent development of a National Health Care Policy by a loose community of advisors communicating to a great extent over the Internet illustrates this dramatically. If our citizens do not reach a deeper appreciation of the need for evidence in the emerging "electronic democracy," the rubric will rapidly become a misnomer. I believe that archivists have a responsibility to put the issues more squarely before the public. In not taking a political stand and clearly articulating the responsibility of government administrators for the creation and maintenance of an accountable record, I fear they have shirked that responsibility and will pay for their timidity with their professional identities and future careers.

In 1993, as I write, archivists have yet to take an official position in the case of the ex-Archivist of the United States who participated in a direct assault on the integrity of the electronic records of the Bush Administration.[31] Four months after being served with a contempt citation (since lifted) the present, acting-Archivist of the United States has yet to respond to the court demand that she promulgate government-wide guidelines for management of electronic mail systems. This case will eventually be resolved on its merits. It will impact how all government archivists will handle electronic records, not only within the federal government but at the state level as well. Despite the profound impact, the Society of American Archivists has not been heard. The plaintiffs include the National Security Archive, the Center for National Security Studies, the American Historical Association, the American Library Association and several individuals including former U.S. Senator Gaylord Nelson. The case for the plaintiffs is being argued by Alan Morrison of the Public Citizens Litigation

Group and Kate Martin of the American Civil Liberties Union Foundation. Where is the SAA?

Archivists must craft a position that will secure public backing for the electronic record and actions taken to preserve it. Archivists should have been on the front lines of a political battle for judicial review of presidential records decisions. As long as archivists lack, or feel they lack, the authority to require appraisal of these records, they should be welcoming judicial review as a step that will result in ordering the archival appraisal of these and similar records. The fact that the Archivist of the United States was a defendant in this case should have been further reason to join the suit in defense of the true position of archives. Instead the executive branch has to legitimate as archival a position that would have effectively placed the president above the law and above judicial review and totally subverted the intention of both the Presidential Records Act and the Freedom of Information Act.

Like the Appeals Court, archivists should reject completely, and publicly, the position taken by the National Archives that records are what the head of an agency defines them to be. They should abandon the pernicious concept that information "rises to the level of a record" which contradicts the archival concept of records as documentation of transactions and has no place in law. Archivists should demand that NARA promulgate guidelines for electronic records which base records retention requirements on documentary requirements of business applications not software utilities. If necessary, archivists should go to Congress with a request to change the authorities of the National Archives in order to be able to effectively carry out electronic records management. The current position of the NARA Center for Electronic Records and Acting-Archivist of the United States Trudy Petersen that no changes are necessary in NARA practice to cope with electronic records is dangerous, deluded, and destructive.

Court cases are important not only for the resolution of the specific issues at hand, but also as arenas in which broad cultural understandings of the nature of responsibilities and technologies can be exposed. *Armstrong v. the EOP* revealed how unresolved a variety of issues having to do with archival accountability are in the minds of government employees and how common misunderstandings of electronic records requirements are among information systems administrators. If archivists do not use this and other opportunities to articulate forcefully what we expect from records creators and systems designers and to extend their mission and authorities both legally and in practice, we will lose most of the archival record of the next decade and squander our role as protector as of the public interest in documented accountable government.

NOTES

[1] The *Presidential Records Act of 1978, U.S. Code,* vol. 44, secs. 2201-2207, is referred to here as the PRA. The *Federal Records Act, U.S. Code* chapters 21, 29, 31, and 33, is referred to here as the FRA. Often separate chapters are referred to by their own names, specifically the *Records Management Act* (chapters 29 and 31) and the *Disposal of Records Act* (chapter 33).

[2] *Armstrong* v. *Bush,* 721 F.Supp. 343 (D.D.C. 1989).

[3] *Armstrong* 1 924 F.2d.

[4] *Armstrong* v. *the Executive Office of the President* 810 F.Supp. 335 (D.D.C. 1993).

[5] *Armstrong* v. *the Executive Office of the President,* U.S. Court of Appeals, District of Columbia Circuit, #93-5083. This decision is referred to throughout this chapter as "the appeals court decision," or is implied whenever I use the phrase "the court" without further qualification.

[6] *U.S. Code,* Sections 3101 and 3301.

[7] The term "documentary materials" is defined to include "electronic or mechanical recordations" [44 USC 2201(1)]. Documents exempted from, the PRA include only: 1) agency records subject to FOIA, 2) personal records, 3) stocks of publications or stationery and 4) extra copies of documents produced for convenience [2201(2)(B)]. Finally, personal records are defined as material of a "purely private or non-public character which do not relate to or have an effect upon the carrying out of the . . . duties of the President [2201(3)] . . . and these are further identified as "diaries, journal, or other personal notes serving as the functional equivalent of a diary or journal which are not prepared or utilized for, or circulated or communicated in the course of transacting Government business."

[8] *U.S. Code,* Section 2201(3).

[9] *U.S. Code,* Section 2203(6).

[10] *U.S. Code,* Section 2203(c).

[11] *U.S. Code,* Section 2203(f)(1).

[12] *U.S. Code,* Sections 2904(a) and 2904(c)(1).

[13] Luciana Duranti, "Diplomatics: New Uses for an Old Science (Part VI), *Archivaria* 33 (1991/2): 6-24; Barbara Reed, "Appraisal and Disposal" in Judith Ellis ed., *Keeping Archives,* 2nd ed. (Melbourne:

Thorpe, 1993), especially pp. 185-200; Glenda Acland, "Managing the Record Rather than the Relic," *Archives and Manuscripts* 20 (1992): 57-63; David Bearman, "Archival Principles and the Electronic Office" in *Information Handling in Offices and Archives*, Angelika Menne-Haritz ed. (New York: K.G. Saur, 1993): 177-193, reprinted in this volume as Chapter 5; David Bearman, "Archival Data Management to Achieve Organizational Accountability for Electronic Records," *Archives & Manuscripts* 21 (May 1993): 14-28, reprinted in this volume as Chapter 1.

[14] David Bearman, "Electronic Office Records: Report of a Meeting Held at the Brookings Institution, 11 January 1990," *Archives and Museum Informatics* 4:1 (Spring 1990): 12-15.

[15] National Archives of Canada and Treasury Board Secretariat, *Information Management: Managing Your Computer Directories and Files* (Ottawa, 1993).

[16] United Nations, Advisory Committee for Co-ordination of Information Systems (ACCIS), *Management of Electronic Records: Issues and Guidelines* (New York: United Nations, 1990), of which parts of Section II are reprinted in this volume in Chapter 3.

[17] Transport Canada Integrated Office Services, *Model of Generic Office Functions Summary Report*, DMR Group Inc., 20 December 1989.

[18] National Archives of Canada, *The IMOSA Project: Information Management and Office Systems Advancement Phase I Report* (Hull, 1991); *The IMOSA Project: Functional Requirements for a Corporate Information Management Application (CIMA)* (Ottawa: November 1992).

[19] National Archives of Canada, *The IMOSA Project: An Initial Analysis of Document Management and Retrieval Systems* (Hull, November 1992).

[20] Charles Dollar, *Archival Technologies and Information Theory: The Impact of Information Technologies on Archival Principals and Methods* (Macerata, Italy: University of Macerata, 1992); Angelika Menne-Haritz, ed., *Information Handling in Offices and Archives* (New York: K.G. Saur, 1993): 177-193; Dagmar Parer and Ron Terry, eds., *Managing Electronic Records: Papers from a Workshop on Managing Electronic Records of Archival Value* (Dickson, New South Wales: Australian Council of Archives and Australian Society of Archivists, 1992).

[21] National Historical Publications and Records Commission, *Research Issues in Electronic Records* (Washington, D.C., 1991).

[22] David Bearman, "Record-keeping Systems," *Archivaria* 36 (1993): 16-36, reprinted in this volume as Chapter 2.

[23] Reports of *Archival Administration in the Electronic Information Age: An Advanced Institute for Government Archivists* were prepared by Richard Cox in 1989, 1990, and 1991. The Institute was organizes and conducted by the School of Library and Information Science, University of Pittsburgh. They were cosponsored by the National Association of Government Archives and Records Administrators with support from the Council on Library Resources (1989 and 1990) and the National Historical Publications and Records Commission (1991).

[24] United Nations Administrative Coordinating Committee for Information Systems, *Management of Electronic Records: Issues and Guidelines* (New York: United Nations, 1990), especially pp. 17-70.

[25] National Institute of Standards and Technology, *Framework and Policy Recommendations for the Exchange and Preservation of Electronic Records*, a report prepared for the National Archives and Records Administration (Washington, D.C.: National Institute of Standards and Technology, 1989).

[26] David Bearman, "The National Archives and Records Service: Policy Choices for the Next Five Years," *For The Record* (December 1981): 1 *ff*.

[27] David Bearman, "Documenting Documentation," *Archivaria* 34 (1992): 33-49, reprinted in this volume as Chapter 8.

[28] Alan Kowlowitz, *Archival Appraisal of Online Information Systems*, Archives and Museum Informatics Technical Report #7 (Pittsburgh: Archives and Museum Informatics, 1988).

[29] David Bearman, *Archival Management of Electronic Records*, Archives and Museum Informatics Technical Report #13 (Pittsburgh: Archives and Museum Informatics, 1991).

[30] David Bearman and Margaret Hedstrom, "Reinventing Archives for Electronic Records: Alternative Service Delivery Options" in *Program Strategies for Electronic Records Management*, Archives and Museum Informatics Technical Report #18 (Pittsburgh: Archives and Museum Informatics, 1993): 82-98.

[31] David Bearman, "Archivist Abdicates Responsibility," *Archives and Museum Informatics* 7:1 (Spring 1993): 1-2.

SECTION III

Design and Implementation

❖

CHAPTER FIVE

Archival Principles and the Electronic Office

❖

CHAPTER SIX

Managing Electronic Mail

CHAPTER FIVE

Archival Principles and the Electronic Office*

Electronic information systems are capable of capturing substantial amounts of information about the provenance of records they contain. These systems can track specific functions, activities, and transactions and which individuals contributed to or modified each item. As currently implemented, however, records are often striped of contextual information, thereby greatly reducing their value as evidence. Contextual information is most often lost during data migration as systems are upgraded or data is communicated from one system to another. A cost/benefit plateau determines the degree of contextual evidence that will be retained. Archivists must articulate what evidential detail is required or desired for each transaction. The author examines the specifics of contextual data capture and retention in the principal software applications: word processing, electronic mail, spreadsheets, database management, and graphics.

* Originally published in *Information Handling in Offices and Archives*, ed. Angelika Menne-Haritz (New York: K.G. Saur, 1993), 177-193, which contains papers presented at the Symposium on the Impact of Information Technologies on Information Handling in Offices and Archives in Gladenbach, near Marburg, Germany, in October 1991. An earlier version of this paper was presented at the National Archives of Canada, 26 February 1991. The author wishes to thank Terry Cook, Richard Cox, John McDonald, and Lisa Weber for their thoughtful critiques which contributed to improving the presentation.

ARCHIVES AS EVIDENCE

Responsible corporate management of electronic records, whether for ongoing operational purposes or for long-term retention of corporate memory,[1] depends upon an understanding of the fundamental archival principle of provenance. This principle is central to the concept of archives as evidence of activity and pertains with equal relevance to all forms of documentation. Two derivative archival methods, "respect des fonds" and "respect for original order" which are also often referred to as principles, are in fact only implementations of the principle of provenance which reflect the nature of record-keeping in bureaucratic organizations during much of the era of paper records. Ironically, electronic records systems make it both possible to more fully capture provenance than paper records systems did and, at the same time, make it more likely that provenance will be lost and that archives, even if they are preserved, will therefore lack evidential value.[2] This chapter explores the relationship between provenance and evidence and its implications for management of paper or electronic information systems.

Archives are recorded transactions created in the course of organizational activities that have continuing evidential value. The criteria which distinguish archives from all of the information ever created or received in an organization are that:

(1) archives are records of transactions;

(2) archives document activities or functions reflected in the mission of the organization, not just incidental to it; and

(3) archives are retained for their continuing value as evidence.[3]

These three criteria contribute to an implementation guideline which has been central to records management and archival practice but is rarely made explicit: because the meaning of archives derives from the context in which they were created, and their evidential value is determined by the degree to which that context is still discernible, records management seeks to capture, and archives management to preserve, recorded transactions, their original form, and information about the historical nexus between creation and use.

Archivists select records for their "evidential historicity." Evidential historicity is the sum of all information that can be determined about an accountable transaction, which is defined as the relationship between a record and an activity determined by archivists to require evidence. The information which contributes to evidential historicity is derived from analyzing the data, the structure, and the context of records, each of which testifies explicitly and implicitly.

• The **data** of the record are the words, numbers, images, and sounds actually made by the creator of the record.

• The **structure** of the record is the relationships among these data as employed by the record creator to convey meaning. One kind of structure is the stylistic formalisms which we use to recognize the "address," "salutation," or "body" of written documents. Another kind of structure is the pointers between physically or logically distinct groupings of information as is the case with forms or databases where one aggregation of data elements is related to another aggregation in a separate record, but kept together in the same case file or in a "relation" in the database definition. Often structural information will be both indicated structurally and recorded explicitly in the data content of a record, as it is in the standard memorandum with the headings "To:," "From:" and "Re:."

• The **context** of the record is the testimony it provides about the nexus of activity out of which it arose and in which it was used and about how it appeared and behaved in that setting. Archivists recognize that a body of records that has lost its provenancial link has little or no value as evidence, but they have not analyzed the sources of information that reveal the relationship between the record and the activity out of which it arose. The most unimpeachable contextual information from which records derive their evidential value resides in the record system, not the individual records. Although this is the acknowledged reason why archivists retain record systems (which in paper-based systems means "original order"), there is little analysis of how to read the evidence of records systems in the archival literature. As with structural information, it is also possible for contextual information to be carried as data in the record, as it commonly is in the case of dates on correspondence or reference codes in registry systems.

It is important to note that, when information which purports to provide structure or context is carried as data, it can be purposefully or accidentally misleading. The date on a document (data) may not be the date the communication was written or sent (context), and the distribution list may or may not be the same as the people who actually received a memorandum. Authors are free to invent data that purports to be context, and may even do so after the fact.

EVIDENCE AND BUSINESS APPLICATION REQUIREMENTS

Businesses maintain record systems to meet the requirements of ongoing operations for evidence. Archivists retain those records required for ongoing accountability. Archivists recognize the importance of contextual information to the quality of evidence in their appraisal practices when they consider the "evidential value" of the information in deciding about its disposition in their practices of arrangement and description. Archivists reflect the belief that they can say significantly less about the meaning of records that are no longer in their "original order" than of those whose connection to the organization and activity which generated them. But archival theory has not articulated the link between the information conveyed by original order, which suggests how the records were used in the course of business, as a contextual information requirement of evidence even though courts have set such standards. For example, archivists and records managers know that only the systematic microfilming of records in the normal course of business, in which each record retains its contextual relationship to other records received and sent the same day, can assure the admissibility of a microfilm surrogate as evidence in a court.[4] Similar structural and contextual information requirements for evidential historicity are present also in all records systems. Here we argue that they can be made explicit and that doing so is essential to defining the requirements for records management.

Different business applications will have differing requirements for evidence. The character, or degree, of requirements for creation and management of contextual information is directly related to the particular functions of each business. Once created to carry out a transaction, records are managed by organizations according to procedures dictated by ongoing needs of the application. In paper-based records systems the primary need of an office can be implied from their filing sequence or "original order" of its records; secondary needs can be implied from the existence of indexes to those records. Thus contextual evidence tells us whether the critical organizing principles of daily work were time (if so we will find chronological files), responsibility (where we find project files), client (case files), or intellectual context (subject files). It is instructive to examine both the actual filing sequences required by given functions and the practices of recordkeeping surrounding some functions in which a greater degree of contextual information is kept in order to understand better the importance of contextual data to evidence. This will also help us to appreciate why contextual data are of such great importance to electronic records management.

In an office conducting a single routine function, paper records are often filed according to a single salient feature such as the license number, plot identifier, or date of application. "Line" offices, which are responsible for carrying out a single function of the organization, will have procedures that assure the capture and retention of necessary evidence of their activity. If the service they perform is based on priority, for example, the date on which an application was submitted or a fee was paid will very likely also be explicitly maintained by the filing system. In such an office, incoming material will be subject to a transaction (receipt) which involves stamping the documents with the date of receipt in the office performing the application review function. Subsequent steps in the procedure will be subject to similar documentation, which could be recorded or stamped on the original document, or on the folder containing the case, or on an accompanying transaction slip. The consequences of transactions may be recorded by filing the documents in a distinctive file based on the outcome (approved, rejected, continuing under review, etc.) or such information may be reflected in data on the transaction slip and all records interfiled. In this hypothetical case, we can see the accumulation of data from a number of transactions (the original letter of application, each entry acquired along the way), along with structural information (the linking of an application to a license number), and contextual information (the form of the record revealing its provenance, the stamping on the record or file revealing the time of its receipt, and the folder in which the document is found) suggesting, but not explicitly revealing, the activity locus and its relationship to other documents with which it is filed.

Since the late nineteenth century, client-oriented functions have maintained case files for each client. These will typically contain both information about the client and information about the handling of the clients' case by the organization. Much of the latter, contextual, information about handling the case may take the form of dates and initials of various people who collected information, evaluated it, and made recommendations, approved courses of action, and communicated actions to clients. It may also include notes indicating who has viewed the folder. These contextual data are not the text of documents in the folder, but may be marked on the folder it-

self or attached to documents in a variety of routing or transaction slips. They are reflections, in a "paper trail," of the procedures employed by the agency, and hence provide evidence
of what procedures were followed.

For example, in the Office of the President of the United
States, dossiers containing many briefing papers were routinely marked with their drafting history, the history of their
review and approval, and indications of their dissemination.[5]
In such application environments, we must presume that the
requirements of the function dictated that detailed contextual
information about the use of records be maintained. The fact
that we do not keep every draft of paper documents or every
copy of a document sent for information in most offices reflects the fact that organizational and economic costs of implementing such a degree of contextual data capture exceeds
the business requirement for it.

RECORDS SYSTEMS AND EVIDENTIAL HISTORICITY

Evidential historicity is captured in records systems which
reflect the social and mechanical technology of the time. It is
then retained and retrieved by archivists whose selection of
records shapes the archives. Explicit recording of contextual
evidence is rare in paper-based environments because it is
costly, inefficient, and, given the amount of implicit evidence
provided by paper-based systems, often unnecessary.

A cost/benefits plateau determines the degree of contextual evidence that will be retained. The contextual data capture plateau in paper-based environments typically excludes
data on the intermediate transformations of documents; the
bulk of paper that would be required to retain "version control," and the lack of means to link changes made within individual drafts to the individuals or offices making them, have
generally prevented the long-term retention of drafts of all but
the most important of documents. A different equation operates in electronic records environments where a multiplicity of

versions will require incrementally more storage if the software environment stores only changes as it creates subsequent drafts.

In paper-based systems, evidence may be explicitly recorded for accountability as a matter of regular business practice, but still have very limited utility due to the limitations of retrieval. Such information is often retained only until an audit is performed. For example, in the licensing application discussed earlier, dates of application or final approval may be retrievable while intervening procedural states will probably not be. Thus, in this system, the question of who worked on a given case may be answered by the record system (retrieve by case, examine initials), but the question of what cases an individual member of the staff worked on in a given week may not. As a result, archivists may decide to discard contextual data about transaction handling history which are recorded on the file folders when refoldering the files themselves to better preserve their contents for archival retention.

Archival cost/benefits are not isolated, but rather reflect the cost/benefits of the implementation context. In the examples of version control and work analysis, an important consideration in guiding archival retention of evidence is the degree to which it was available, and used, in the course of the work of those who created the records. In the paper-based environment such data was also not used regularly in the course of decision making while in an electronic office it might well be.

But moving from paper-based to electronic systems is not a one-way street towards greater ease in using and retaining contextual data. It is often not necessary to explicitly record much contextual evidence in paper-based record systems because they provide such a wealth of evidential historicity from implicit clues. Scholars working on pre-twentieth century records are frequently able to distinguish entries made by different hands and estimate the date by the ink used. In twentieth century paper-based case files, the context of origin of records can often be inferred from the forms provided by different offices or functions. No one consciously designed the nineteenth century ledger to take advantage of the changes in handwriting and ink that serve the scholar in the construction of evidence, but these are nonetheless features of its design. The evidential historicity of these records derives from the immutability of the structural connection between entries on a page and the identifiability of handwriting and ink. Probably the handwriting and ink were used by the makers of the ledger, just as they are by the scholar, to retrieve records entered by a particular person. Although such evidential historicity could be captured in electronic systems where the invisibility of the evidence prevents us distinguishing the writer's hand or ink, and tools may be developed to allow authorship to be used as an attribute for retrieval, it is unlikely to happen unless we are conscious of the evidential historicity that will be lost without such design intervention.

Whether explicitly recorded or not, evidential historicity may be subject to loss if the record system is disrupted. In the case of the nineteenth century ledger, a decision to microfilm these records might result in losing the identifiability of the ink. In the case files of license applications, refoldering will dispose of much of the contextual data now recorded on the folder itself, while almost any unsupervised use of the materials will disrupt the order of the documents which were originally filed according to a consistent filing procedure (such as "last to front"). In the case of electronic systems, the meaning of the pointer between a transaction record from 1980 and a client record updated in 1982 is obscured when both are written to a flat file for archival retention in 1985.

The costs of explicitly recording evidential historicity, the limitations in paper-based systems on retrieving information based on any recorded data, and the "eye-readability" of the residual evidence of activity in traditional office settings have collectively minimized the attention given to evidential documentation in the design of paper-based records systems. Because paper-based records systems lack methods to automatically capture, easily keep, or systematically analyze evidential information, business requirements have accepted a low plateau of evidential data capture, retention, and access.

Electronic records systems do not have these limitations. They provide the opportunity to capture larger amounts of evidential historicity, and they create a need to do so. Greater amounts of contextual and structural information must be retained from electronic systems in order to assure that electronic records have evidence of equivalent value to that which was obtained from paper systems. In part, this reflects a greater degree of need for contextual information when records are not eye-readable. If we cannot see the documents then we need to have an external description of them. Not surprisingly, such descriptions, or indexes to records, were most often prepared in paper-based systems only when the records themselves could not be directly inspected for reasons of remote storage, security, etc. But in the electronic systems that serve today's offices, we cannot inspect the records directly so we must rely on information about them which is captured and retained by the system. As a consequence we must ask what evidential historicity should be captured by an appropriately designed system and how it should be retained.

An electronic system can track what function, activity, or transaction, and what individual, contributed to or modified each item of information if only archivists articulated what evidential detail is required or desired regarding any given type of transaction. For example, in the electronic office we can easily track every modification made to a record during its drafting life, every recipient of an electronic message and when they read it, and even every time a document was consulted. However, the potential for automatically capturing large amounts of contextual information from electronic records systems is not simply a boon to archives. It is accompanied by a host of new problems, of which the most obvious is to determine what amount of evidential historicity is required and how to capture and retain it. Less obvious is the problem that much of the evidential historicity in electronic systems, just like the arrangement of records in a paper ledger or the use of different handwritings and inks, is hardware and software dependent but the systems in which it is implemented are less easily preserved than paper-based systems were. Retaining evidential historicity also increases the complexity of the information system design and the amount of data that must be retained and hence raises the cost of preservation both for storage and migration.[6]

To design records systems that meet organizational and archival needs for accountability requires that we understand not only that evidential historicity is found in data, structure, and context, and that its character and degree reflect business application requirements, but also how records systems capture this information and the threats to its preservation. In the emerging electronic office environments that serve as the vehicles for creating and communicating the recorded knowledge of organizations today, the same relationship between raw data, structural information, and contextual information can be identified.

The raw data of today's electronic office is the text of its documents. This text does not reliably tell us anything about the provenance of the information or the order in which it was kept or used. Like paper documents, electronic records may have data provided by their creators which are intended to tell us about context, such as the date of a letter, but which does not actually assure us that the letter was written on the date indicated or that it was sent. Indeed, in their ASCII form the data does not even tell us what the documents looked like to those who read them. This kind of structural information, corresponding to that provided by the form and filing of paper records in the past, comes from the documentation of the system in which the data reside. Contextual information about the actual use of data in the system and its communication to others (e.g., transactions) may or may not be kept by the software application based on whether there is a technical requirement to do so in order for the software to function and whether there was a business functional requirement dictated by the client(s).

APPLICATION SOFTWARE AND INTERCHANGE STANDARDS

To provide concrete guidance on the capture and retention of evidential historicity in electronic records environments requires that we distinguish between the way in which evidential historicity resides in data, structure, and context information in a variety of different applications. Specifically, we need to identify that evidential historicity which is a minimum technical requirement to support each application and that which is the maximum observed evidential historicity implemented to support client functional requirements. This will enable us to develop strategies for capture and retention of evidential historicity and to identify that evidential information which could be interchanged between software systems using existing standards and that which is not covered by existing interchange standards and must therefore be represented in proprietary ways. This in turn enables us to estimate the cost and effort involved in achieving certain plateaus of evidential historicity within a range of applications, thereby making it possible for archivists to return the decision about how much to capture and retain to the organization where the risks and requirements for accountability can best be addressed.

Electronic records present one management challenge less frequently encountered in paper-based systems: retaining records for whatever period of time they have continuing value necessarily means moving them from one software environment to another.[7] Because the data must be moved, and because their value as evidence depends upon their evidential historicity, the migration of records to future implementations including, but not limited, to archival implementations requires that structural and contextual information be moved as well. Interchange standards which accommodate necessary evidential historicity are essential to the survival of archives.

Interchange standards for data and for structural information are critical for organizations conducting their business electronically. Such standards have therefore received significant attention from information managers and the software industry. The case for migrating contextual information is most evident to those who need to keep information for a very long time, and who are concerned for its evidential value. Unfortunately, archivists have not yet articulated clearly the requirements for evidential historicity associated with particular types of information systems applications. As a consequence, such requirements have been inadequately addressed in the definition of data interchange standards. At the present time, as the requirement for evidential historicity increases, the standards governing the representation of the data become less adequate for migrating records and the degree of proprietary information structuring is increasing.[8] Archivists, records managers, other information managers, and, to a great extent, program managers dependent on electronic information systems must become aware of the gap between the evidential information available to electronic application systems and the information that can be removed from the proprietary environment and maintained over time.

The degree of difficulty associated with contextual data capture and retention, and the types of information that could be captured in addition to "raw data," differ from one application software system to another. The way to begin to understand the implications is to analyze some generic characteristics of a variety of software application environments. Ultimately, specific software applications and implementations will need to be studied in order to derive the data required to define concrete cost/benefit plateaus.[9]

Word Processing

The most common office application of electronic information systems is word processing. The word processing file as created by the user (e.g., the data of the record) consists of ASCII text interspersed with display instructions such as punctuation, type size and font, tabs, and paragraph breaks. If users save the file, they must typically enter the document name into the appropriate component of the header. The display instructions indicate the logical structure of the file using typographical conventions which are familiar to readers of paper documents. The header consists of contextual information which is mostly supplied by the software system including, for example, the date and time of creation, the file size, and location of the first physical data segment. In some software systems, especially in multi-user systems, the header might also include update history of the file, access rules, output format definitions, and links to distribution lists.

An office system need not maintain a great deal of evidential historicity to manage word processing files if the word processing system is simply a means of making paper output products. But from an information management perspective, if the system serves as a repository of textual records created and maintained in the course of business, it is essential to retain evidence of the structure and context of the data, including information about the creation and use of the record.

Contextual information must be retained for operational as well as archival reasons. In electronic networked office environments that are now becoming the norm, there is a technical requirement to preserve evidence of what changed between versions of a document. This responds both to the business requirement to be able to return to prior drafts and to the audit requirement to identify who was responsible for all changes. The system may also have a technical requirement to identify the authors of each change in order to support security (permission) controls. Finally, the client may impose functional requirements on the software designers to create and retain information on the users and uses of documents. This kind of information is especially critical for records to serve as evidence in a shared filing system where many individuals have access to records and where "sending" the document in a transaction actually involves only making it accessible to another.

It is possible to design electronic office systems which record the evidential historicity associated with each transaction that creates, communicates, uses, or modifies a document. For example, each transaction that is recorded and communicated beyond the boundaries of an individual workstation, a workgroup, an organizational unit itself or the organization (depending on what boundary the institutional policy decides is evidentially significant) could be captured in an audit trail and written out as a data file. But in order for the system to use data of this sort, the information must be active with respect to the application software, as it is in a document header, rather than passively recorded as data of the document itself. Unfortunately, existing standards for office systems do not provide for interchangeability of header information regarding permissions, or file locations, of such documents. Existing standards do not even define methods of explicitly writing such header data to the file being kept as evidence.

Structural information must also be retained if we are to have adequate evidence and conveying such structural information beyond the confines of the creating software is becoming more, rather than less, problematic. As the means of exchanging information created in electronic systems on media other than paper become widespread, we are witnessing a rapid evolution in "forms of material" which reflect new structural relations between data. Forms of material are socially or culturally constructed information containers with which we communicate.[10] It is as a result of these structural signals that literate people in our culture can immediately recognize the difference between a job application, a greeting card, or a legal summons without reading the words which appear on each. We are currently witnessing a rate of change in forms of material that has not been seen since the advent of writing and the subsequent introduction of printing.[11] Because the appearance of electronic information is governed by software control of the application in which the information is made to appear, common conventions for rendering structural information are essential for the full meaning of records to be transferred.[12]

Electronic technologies are now being used to generate an entirely new form of material called hypermedia or compound documents. These non-linear "documents" are composed of data objects in the form of text, image, and sound that are linked by pathways defined by the author. The pathways are made manifest on being "played back" through software which is at this point still non-standard. Hypertexts and compound documents may, like the graphics generated from spreadsheets contained within word processing documents, point to dynamic data objects which take on characteristics of a changing environment, thus they may be different each time they are viewed. The implications for archivists are obvious: with these forms of material the transaction, and not the data of the document, is the archival record. Standards efforts for hypermedia have not yet succeeded in defining all the terms with which they must deal (the second NIST conference on hypermedia standards in the summer of 1990 had to be canceled because of this), to say nothing of dealing with the contextual data questions raised by archivists.[13]

The challenge of retaining the evidential historicity of dynamic forms of material goes beyond what has been recognized by the standards efforts of today. These efforts have focused on the interchangeability of the data content of documents and to a lesser extent on interoperability based on structural information. They have not had adequate regard for the need to capture and interchange contextual data about the particular transaction in which a user encounters a dynamic document. To do so, the standards efforts would need to address documents comprised of data objects that are brought together under user control through the functionality provided by one application, but which might themselves be created by other applications. In the moment of being brought together they have an evidential historicity which the systems designer could have designed to adhere to them. But the methods of representing the evidential historicity of the document would, by necessity, have to be non-standard because no such standards have yet been developed. Yet the new forms of material with which we are increasingly dealing require precisely such standards, operating above the application level, in order to survive with their evidential historicity intact.

Electronic Mail

Electronic mail is a deceptively non-traditional technology which can illustrate some of the problems and potentials of electronic environments. The speed with which electronic mail is delivered seems to reduce the length of individual messages within the communication. With electronic mail, numerous messages will be exchanged as a dialogue where previously the participants would have written a finished argument in a single exchange of letters. The velocity of electronic mail exchanges (the time between a message and the response) in many organizations is 2-3 times per day, thus the equivalent of a full complex exchange can take place incrementally over several days (in the length of time it would have taken to send a letter).[14] All the messages in the exchange can be sent to numerous individuals who respond asynchronously. It is necessary to know what messages have been received by whom and at what point in a discussion in order to fully understand the responses. In other words, the evidential historicity of the documents is essential to the reconstruction of the transaction.

In contemporary implementations of electronic mail, the "envelopes" of the messages are defined by the ANSI standards X.400/X.500 to carry the address to which they will be sent, whether acknowledgment is required, and other information relating to the context of the exchange. Archivists require that additional information about the communication context be preserved for the record to retain its evidential historicity but they have yet to examine envelope headers to determine specifically what additional information would be required to establish the provenance, or originating context, of electronic messages. Systems designers have, to date, paid little attention to capturing the envelope data in their attempts to archive electronic mail. Thus we find ourselves in a world in which we have the technological capability to capture a level of context-based information surrounding records that surpasses greatly any data we had in traditional archival provenance, but have settled for a plateau of data interchange that does not satisfy archival requirements. Higher plateaus can be easily envisioned, and the economic and technological costs (including the potential explosion of the size of information bases as they carry evidential historicity data concerning all their objects) can be calculated. Archivists need to participate in such efforts in order to articulate the functional requirements of archivally acceptable electronic mail environments.

Spreadsheets

If we look briefly at the spreadsheet, another common office application, we encounter these and other issues. The cells of electronic spreadsheets contain formulas relating to the nature of work in the organization. These formulas embody a great deal of knowledge about the organization, as anyone who has ever tried to use a spreadsheet developed for a specific office accounting function will recognize. However the nature of the data being cited and the history of the expression or formula are not documented in the application itself unless individuals make a concrete (and rare) effort to document it.

Transactions involving spreadsheets are even more complex. In addition to hiding their operative formulas, spreadsheets may draw their data from numerous active databases and they may be displayed to those making decisions as a series of graphs rather than as textual data points. Evidence of this transaction is not currently represented in application software except as the resulting graph, which is a print record surrogate, but which disguises the calculations as well as the raw data on which it was based. In short, the spreadsheet is rife with contextual data without which the "raw data" is hardly meaningful. In this and other many layered application software environments, standards for information interchange barely address the transfer of the data content and the structural information that assigns a calculation to the appropriate cell from one system to another, and none have addressed the contextual information interchange issues.

A spreadsheet displayed as a graph, drawing data from a variety of contemporaneous database states, may, furthermore, be displayed in a word-processed document in which it resides as a pointer, rather than as a fixed manifestation. If such a document is used for decisionmaking, archivists will want to know what it said at the time the decision was made, because if they save the document with its pointer, even if they could succeed at the task of keeping the associated information systems intact, they would view a different image when the document is next displayed.

In the spreadsheet we are beginning to encounter a new kind of data -- intelligent data -- which could be major contributors to the productivity of the office in the next decade and which pose a serious threat to archives.[15] "Intelligent data" are aggregates of raw data created in a system which imbues them with contextual information that instructs them how to behave in that system; for example, a text given the "intelligence" assigned to a memorandum would "know" when to send itself and to whom to send itself. A word or two assigned the intelligence of a future date would "know" to remind the creator on or before that date. Creators need not assign this intelligence themselves, because in intelligent systems some of this work can be done automatically. Thus a program could determine the keywords under which to file a document, build a table of contents and an index, and screen readers for security requirements which it determined from reading the text. In the spreadsheet, each cell contains the formulas which it uses to analyze the raw data provided to it.

Database Management Systems

Database management systems are the next most common office applications. When we examine them from an archival perspective, some contextual information retention requirements present themselves immediately. The raw data in a database has some informational value, but it has little evidential meaning. The transactions in a database environment are input records, queries, and output instructions. Without the documentation of the system, we do not know what data any given individual or office had included in their "view." Without update records, we cannot tell the state of a given piece of data at a given time. Without links to other systems that might have been provided to active users of the system, we cannot tell what use might have been made of the data. This kind of documentation of the "potentialities" of the data is recorded in metadata systems called data dictionary/directory systems and Information Resource Directory Systems to which archivists need to pay greater attention. In addition, we could capture documentation of the actual uses, the actual updates, and the actual data participating in specific transactions. In principle a transactional audit trail could document changes so completely as to make possible a "time-travel" database, but the practical implications of maintaining a system so that it can back itself up in time are formidable. Therefore, archivists will need to work with systems designers to assure that database systems create certain transactional records (for particular types of transactions initiated by certain functions within the organization) that otherwise would not be created.

To get a complete picture of what the database does we need to document also whether it acts under human control at all times or if the database management system sometimes takes action (and creates records) on its own. For example, does it have a "tickler" report, or does it generate warning notices when someone tries to breech its security, or does it generate weekly, monthly, and quarterly reports at the appropriate time without specific human request? Increasingly, software is being implemented in organizations so that the database serves each office differently and so that distinct facilities are provided for different functions. The trend in information processing is towards more and more "intelligent" systems. These include systems using "object-oriented languages" and "artificial intelligence" but very traditional programming is also embedding growing amounts of intelligence in software. Unfortunately, the methods of representing this "intelligent" information surrounding the raw data, like those for representing contextual information, are non-standard. Nevertheless, the system rules are context to the transactions, and without them we can only poorly comprehend the evidential significance of a record.

Graphical Software

Beyond the office, a class of applications which include Geographic Information Systems (GIS), Business Graphics and Statistics and Computer-Aided Design (CAD) systems are growing in importance. These applications are characterized by a graphical presentation of data. They enable users to envision the relationships between large numbers of discrete data points by displaying them visually. As such they enable effective communication of complex information, and their outputs are records in such communicated transactions. But in order to employ these outputs as evidence, the underlying data are required in addition to the visualization.

Geographic Information Systems (GIS) can serve to illustrate this. GIS environments are one of the most rapidly growing applications created by and used in government today because so much of the function of government involves delivery of services to the population of a geographic region. That population, and the infrastructures that serve it, must be envisioned by those delivering and receiving services.[16] Geographic Information Systems are databases whose records are data points in a spatial linking structure (e.g., a map). They constitute a powerful application environment precisely because data points derived from one source can be retrieved in conjunction with data points from other sources, thus building a comprehensive view of what is known about any space on the face of the earth (or under water). For government, the organization of databases by geographical locus is an important tool for management. However, the data points contributed to a geographic information system will have been established at different times, by different agencies, and for different purposes. From an archival perspective, this means that they will have different provenances. Archivists need to decide both what data to retain about the context of creation and use of each discrete data point with respect to its original relation (which becomes simply another retrieval set within the operational GIS application) and what contextual data needs to be preserved as evidence of functions that subsequently use that data point in creating records (transactions) in other applications employing the GIS. Even if there were standards for the interchange of GIS data, or the interoperability of GIS systems, they would not address the retention of the evidential historicity of these new forms of material.

Another increasingly important software-dependent data object is being created by Computer-Aided Design and Computer Assisted Manufacturing (CAD/CAM) systems. These systems employ vectorized information (formulas for lines) to generate displays of three-dimensional objects such as buildings or machine components. CAD/CAM files are used to make decisions about construction and maintenance of increasingly large portions of the capital assets of governments, but they are highly software dependent. Changes to drawings in CAD/CAM systems may or may not be documented and the contextual significance of the source of the data are not generally considered important by the architects, electricians, manufacturers, etc. who make and use the latest version of this data. Hence the implementation plateaus in these systems are set far below the levels regarded by archivists as important to record for evidential historicity. Meanwhile standards, such as IGES (Initial Graphics Exchange Environment), are focused on interchange and interoperability below the application level.

ELECTRONIC RECORDS MANAGEMENT GUIDELINES

Electronic information systems, therefore, present at least two challenges to archivists. The first is that the designers of these systems may have chosen to document less contextual information than may be of interest to archivists when they designed the system. The second is that the data recorded in any given information system will, someday, need to be transferred to another system. As long as the information created in the course of work in an electronic environment remains in the software and hardware system in which it was created, it loses none of the contextual information which is critical to its meaning, but the transition, or "migration," of data to a new environment threatens to change the way the information looks, feels, or operates, and hence what it means.

Archivists have always been dependent on the information systems implemented in working offices for the amount of contextual information that would be available as evidence. What has changed with electronic records is both that a greater degree of evidential granularity is possible, and that it may not be retained because program managers are less aware of its value, or of their ability to require its retention, than they were in paper-based office systems.[17] Archival retention of contextual data at appropriate levels of granularity is likely to depend, in the future, on program managers insisting on their requirements for this contextual data for information management within their functions. For this to happen, archivists need to articulate what contextual data are required as evidence, how it might be captured, and at what cost.

Although archivists accession records at the level of the record series, we found very little contextual documentation at the series level in paper-based records environments. As a consequence, documentation of the paper-based records systems by procedures manuals rarely answers questions such as:

- What functions and transactions within functions created records in the series?

- What functions filed into the series and how did they exercise their judgment?

- Which offices had access to information in the series and could they alter it?

Instead, in paper-based environments we find evidence of creation and use at the individual document or transactional entry, or at the level of file folders which detail who saw their contents, the time at which they received them, and what they did with them (forwarding, taking action, etc.). In electronic information systems, metadata systems should explicitly document the activity context out of which records arise, and policy should be implemented to define forms of documents created in such contexts and the organizational retention requirements for each. Systems can then be implemented so that when a record is identified by its origin and date, appropriate retention policy can be automatically executed. Records which need to be retained for their continuing value can be protected from alteration or deletion.

The second threat is more insidious. It is expensive to transfer data from one system to another, especially as the information we are trying to capture in these transfers is the most system-dependent and the least standard. Each system migration is accompanied by extensive planning. Often it must include making modifications to both systems in order to preserve functionality associated with the old system and to retain contextual data, including that upon which systems functionality depends. In an operational environment, the decision is usually made to "migrate" as little data as possible into the new system and to preserve a minimum of contextual data. Archivists must realize however that data loss in migration, like data loss in copying, is a one-way street. As decisions are made to leave some contextual data behind, the evidence provided by the information that is transferred will be lost.

The current state of standards does not permit functional equivalency (by and large) to be communicated across systems. Only the "data" content of texts, images, and sounds are accommodated by existing standards. New standards will eventually be developed (ideally with archival input) to bring more and more contextual functionality across systems barriers. However, new methods of data organization and new concepts in computing will also continue to emerge and will always lack standards when they are new so the problem will not go away. Archivists will have to continue to face the questions of how much functional equivalency they will try to transfer and how software dependent they will permit the data they manage to be. In other words, archivists will need to confront, on an application-by-application basis, the potential for capture of data with various degrees of evidential historicity.[18]

In each case, archivists will need to return to fundamental archival principles to determine just what they really wanted to save anyway. And they will need to look forward into the management of the current technologies to determine how practical it is, or will be, to save data of evidential value. It may be that archivists will be satisfied with the degree of evidential historicity they were able to achieve in paper-based record systems, in which case there are very few barriers to implementing successful electronic-based archival environments. Or archivists may decide that the fuller capability of tracking the actual participation of electronic data objects in organizational activities needs to be documented by archivally satisfactory information systems, in which case they will need to define those levels of evidential historicity that must be attained and specify the systems requirements for such environments.

At a meeting on electronic records management research issues sponsored by the National Historical Publications and Records Commission in January 1991, participants identified the concept of technological and economic plateaus in electronic data capture and archiving as an important arena for research. They proposed research efforts to identify such plateaus in existing applications and to define the technical challenges associated with the retention of greater degrees of evidential historicity within applications as well as the problems and prospects for long-term preservation of data representing different plateaus.[19] Their proposal would, for example, bring sociological evidence about transactions in organizations together with technical specifications of different degrees of evidential historicity of records to generate preliminary estimates of the increases in data volume required to satisfy different levels of requirements imposed by the archival principle of provenance. It is hoped that this research will produce information to help archivists make decisions regarding the amount of contextual information they can afford to capture and the requirements of systems designed to document context along with managing data content. In any case, the analysis to date has enriched the concept of provenance and reinforced its direct link to missions, functions, and ultimately the activities or transactions of an organization rather than to organizational units, as was predicted by Richard Lytle and me in an earlier article.[20] I will not be surprised as we refine our concepts of evidential historicity to discover that the concept of provenance takes on even greater granularity and is associated with the particular actions.

NOTES

[1] The term "corporate memory" is used extensively in the writings of John McDonald and the policies of the National Archives of Canada to refer to that evidence which it is important for an organization to retain for its ongoing operations and legitimacy. See for example, National Archives of Canada, "Strategic Framework for the Information Management Standards and Practices Division" (unpublished manuscript, April 1991).

[2] These concepts were originally developed in a discussion with Richard Cox, Margaret Hedstrom, John McDonald, and Lisa Weber in January 1991 following the NHPRC-sponsored Working Meeting on Research Issues in Electronic Records Management.

[3] Note that *archives* as used throughout this chapter refers to a kind of records not to an institutional setting. The institutional setting called an *archives* may contain materials that do not fall within the scope of this definition of archives, such as personal papers, materials kept for their "informational value," and information generated by archivists. The narrow sense of *archives* as evidence is explained further in Chapters 2 and 3 of this volume. See also Sue McKemmish and Frank Upward, "The Archival Document," a submission to the Public Inquiry into Australia as an Information Society, *Archives and Manuscripts* 19:1 (May 1991): 17-31.

[4] *Digital Image Application and Optical Media Systems: Management Issues, Technical Trends, User Experience: Guidelines for State and Local Agencies*, A Joint Report by the National Archives and Records Administration and the National Association of Government Archives and Records Administrators (July 1991). See also Association for Information and Image Management, *The Use of Optical Disks for Public Records*, Technical Report #25 (Washington, D.C.: AIIM, 1990).

[5] These paperwork practices in the office of the president were common in the Kennedy Administration as reflected in records at the Kennedy Presidential Library. Similar practices probably were not followed in the Reagan administration use of the IBM Profs electronic messaging system because the system provided some of these features as long as the records were active within it. Chapter 4 in this volume further describes the implications of the suit by Scott Armstrong, et al., to prevent destruction of the Reagan administration White House Profs files.

[6] Even though storage costs may prove to be insignificant in the future, it is evident that migration costs will not be trivial in the absence of complete interoperability standards.

[7] The half-life of software products is less than three years and less than one year between releases. In an environment in which several layers of software will run between the operating system and the application, maintaining all these functional capabilities "as they were" would be technically impossible even if it were not the case that the software licenses do not transfer with the data if it comes to the archives, thus making it legally impossible to maintain commercially developed application software.

[8] As the user's mental model departs from traditional paper models, the complexity increases. Hence databases and GIS systems require greater contextual data capture to represent transactions that word processing or electronic mail where the transaction is essentially like that conducted in the course of business in a paper-based office.

[9] At present, I know of no reliable studies of the costs of these migrations that can be used for archival cost-benefits analysis.

[10] The definition I wrote for the NISTF data element dictionary has been used in the archives community but few have followed its implications. See David Bearman and Peter Sigmond, "Explorations of Form of Material Authority Files by Dutch Archivists," *American Archivist* 50 (Spring 1987): 249-253; and Luciana Duranti, "Diplomatics: New Uses for an Old Science," *Archivaria* (1988-1992), Part I, 28:7-27; Part II, 29:4-17; Part III, 30:4-20; Part IV, 31:10-25; Part V, 32:6-24; Part VI, 33:6-24.

[11] Forms of electronic records are discussed in David M. Levy, Daniel C. Brotsky, and Kenneth R. Olson, "Formalizing the Figural: Aspects of a Foundation for Document Manipulation" (Systems Sciences Laboratory, Xerox Palo Alto Research Center, 1988).

[12] The Text Encoding Initiative, an undertaking of numerous text-oriented humanities disciplines, is developing methods of indicating the structural aspects of texts going back to the middle ages using Standard Generalized Markup Language (SGML). Twentieth century documentation practices are generally covered by a smaller set of declarations developed by the American Association of Publishers. More complex modern Document Type Definitions (DTDs) are being implemented for multimedia documentation for airplanes, battleships and like systems following the specifications developed by

the Department of Defense Computer-aided Acquisitions and Logistical Support (CALS) initiative.

[13] The National Institute of Standards and Technology (NIST) called a conference on hypertext standards in the early spring 1990. A follow-up meeting to have been held in the summer 1990 was canceled because there was too little agreement about how to proceed to make progress possible. Currently two efforts are underway which emphasize different aspects of hypermedia interchange: HyTime, an extension of the SGML approach, declares the logical functions and links of objects being interchanged while MHEG defines the technical specifications for data representation in those objects.

[14] Tora Bikson and J.D. Eveland, "The Interplay of Work Group Structures and Computer Support," in *Intellectual Teamwork*, ed. Kraut, Galagher, and Egido (Hillsdale, New Jersey: Erlbaum, 1990). Observations on university campuses where electronic mail is widespread confirm that the medium is leading to the evolution of a truncated form of communication, sometimes resulting in exchanges analogous to the nod or grunt in face-to-face communications.

[15] Timothy J. Heintz, "Object-oriented Databases and Their Impact on Future Database Applications," *Information & Management* 20:2 (1991): 95-103.

[16] Kentucky Information Systems Commission, *Current Issues in Government Information Policy Conference Proceedings* (Frankfort, Kentucky: KISC, June 1991).

[17] The practice of associating provenance with the governmental agency responsible for the creation of an entire body of records, which led to the establishment in the United States of the "Record Group" concept, has largely been superseded in the U.S. and Australia anyway by the link between the record series and its functional provenance, or the activity of the agency that gave rise to it. The seeds for this move are found in the writings of Peter Scott in Australia in the 1960s and 1970s; of David Bearman, Max Evans, Richard Szary, and others in the U.S. in the 1980s; and in the practices surrounding the implementation of USMARC AMC and APPM. The increasing granularity of provenance may be a trend that will carry the assignment of provenance down to the contextual information in particular documents in electronic information systems.

[18] The identification of the business application as the locus of intervention by archivists is based on the realization that requirements for data retention derive from the combination of requirements by

ongoing offices for information regarding their functions and the requirements of the organization for evidence of its activity over time. Both of these requirements are focused at the program level and must be achieved through the implementation of software to support concrete functions of the organization. For further discussion, see Chapters 2 and 3 in this volume.

[19] The National Historical Publications and Records Commission, *Research Issues in Electronic Records* (St. Paul: Minnesota Historical Society, 1991).

[20] David Bearman and Richard H. Lytle, "The Power of the Principle of Provenance," *Archivaria* 21 (Winter 1985-86): 14-27.

CHAPTER SIX

Managing Electronic Mail[*]

Electronic mail is a new way of transporting communications which creates a new documentary form of record. The question of how to manage electronic mail as a record is one that will confront management in every contemporary organization within the next few years. This chapter explores the issues associated with the management of electronic mail which combine the requirements for correspondence control and filing present in paper-based communications systems with the functional requirements for managing any electronic record-keeping systems. The author applies a generic framework for managing electronic records to define an approach to accountable corporate management of electronic mail. He notes in conclusion that the resultant system provides advantages over traditional paper-based systems in the archives and records management arena as well as for users.

[*] Originally published in *Archives and Manuscripts* 22:1 (May 1994): 28-50. Previous versions of this paper were delivered at the Society of Canadian Office Automation Professionals, Ottawa, 31 March 1993, and the National Association of Government Archives and Records Administrators Annual Conference, St. Paul, Minnesota, 22 July 1993. Ideas contained in the paper were refined in workshop presentations at Monash University, Melbourne, Australia, in May 1993, and the University of Texas-Austin in November 1993.

INTRODUCTION

In August 1993, the U.S. District Court ruled that the President of the United States, the directors of agencies within the Executive Office of the President, and the Archivist of the United States were wrong in not considering White House electronic mail as records, in not providing for the systematic retention of electronic mail messages, and in believing that they could satisfy recordkeeping requirements for electronic mail by printing certain messages out to paper.[1] The case will not have explicit applicability to other jurisdictions, but the reasoning of the court in a case with such a high profile will certainly not go without notice. The question of how to manage electronic mail as a record is one that will confront management in every contemporary organization within the next few years. The impetus may be to document what the organization has done to make better decisions, enforce contracts, or avoid claims, or it may be to reduce risks by destroying electronic records as soon as they are not required for operational reasons.

Whatever the purpose, we require a framework that will help us ask the question of how to ensure that electronic mail results the in creation of a record and how to manage records created by electronic mail communications over time. In this chapter, I apply a generic framework for managing electronic records to define an approach for the accountable corporate management of electronic mail.[2] The purpose is both to illustrate the applicability of the framework and to assist records managers, auditors, and archivists in applying appropriate controls to the creation, maintenance, and accessibility of electronic mail. The *constants* in this framework are:

(1) definition of functional requirements for capturing, preserving and providing access to electronic records;

(2) identification of four tactics used to satisfy any given functional requirement: policy, design, implementation, and standards;

(3) rigorous exploitation of the Open Systems Environment (OSE) model developed by the National Institute of Standards and Technology[3] to identify loci for intervention; and

(4) use of the formal methods of the information science disciplines of data administration and configuration management.

In addition, the framework references the effect of three classes of specific environmental *variables*:

- the business function for which the electronic record is created,
- the software in place to support the business application, and
- the corporate culture of the organization.

The appropriate methodology is to employ one or more of the four tactics to achieve the required degree of control over electronic records throughout their life. The choice of tactics to apply is determined by the variables -- based on an assessment of the ability of each approach in the specific context -- to affect hardware, software, or procedure in a fashion that will result in electronic records that satisfy the functional requirements.

To operationalize this method, the functional requirements are viewed as metadata documentation specifications.[4] In this way it is easier to see how they can be satisfied at different points in the overall hardware and software architecture (using the Open Systems Environment model of software architecture) and in the information flow. In consequence, we can express each functional requirement as consisting of a requirement to capture and keep particular metadata at a given layer of OSE ("a switch" in the hardware configuration) and to apply data administration and configuration management techniques to their control.

THE PROBLEM

We are moving rapidly into a future in which virtually all workers will be linked by networked computing. A decade ago I, and most other automation experts, predicted that white-collar information workers would lead the way towards this future, but in fact they have held back. Today grocery clerks have networked cash registers, package delivery and messenger services employ networked hand-held receipt pads, and production workers on the shop floor have networked cutting tools, but many office workers are not yet connected. The economic drivers which have led to value-added information processing in the grocery, the factory, and the service industry are, however, about to change the office as well. Before this decade is out, information managers will have to support twenty-four hour a day remote access to a virtual work space. Most organizations will provide traditional white-collar services -- such as advice, regulation, and policy debate -- electronically. The means by which such communications occur is generically called "electronic mail" (e-mail), which refers to an underlying utility of software functionality that actually incorporates a changing set of services. Like the post office and Federal Express, electronic mail services do not interact with the content of the messages and should support interchange of virtually any kind of data. Indeed, electronic mail can carry highly structured messages such as Electronic Data Interchange (EDI) documents or messages containing data formatted in other than ASCII text, such as multimedia.

Does e-mail therefore present a problem for accountability and organizational continuity? No doubt it will unless organizations do something to manage it. Presidents Reagan and Bush ordered the erasure of the electronic mail of the White House on the last day of their administrations only to be greeted in court by citizens who successfully argued that the data in these computer systems contained records and could not be destroyed except after archival review.[5] Electronic Discovery, Inc., a Seattle-based company, lives by finding electronic mail messages on unmanaged disks throughout corporate America, winning cases and large settlements for its clients in areas ranging from product liability to unlawful personnel practices. As organizations use electronic mail systems in the daily conduct of business, they accrue evidence of the conduct of business that is essential in reconstructing how the organization made decisions, what decisions it made, and how they were carried out. As some organizations develop and implement policies and procedures -- and the auditing, archives, and records management professions define "best practices" for management of electronic records -- organizations will find themselves under great pressure to adopt guidelines and implement programs to control their e-mail.[6] Even in the absence of such widespread adoption by others, the Appeals Court in the Profs Case admonished both the Archivist of the United States for dereliction of duty in not providing guidelines and the White House for failure to adopt procedures to ensure the preservation of electronic mail.[7]

In our society, organizations are legal persons. They may be committed to an action by their employees when these commitments are communicated in writing or in other ways which leave evidence. Electronic mail is written communication and will become part of the normal business practice of any institution that uses it. Like all writing, it is "hearsay" evidence but the rules of evidence, business practice, and case law combine to ensure that in any jurisdiction, electronic mail will at least be admissible in legal and administrative proceedings.[8]

Organizations are accountable to society. If private, they must provide a reckoning to governmental taxing, regulating, and reporting bodies; if public, they are accountable to the general public, legislative bodies, and the executive. In all cases, they are responsible for contractual relations and must provide accounting for performance of such contracts. The burden of proof has always been on the organization, but the trend in many jurisdictions -- as illustrated by the adoption of new Federal Rules of Evidence by the U.S. Congress on 1 December 1993 -- is to place responsibility for identification of all relevant records on their creators.[9] While good record-keeping was always valuable in court to defend a company charged with negligence, it becomes essential in a climate in which all records relevant to any corporate activity must be produced within ninety days.

But even if organizations only needed to ensure their own survival, we would need to adopt better practices for management of electronic mail. Operational records are required for day-to-day management when an employee is away from the office as well as to survive disasters such as the World Trade Center bombing.

In fact, electronic mail generates requirements for all of the functions within an organization which are dependent upon recordkeeping, including privacy administration, vital records management, administrative security, auditing, access, and archives. The reasons for managing electronic mail are no different than those for managing internal and external correspondence carried by other carriers, but the functional requirements are quite different.

A THEORETICAL FRAMEWORK

Functional Requirements

The fundamental reason that the functional requirements for managing electronic records seem so different from those for managing records recorded on paper is that electronic records are software dependent. This fundamental property has numerous implications: electronic records are not visible to the naked eye, they require software and hardware to be accessed and used, and they are composed of information created by the integrated use of a variety of software applications.

The most fundamental implication is that not all information systems are recordkeeping systems; indeed, most database systems are designed not to generate records when they are queried and provide information in response to a user request even if the user "writes" a report from that data.

When records are created, software dependency dictates that they must be identifiable by a system, their boundaries must be known to that system, and they must include within their boundaries the complete set of information from whatever software applications is required to ensure that they are evidence of a transaction. The system must also somehow ensure that a record exists which is comprehensive in that it documents every business transaction. None of these requirements tends to be identified explicitly when we think of paper records because they are either self-evident (identifiable, bounded, complete) or nearly impossible to ensure within the design of paper systems (comprehensive).

Software dependency also impacts the functional requirements for maintaining records once they are created. The soundness of records, or their integrity as complete records, must be maintained across software generations which may require representing knowledge of their contents, structure, and context in system-independent ways. Any uses made of them must be auditable -- including not only changes such as additions, deletions, and modifications, but also retrieval, viewing, filing, indexing, or classifying -- because these acts have a significance for the business and affect subsequent use. In addition, records must be removable under appropriate authority and exportable to another system in order to accommodate changes in software and hardware systems.

Finally, software dependence is what makes satisfying the functional requirements for access to records over time difficult. Changes in hardware and software that take place over time can compromise the availability of records to software that will access them and their usability in the ways in which the original record was usable (executing processes along the same relations as the original record when the original record had functionality within a larger system). It may also affect the end users' ability to understand their presentation because software different from that under which they were created may make different use of the contextual and structural information they contain. In addition, the system must provide for the redactability of records over time and the maintenance of records of redactions across the history of changing implementations.

Even when systems architects, policy makers, and designers of business procedures are alert to these functional requirements of recordkeeping systems, it is not easy to guarantee their satisfaction. Success may rest in the ability of the archivist and records manager to identify an appropriate tactic for the satisfaction of each requirement.

Tactics

Assuming a set of defined functional requirements for electronic recordkeeping systems, there are four basic strategies that could be employed to achieve the desired ends. The first (examined at considerable length in my 1990 report to the United Nations) is policy.[10]

First, and most direct, would be able to tell people in your organization to satisfy the functional requirements. If one requirement is to be able to identify the context in which the record was created and the business transaction of which it is a part, you would instruct people in your organization that they must document this information either in the content of the record or in a header or pointer to the record before it can be communicated to another person. Of course it is possible that a policy may not be adhered to. If this is a risk in a given business context it would lead us to examine one of the other strategies.

A second approach would be to satisfy the same functional requirement through design. In this case you would specify the development of software which recognizes the context from which the record was created, uniquely identifies each business transaction, and "stamps" this information on the record before it is sent out of the system to another individual or database.

Alternatively we could decide to use an implementation approach to satisfying this functional requirement. At log on, each individual could be assigned a context extension. Business transactions would be meaningfully coded by employees as part of a filing system; the employees would be instructed to identify these codes in a second subject line of all outgoing correspondence. The second subject would be employed for retrieval but not transmitted to the addressee.

Finally, the organization could establish an internal standard, or work to adopt a national or international standard, for electronic mail envelope structures which required the presence of such information in order to carry a message across networks. They would then acquire only systems which conformed to that standard.

Over the past several years, I have not encountered any approaches to satisfying requirements that use any approach other than these, although most approaches actually combine elements of these four "pure" tactics. If an organization walks through each functional requirement for recordkeeping -- imagining how each of the tactics might be suited to their situation -- they generate a menu of options for action on electronic records which can be presented to program managers and data processing personnel who are searching for answers to the question of how best to manage such records. The solutions they choose are likely to be dictated by local organizational variables.

Variables

There is no rule which defines what tactics an organization should employ to satisfy each functional requirement, but it must be understood that each requirement can, in principle, be satisfied by a different tactic. In fact, because the functional requirements can be further analyzed to derive a set of metadata functional specifications, there is no reason why each element of information that must be managed in order to satisfy the functional requirements could not come from, and be controlled by, a different tactic. The choice depends on the business function which the records document, the organizational culture in which they are created, and the technological environment or systems architecture in which they are communicated, maintained, and accessed.

First, the degree to which each functional requirement pertains must be assessed based on the need to satisfy it in a given functional area. For example, financial transactions involve different risks than personnel transactions. In manufacturing organizations, the background to design decisions are as important as the background to policy decisions are in public organizations. In housekeeping functions, the fact that an action occurred is typically all that it is required to know, and even this may not need to be known for long.

More concrete relationships between business functions and recordkeeping requirements results from specific regulatory and legal requirements for recordkeeping that pertain only to a specific business application domain. Hence rules under which the company operates may dictate the way in which authenticity must be documented or the procedures that must be in place to ensure comprehensiveness of documentation of transactions. Often these external rules or guidelines are not so much statutory or regulatory as they are derived from standards of "best practices" within an application domain or discipline. Thus patient records in hospitals or research records in R&D laboratories are governed by stringent requirements dictated by the practitioners themselves. Sometimes these statements of best practices will be formal, as in the case of ISO 9000 product documentation standards. But more often they have the status of guidelines to a group of professionals but serve as a standard because more formal standards do not exist. When guidelines for recordkeeping exist in a specific business application domain, it is important to incorporate them into the functional requirements adopted for electronic records management in that business context.

Just as the nature of the business functions will influence the approach taken to fulfilling the functional requirements, so will the technical ease of satisfying the requirement through software or system modification. The design of software applications can help or hinder efforts to satisfy the functional requirements through design, implementation, and standards. Within a specific application domain, some software packages will serve better and others worse in achieving the same functional end. In developing a tactic for managing electronic records, however, it is critical to understand that application software boundaries are not business application boundaries. In some case, as in electronic mail, many business applications may be conducted using the same application software (which is, in effect, a utility to the business application). In other cases, a single business application will employ many pieces of application software. In any event, more software than simply application software will be involved in the satisfaction of any business requirement. Strategies for management of electronic records depend on understanding the opportunity presented by the layering of software (the OSE model) and hardware (in distributed systems architectures). Each layer of the software represents a location at which a functional requirement could be satisfied, and every interface between hardware components is a "switch" across which a communicated transaction must flow.

Technical aspects of the systems environment may provide reasons to address those functional requirements being satisfied through systems design or implementation at particular layers in the software or hardware architecture. Characteristics of the functional requirement or of the technical architecture could lead us to choose to satisfy one requirement through the user interface layer, another through modification to the application software, a third at the operating system or Application Platform Interface (API) layer, and a fourth at the front end to a corporate filing system on the network. Later in this chapter, further exploration of these options will illuminate the power of using a system's technical features to implement tactics; the point here is that the same technical characteristics may constrain our choice of tactics as well. In an environment in which the software application functionality is a given and proprietary, we may have to locate new functionality at another layer. In a systems architecture in which there are no corporate storage facilities, the "corporate" view of the local storage may have to be imposed quite differently than in one in which there is a physical corporate store.

Finally, however important technical environmental constraints are, the corporate culture of the organization (or of the specific business area upon which the strategy is focused) will probably be the most important variable in selecting the tactics to use in management of electronic records. Some corporate cultures are simply not amenable to certain tactics while others are so hospitable towards them that there is no need to develop more complex approaches. For example, the privacy act administrators in Sweden, when asked how they preserved the rights of individuals in records collected by the government, explained that they simply identified the original purposes for which the information was collected on each file and that the policy stated that the records could not be used for any other purpose. When I expressed surprise that such a policy would be effective, they related to me the case of a minister in the present government who, wishing to use such information for other purposes, asked the Parliament for such an authority but was turned down. What had surprised me was that anyone with custody over such records would be constrained at all in their use, not whether Parliament might be successfully petitioned to alter a use once it was determined. Policy approaches to satisfying access restrictions on records were, in this case, adequate, but in another corporate culture these might be unlikely to succeed, leading to the choice of one of the other tactics to satisfy this requirement.

PRECONDITIONS FOR ELECTRONIC MAIL MANAGEMENT

Four critical success factors in implementing solutions to the accountable management of electronic mail are:

(1) The identification of electronic records as the information associated with a business transaction.

It is inherent in the concept of a transaction is that the information must be communicated to be a record. Further, to be considered a record by an organization, the communication must cross what that organization regards as a "business boundary." Typically the concept of a business boundary is identical to the boundary of an individual person, so we would say that a record is any information communicated beyond that person. Sometimes, however, because of the corporate culture of the organization, the boundary could extend beyond one person to include that person's administrative assistant, a work team, or even a larger group of people. When this occurs it must be clearly understood by the employees and the systems administrators that records are only created when information is communicated beyond the boundaries of this larger aggregate as a business rule.

(2) Corporate assignment of responsibility for accountability to every employee in the firm.

It must be understood that records are corporate property and a resource of value which cannot be destroyed or misplaced without serious consequences to the employee. Of course this policy must be accompanied by a training effort to convey to employees a mental model or conceptual framework of how systems in the company actually operate which is adequate for them to carry out this assigned responsibility successfully.

(3) Recognition by records managers, archivists, auditors, and others concerned with records creation of the primacy of program requirements.

Not only must program requirements be acknowledged, the records managers and archivists need to communicate that attitude to program managers. Once they have succeeded they can begin to convince program managers that the primary reason for good record-creation and recordkeeping practices is that it is an operational requirement.

(4) It is necessary to understand certain aspects of the software application called "electronic mail" in order to develop a satisfactory approach to managing the records it produces.

Electronic mail is the generic name given to a software functionality which enables users to write a message and "send" it to another person who may see it on their computer at a later time. As a "store and forward" technology it makes at least one copy of a record of the communication and links it both to the act of creation/transmission and of receipt/opening. It also maintains links between a mail item and responses to it which utilize the "respond to" software function and to the path of mail that utilizes the "forward" or "distribution list" functions. The electronic mail application also maintains names given to documents, security attached to them, and other attributes assigned by the creators. Some electronic mail facilities support extensive filing and even indexing attributes assigned by senders and by recipients.

Each of these four critical success factors needs to be explored further if we are to implement electronic mail as a recordkeeping system.[11]

The identification of what constitutes electronic records is arguably the most critical task in their management. Whatever definition is employed, it must be understood by both people and machines since the satisfaction of the requirements will involve a combination of human and system based judgments. In work for the United Nations in 1989, I suggested defining a record as a "communicated transaction." We have found this concept workable for both people and machines. It may be more completely stated as:

A record is any communication between one person, and another, between a person and a store of information available to others, back from the store of information to a person or between two computers programmed to exchange data in the course of business. The important aspect of this definition is that a record is not a collection of data but the consequence of a business event. Records "occur" rather than "are."

Electronic data excluded from this definition of records includes information that remains within the computer/workspace of a single individual or the business functional equivalent of a single individual, inaccessible to others, for private information or editing or information stored in a database, but not communicated in a business transaction to anyone else. When the information is shared with another person or sent to or from a machine accessible to others, the transaction in which it in engaged becomes a record.

The virtue of this definition is the ease with which individuals can understand it and the simplicity of instructing computing and communications systems to capture it. As we will later see in applying the definition, however, it does force people to adopt a more rigorous understanding of what constitutes a record than they have in many organizations to date.[12]

The identification of when a record occurs is only the first step, however, in determining what information becomes part of a record. Obviously the content of what is written in an electronic mail message will be part of what is kept, but electronic mail, because of the velocity of communication in this environment, is notorious for assuming that the recipient knows what the message is about. E-mail that says "sure" or "yes" or "well done" (to quote a rather famous message from Admiral Poindexter to his aide Bob Pearson upon learning that Oliver North had succeeded in lying to Congress) is frequent. These messages are complete in their content but they lack two other necessary ingredients to make them evidence: structure and context. The contextual data about the message -- which tells us who wrote it, when and where it was posted, to whom and with what instructions -- is declared to the software system carrying the message and carried in an "envelope" when the message is posted outside the originating system. The structure is embodied in the relationships -- internal to the message and external -- that link the data. For example, the links with prior messages that constitute a train of communications comprising a single business transaction or the links between text in one file and images in another when both were joined in a single compound document. Content, structure, and context must be joined for a record to be evidence.

While the identification of a record is a precondition for managing it appropriately, it will not result in satisfaction of the functional requirements unless the organization demands -- and individuals accept -- responsibility for accountability. Unlike paper records which would remain essentially as they were created and interpretable over time even if individuals and their managers did not do anything proactive on their behalf, electronic records are not visible except under software control and are subject to accidental destruction or loss of structural and contextual information if no one takes responsibility for them. Developing policies and promoting consciousness of the need for management of electronic records is only the first step in promoting better practices; it may be necessary to introduce oversight and rewards for information resources management similar to those employed for management of financial, personnel, or property resources.

One of the major impediments to employees taking appropriate care of electronic records is that they have a "mental model" of the way the system works which does not correspond to the way it works in reality. It is no use to insist that employees create or delete records if they do not understand the ways in which the systems on which they work create and delete records. Thus employees may believe that a record which exists on another machine and to which they are pointing is actually in their computer's hard disk or that a record which they have "deleted" from their system is actually gone when neither is in fact true. Organizations which want their employees to behave responsibly with respect to electronic records must teach them how their system really works so that their mental models will correspond to practice.

Furthermore, no program of records management will succeed unless it is completely clear to everyone involved that the major business of the organization is the achievement of its mission and that the responsible management of electronic mail is an adjunct function that should in no way interfere with, and may in some ways contribute to, the achievement of the central programmatic missions of the organization. Functional requirements for electronic mail must not result in the loss of functionality required to perform central missions, produce necessary products, deliver essential services, or develop critical policies. At the same time, recordkeeping requirements are derived from the needs of organizations for continuity of operations and accountability; they are not something external to the organization and must be weighed in considering the overall costs and benefits of adopting new methods of work and new information flows.

Finally, although the requirements for electronic mail systems are no different from those of traditional correspondence control systems, the fact that electronic mail produces virtual documents (documents whose logical boundaries are not those of a given physical file) does require us to develop some rigorous intellectual constructs to understand these traditional requirements.

To begin with, we need to understand that a record consists of information derived from its content (what the creator writes), structure (relationships between data items maintained by the computer for display and linkage), and context (information documenting the provenance and use of the record).

In terms of content, we need to define e-mail records as is what is received. The content of electronic communications may be edited until they are received by the addressee, but subsequently they must be preserved inviolably.

With respect to structure, mail looks like and acts like what the recipient gets. The record is both what the recipient sees and the software instructions which produce the record in that form from the raw data which is sent. Electronic structural links are analogous to page layout and they may consist of nothing more than formatting instructions, which, while software dependent, do not result in data management problems for which there are not reasonably straightforward solutions. However two other types of structural requirements have been identified which are considerably more challenging to manage over time.

Functionality to link items of correspondence with replies, forwarded materials, enclosures, and any other capabilities supported by the particular application package must be preserved to form meaningful business transactions. The full web of relationships between records within a business process was once reflected in the collation of all the records having to do with that process in a "project" file or "cover" but the interpretation of the actual relationships was left to human beings processing visual and textual clues. In electronic systems these relationships must be managed in part because the business conventions for referencing such relationships are as yet under-developed and in part because they will, in any event, be software dependent.

Functionality to reconstruct active relationships within the data must be retained whether these are supported by the electronic mail software (which is still very rare) or by the underlying Application Platform Interface (API) layer (which, because of object-oriented toolsets, is becoming quite common). The problem can be illustrated by what is often called a "dynamic document," or a document which embodies active content. In this kind of document, the recipient might see a graph drawn from a spreadsheet created from a database search without necessarily being aware that the graph is not an output product with fixed content, but instead is stored in the e-mail message as a search query to a database which exports its result to a spreadsheet with embedded instructions. Structural data such as the user permissions set and other limitations on the view of the search database, as well as the database state itself, all go into determining the content of the record.

In relation to context, mail is meaningful and acted on because of its source. The context of communications must be preserved with them but it cannot simply be the context which is asserted by the sender (for instance, the date or the distribution). Much attention has been paid to validating of signatures to ensure correct attribution of authorship, but the more significant aspect of authorization is whether the individual who signed has the authority to conduct the underlying transaction. Electronic correspondence must be authenticated in part because the contents of some electronic mail messages can be designed to take direct effect in the receiving system without being previously assessed by humans.

Second, electronic mail is a store-and-forward technology. A communication is written by a user at one workstation that has the ability to communicate outside itself and is sent to another user at a different workstation, often through many intervening computers. In the simplest manifestation, a user at one workstation attached directly to one computer leaves a message (creates a pointer) for another user at a workstation attached to that same computer. Even here, both users employ all software layers and hardware connections on the way to utilizing the mail although the original message is stored on the same computer which grants access permission. This aspect of electronic mail provides us with significant advantages over paper systems because the entire process exists under the control of a computing technology capable of tracking the mail at every step. In fact, the "electronic" aspect of electronic mail actually is a great advantage in its management because it provides numerous opportunities for solutions which are not present in manual systems.

DESIGN AND IMPLEMENTATION-BASED TACTICS

The problem with managing electronic mail, like that of mail received through the postal system or inter-office mail, is that electronic mail is a utility. As such it carries undifferentiated types of records for which we have very different business requirements. Since our reasons for keeping records have to do with business requirements for records for ongoing activity or long-term accountability, the fact that we do not know what mail contains, or more accurately what business transaction it carries out, means we do not know how it needs to be managed. We can not make any progress in managing electronic mail unless we can make the system identify the business transaction involved; ideally we would signal this information on an "envelope" so that the system could avoid having to "open" the mail and read it in order to make the decision about its management.

One approach that has been taken to identify the business application source of electronic mail is similar to that used in paper-based systems: employees categorize their correspondence by assigning it a classification number. While the specific method might vary, the implementation is to bring up a screen that the user must fill in before the mailing can go forward. The effect of this kind of approach is that the designation of appropriate management and retention practices is the responsibility of the records creator who is fully conscious that this is what is being requested.

A slightly different approach is to design the user interface so that users do not see "electronic mail" as an option, but rather view their systems options as business tasks such as "report on sales," "send policy directives," "assign work" or "make appointments." The choice of a business task brings up the electronic mail system with appropriate software functionality, pre-designed distribution lists, and style sheets for that task. It also schedules the electronic mail transaction and determines its appropriate filing. Under this scenario, the end user is responsible for the effect of scheduling but does not consciously make the decision.

A similar approach using the application software layer rather than the user interface is to develop style sheets for different genres of business transactions which carry their scheduling requirements with them. When the user selects an appropriate style sheet, reformatted aspects of the message structure are brought onto the screen and the hidden scheduling information is conveyed along with the transmission.

Combining these approaches, the best solution would be to have users, instead of using software applications directly -- open facilities in their user interface for their business purposes such as sending directives, making appointments, or scheduling staff work. Each user would have an interface designed to support the specific functions of their job. By opening a business application rather than a software application, the use would be declaring, in effect, what the purpose of the message was and how it should be managed. The reasons the user would select the appropriate facility for the proper purpose are both the push that the policy and the pull that the software capabilities each has already attached. When writing a directive, the style sheet for directives comes right up, the distribution list for directives is immediately invoked, and the requirements to acknowledge result in the receipt of each directive being audited. Directives properly handled in the directives distribution function are tickled for review prior to their expiration date and can be cited as authority in other actions (e.g., they are linked to validation tables used elsewhere). Directives cannot be copied locally, but are saved only in the central files where they are available for all to see. Out-of-date copies are never found in offices. Personal notes, on the other hand, may be secured for viewing by only one person and will be deleted from local spaces after user specified times, but they cannot be saved to corporate storage and may not use corporate styles. Staff schedules use a corporate style sheet, are incorporated into group and individual calendars, and may be answered formally by using calendaring acceptance functions.

Each type of communication employs a variety of other software with preset configurations, thereby facilitating work flow. It also declares the contents of messages for purposes of retention without requiring records managers or archivists to read the contents of each message. Occasional audits can be used to ensure that employees are correctly using the functions provided, with training and ultimately reprimand directed towards those not employing the facilities in line with policy.

In addition to being identifiable by the business process for which they were created and in which they served as a transaction, electronic mail must satisfy the functional requirements applicable to all electronic records creation of being comprehensive, complete, and authentic.

To be able to prove that the records in the system are comprehensive, the inventory of records in storage must conform to the log of records communicated. Any such log would have to be created by layers of software system below the application, whether the Application Program Interface (API), the Operating System, the External Environment Interface, or software at the external communication switches. The inventory would have to be created either as records were read onto a remote storage device for filing or as a report from the corporate file management software.

To ensure that records are complete, a metadata model of the contents of a complete business transaction of the sort conducted under each process would be compared against the contents and envelope of the electronic mail message, perhaps using Standard Generalized Markup Language (SGML) markup, to ensure that all the necessary structural and contextual links for that type of transaction were present. A content data model of a complete transaction would, for example, require data for the sender, the recipient, the distribution list, the time of transmission, the time of opening, the response to link, the response from link and any forwarding links.

Figure 6.1
Layers in the Open Systems Environment Model

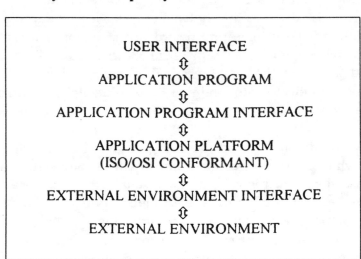

Authentic transactions are those which originate with the author who claims to be the originator and who has the authority to launch transactions of that sort. Both of these criteria can be validated using the information collected to ensure completeness or comprehensiveness. The satisfaction of these requirements could be enforced at the level of the API, where most requirements reflecting security and requiring definite identification of users are resolved, or at the level of the operating system where data is routed to appropriate files. See Figure 6.1.

"Software engines" at communication nodes can stamp electronic mail as it crosses boundaries, i.e., those defined by the organization as significant for record purposes. These "boundary crossings" define record transactions in a way consistent with the UN ACCIS report. Similarly, locating such engines at servers, at telecommunication gateways, and in DBMS information retrieval facilities could capture specified types of transactions for forwarding to file rooms. There they would be documented complete with the content, structure, and context of the transaction. The documentation would also include the configuration management data required to reconstruct the information a user would have seen and what functions they would have had available to them. See Figure 6.2.

When each functional requirement is reduced to a specification for particular metadata, the system designers and systems administrators can select which "openings" provided by the software and hardware architecture to employ in a specific mechanization of its audit. In principle, each functional requirement could be satisfied by solutions found at nearly every layer of software and hardware. The selection of an actual location at which to intervene should reflect the requirements of the specific organization and its actual architecture.

It will often be easier to obtain the same result at one layer or another because of the tools available in an organization or the assignment of responsibility for control of different portions of a system to different agents within the organization. If the tools for user interface design are not flexible enough to support the proposed solution of structuring the interface to reflect the business transactions of the organization (and hooking the appropriate software functionality to those functions), we could turn to another layer. For example, it might be more viable to build software to monitor communications traffic from the user workstation as it enters the network (thereby becoming available as corporate records). Also it may be necessary to use solutions at communication interfaces if the network administration control is tight but the local workstation

Figure 6.2
Technical Environment Model

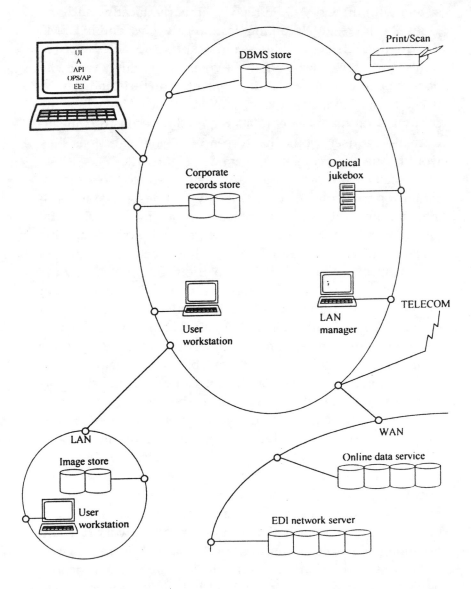

use control is weak. Or it may be desirable to build the functionality into corporate file rooms and ignore local filing and storage facilities if there is little corporate ability to influence naming conventions used by those with control over local workstations.

Implementing responsible solutions to electronic records management can be made easier in the future by adopting architectures that take advantage of some relatively new approaches to computing. Object-oriented systems, when they are implemented, will allow us to attach object attributes to records that cause them to be filed, retained, and accessed in the ways that a sound records policy would dictate. Client-server architectures allow us to built servers that will continue to perform their role across generations of clients that can address new servers, making for easier and less costly migrations. Open systems standards, if adopted, will generally make the task of managing distributed information resources over extended periods of time much easier and may lead to areas of interoperability even if complete interoperability eludes us. Existing standards in the electronic mail area have already made inter-network interchange more possible. With appropriate extensions, the X.400/X.500 standards could accommodate contextual and structural information needed for reconstruction of evidential historicity.[13]

One of the outstanding issues in the management of mail and other electronic records concerns whether to write a representation of the structural and contextual information to the record or retain it in the external environment. If we write a representation to the record, essentially adding the information as an extension of the content of the record itself, we can take advantage of the software independence of ASCII code to convey structural and contextual information. The disadvantages, and the advantages of retaining it in its original software environment, are that we have to open the message to identify its author, programmatic or business application source, date, the web of interlinked messages, and other structural and contextual meanings. We will have to use great care in selecting a method of representation that will preserve our ability to manipulate the representation for purposes of automatically reconstructing structural links.

In an ideal world, the envelope defined by the standard interchange protocol X.400 (used today in many electronic mail systems) would accommodate this necessary data. But because the need for this metadata relates to post-receipt understandability and usability rather than to transmission, the X.400 protocol, which restricts itself to carrying data essential to successful transmission, does not provide this facility. On the other hand, the contextual and structural data is directly related to the success of the directories defined by X.500. The archival and auditing professions have a strong position with respect to the viability of such directories over time if they care to make the case to appropriate standards bodies. It should be noted, however, that within our community we have not yet accepted definitions of the essential contextual (provenancial) metadata nor developed methods of representation that could be commonly employed to indicate the kinds of structural links we believe it must represent.

Defining the essential metadata for structural and contextual documentation of electronic communications is one of the tasks being undertaken in a research project to which I am a consultant at the University of Pittsburgh.[14] One purpose of such metadata would be to permit the management of "corporate memory,"[15] whether in central corporate files or distributed systems by identifying the attributes that would serve as filing headers such as project titles, names of recipients, dates, or accounting codes as well as file classification numbers where registry office file classification practices prevail.

Once filed, the issues respecting the management of electronic mail become those of managing electronic records in general. The requirements which must be satisfied in their maintenance are that they remain sound, auditable, exportable and removable. These properties are largely ensured through standard data center system security and auditing applied with an understanding of the boundaries of the original electronic record, boundaries which incorporate content, structure, and context information.

Similarly, access to electronic mail stored as a corporate record involves the same measures to satisfy requirements that the record be available, usable, understandable, and redactable as would be applied to other records. These measures rely on systematic and continuous configuration management practices applied to both software and hardware with an understanding that records can only be made available, usable, and understandable over time if they are migrated to current systems. It also recognizes that migration is extremely dangerous both because it risks accidentally changing record linkages and functionalities and because it necessarily takes place in an interstice between two auditable systems.

CONCLUSIONS

Electronic mail is a new way of transporting communications which creates a new documentary form of record. The issues associated with its management combine the requirements for correspondence control and filing present in paper-based communications systems with the functional requirements for managing any electronic recordkeeping system. The tactics available for managing electronic mail are those which are generally available to managing electronic information systems and the conceptual framework developed for the management of electronic records of any sort can be applied to e-mail. When we apply this framework it becomes clear that e-mail is a utility that can only be managed when the business application which the communication supports is clearly identified up front. The requirements we place on the subsequent management of the record are a product of the scheduling and appraisal of records of that business application.

As a new documentary form, electronic mail is not governed by many conventions. We are therefore forced in its management to educate users about how these systems and our in-house files work; design systems that recognize records of specific business functions and treat them accordingly; implement systems which segregate the creation and storage locations so that records must cross over software switches that can assess how they should be managed; and deploy standards that contribute to better documentation of the content of electronic mail, particularly metadata documentation standards.

When this framework is applied to electronic mail, the resulting system should be more manageable than traditional paper-based systems both from the perspective of executing appropriate dispositions and from the view of users who want to retrieve records in the future.

NOTES

[1] David Bearman, *Archives and Museum Informatics*, Special News, "Federal Appeals Court Rules Against White House in Profs Case" 7:3 (Fall 1993); and Bearman, "The Implications of *Armstrong* v. *the Executive Office of the President* for the Archival Management of Electronic Records," *American Archivist* 56 (Fall 1993): 674-689, which is reprinted in this volume as Chapter 4.

[2] Other papers by David Bearman explaining this generic framework include: "Archival Data Management to Achieve Organizational Accountability for Electronic Records," *Archives and Manuscripts* 21 (May 1993): 14-28, reprinted in this volume as Chapter 1; with Margaret Hedstrom, "Reinventing Archives for Electronic Records: Alternative Service Delivery Options" in *Program Strategies for Electronic Records*, Margaret Hedstrom ed., Archives and Museum Informatics Technical Report #18 (Pittsburgh: Archives and Museum Informatics, 1993), 82-98.

[3] Gary Fisher, *Application Portability Profile: The U.S. Government's Open System Environment Profile*, NISTSP 500-187 (Gaithersburg, Maryland: National Institute of Standards and Technology, April 1991).

[4] For a useful overview of the concept of metadata in archival documentation, see David Wallace, "Metadata and the Archival Management of Electronic Records: A Review," *Archivaria* 36 (Autumn 1993): 87-110. See also David Bearman, "Documenting Documentation," *Archivaria* 34 (Summer 1992): 33-49, reprinted in this volume as Chapter 8.

[5] Bearman, "*Armstrong* v. *the Executive Office of the President*."

[6] Canadian General Standards Board, "Microfilm and Electronic Images as Documentary Evidence," CAN/CGSB-72.11-93; also note ISO 9000/9001.

[7] In their decision in *Armstrong* v. *the Executive Office of the President*, the U.S. Federal Appeals Court stated that under the Federal Records Act, the Archivist's duties are not limited to judging the suitability of records for disposal. In addition, the Archivist must "provide guidance and assistance to federal agencies with respect to ensuring adequate and proper documentation of the policies and transactions of the Federal Government and ensuring proper records disposition." *U.S. Code*, section 2904(a).

[8] The Federal Rules of Evidence and the Uniform Rules of Evidence used by most states, as well as the Federal Business Records Act and Uniform Photographic Copies of Business and Public Records as Evidence Act (UPA) used by most states in the U.S., essentially support the use of electronic records if they are employed in the normal course of business, in a manner that is compliant with law and are used in an accountable fashion (responsible, reliable, and implemented).

[9] The Federal Rules of Evidence, as amended 1 December 1993, require records creators to reveal, within ninety days of the filing of a case against them, all records that might be pertinent to the case without having opposing counsel request them under discovery procedures. Freedom of information and privacy laws in many countries which are beginning to require governmental bodies to list the records which they create on citizens or the record systems they maintain for FOI queries are consistent with a trend towards up front declaration as are proposals such as the U.S. Government Information Locator System (GILS).

[10] My report, in a slightly edited form, was published as Chapter II and Annexes I, II, and V, in United Nations Advisory Committee for Coordination of Information Systems, *Management of Electronic Records: Issues and Guidelines* (New York: United Nations, 1990), 17-70, 89-107, 135-189. A somewhat abridged version of Sections A, B, and C of Chapter II is reprinted in this volume as Chapter 3.

[11] David Bearman, "Record-Keeping Systems," *Archivaria* 36 (Autumn 1993): 16-36, reprinted in this volume as Chapter 2.

[12] For a fuller elaboration, see David Roberts, "Defining Electronic Records, Documents and Data," *Archives and Manuscripts* 22 (May 1994): 14-26.

[13] The concept of evidential historicity is developed further in David Bearman, "Archival Principles and the Electronic Office" in *Information Handling in Offices and Archives*, Angelika Menne-Haritz ed. (New York: K.G. Saur, 1993): 177-193, reprinted in this volume as Chapter 5.

[14] Further information, including a bibliography of publications of the research findings of the project, can be obtained from Richard J. Cox, Assistant Professor, School of Library and Information Science, University of Pittsburgh, Pittsburgh PA 15260 or via the Internet from rjc@lis.pitt.edu.

[15] The term "corporate memory" is widely used by the Canadian government in its policy frameworks for management of electronic records, in particular by John McDonald of the Information Management Practices and Standards Branch of the National Archives of Canada and by the Treasury Board Secretariat.

208

SECTION IV

Standards

✤

CHAPTER SEVEN

Information Technology Standards and Archives

✤

CHAPTER EIGHT

Documenting Documentation

CHAPTER SEVEN

Information Technology Standards and Archives*

Standards are designed to overcome boundaries. The boundaries presented by information technologies have been envisioned as a series of seven steps (the OSI model) each of which provides a platform for communications across systems. Archivists are most concerned with interchange standards on the application (seventh) level. These standards, if appropriately formulated, could convey the context in which information is created and managed and the structural relationships between components of the data content as well as the raw data in the system. This chapter discusses the archival requirements for interchange standards at this level. It suggests that archivists have employed tools in their discipline that give them a valuable insight into requirements for accountable management of these new forms of cultural communications. The implications of these for new technology standards will be elucidated.

* Originally published in *Janus* (1992.2): 161-166.

INTRODUCTION

Archivists are confronted by rapidly changing methods of work made possible by the use of electronic information technologies. Often they are told that the only way they can hope to preserve the information generated by these technologies is to employ and influence information systems standards. But when they look for ways to become involved in the definition of standards, they encounter a vast array of information systems standards and discover an inchoate universe of standards development activity. Which standards are important to implement or to influence?

Without criteria by which to evaluate what is most important, archivists will have little impact on information systems standards, even if they try to become involved. In this chapter, I present a framework for evaluating the potential significance of an information systems standard to archives based on an analysis of what makes a record archival. I suggest how this criterion can be employed to effect standards development and in what way that would have an impact on the documentation of the twenty-first century.

THE CHANGING CHARACTER OF WORK

In order to understand the potential significance of successful intervention in the definition of information systems standards, we must first appreciate the changes that are taking place in the conduct of work in modern bureaucracies. To illustrate these, I will present a hypothetical, but by no means unlikely, case study of how the Office of the Attorney General of one of the states in the United States would defend a newly legislated method of statewide school funding being challenged in a state Supreme Court. The Attorney General is the principal legal officer of the jurisdiction and, until recently, most states funded education through local (county level) taxation. Recently, however, the Supreme Courts of some of these states have recently required state legislatures to adopt different methods of funding on the grounds that local tax bases differ and thereby result in discrimination based on property values, or on wealth.

The advantages of this case study is that archivists will have little difficulty agreeing a priori with the presumption that the evidence of such a high level and critical governmental activity should be archival and that in the United States we have witnessed dramatic changes in the way in which lawyers, in and out of government, conduct their work since the advent of electronic information systems.

In this hypothetical case, a team of several lawyers would probably be assigned to work together on researching and writing a brief representing the government's position. They would use a "groupware" writing tool which tracks versions and revisions and permits several individuals to write, comment on, and revise the same document. To prepare their arguments, they would first search online databases for references to prior case law and download these references into a local database making them available for citation in their legal brief. At some point in the preparation of the case, they would also search census data and other demographic databases maintained by the state in order to demonstrate how statewide funding would serve the larger social good of providing equality in educational services. In addition to retrieving statistical data, they would probably view their retrieval results through a Geographic Information System, in order to illustrate graphically the equity issues involved in statewide financing.

During the period devoted to drafting the brief, some members of the team would be out of town on other business or gathering evidence for this case. This would not impede their use of the groupware environment or online databases which they would access by telecommunications. In addition, they would communicate with the other members of the team by voice mail and fax. The voice messages (digitized analog signals) and the fax communications (digitized raster data) would be received on computers where they would be stored in software-controlled voice and fax mailboxes and indexed for subsequent retrieval. Some might also conduct depositions taped on audio or video tapes to provide evidence of school disparities. These tapes would also be indexed and stored. Evidence would include still frames captured from video clips and digital sound from interviews. These sounds and images could be directly incorporated into multimedia documents. While it is rare now, in the near future the legal team would submit their briefs to the court electronically. Such briefs could consist of hypermedia rather than just linear multimedia segments.

INFORMATION SYSTEMS STANDARDS

The archival interest in this case is to assure the preservation not only of the raw data of the brief submitted to the court, but also evidence of the way in which the government conducted and built its case. This objective requires that archivists be able to rely on standards for interchange of data, of information about data structure, and of information about data context.

The data (text, image, and sound) actually created by the government legal team, or recorded by it as evidence, needs to be usable, understandable, and available to future researchers. This requirement would be satisfied by data representation standards such as ASCII for text, JPEG for images, FM or CD sampling rates for audio, CCITT Group III or Group IV protocols for fax, and VHS/NTSC, PAL, or SECAM standards for video. While data representation standards today almost universally accepted for data interchange do not absolutely assure that the data will be usable 100 years from now, we can assume that they define a sufficiently widespread usage that a migration path will be provided between them and whatever standards prevail in the future. Vigilant archivists will be able to move their data along this migration path without loss of information content.

It is important for archivists to realize that they can depend on these standards for data interchange because system designers will implement this level of data interchange capability in response to widely expressed operational requirements of business and government. The need archivists have to transfer this data outside the systems in which it was created do not differ from, and have nothing to add to, the requirements of the business community. It follows that archivists can have little impact on the evolution of such data representation standards.

However, simply transferring the words and symbols created by the lawyers and witnesses in this case will not preserve the archival record as generally understood. Archivists must also capture and preserve structural and contextual information which gives the data created by the legal team its significance as evidence.

Contextual data is information about the creation and use of information. It is not resident in the texts, images, and sounds of the "documents," but it is acquired and/or created, by the information systems in which these reside and used in those systems to manage documents. A simple example of contextual data is the information maintained by an electronic mail system which records the sender, addressee, security assigned by sender, time/date sent, time/date opened, and reply, forwarding, and/or filing history. Within an operating e-mail system, this information must be created and managed by the computer, but it is largely recorded and stored in a proprietary way and will not be interchanged with other systems unless the interchange protocol employed by the two systems requires it.

Business requirements for contextual data interchange are quite limited. In the case of electronic mail, for example, they are reflected in the interchange standards defined for e-mail headers and directories (IEEE X.400 and X.500) which name the addressee and the response requested. They do not reflect the full range of archival concerns, however, as they do not provide for interchange of information about the provenance and revision history of the records in question. Other contextual information in our legal case study relates to the legal and demographic databases searched for citations and evidence and the GIS systems used to represent the demographic information. In order to use information as archival records, we need to be able to represent what data in these databases was available to the searchers (e.g., their permissions and views), what questions they asked (e.g., their search strategies), and what algorithms were used for the geographic representations. This information includes that which is called "metadata" about these systems (covered by standards for Information Resource Directory Systems); "information retrieval commands" using languages such as Common Command Language (CCL) or Structured Query Language (SQL); and representations of user access rules, security, and database views. We also need to retain data about the actual state of the databases at the time they were searched.

Requirements for a complete archival record do not end with capturing contextual data, however, because information is also conveyed by the structure of the records which are retained. Structure has long been recognized by archivists as a conveyor of meaning[1] but the importance of standards for conveying structural relations of electronic archival records -- including internal documents markings which graphically convey meaning -- has not been alluded to in the archival literature. This structural information might include both the internal structures of documents and the structural relations between records in a database which are used to the software to construct the equivalent of the physical record in the paper file. In automated systems, the "logical" record (for instance the case file of an individual) may consist of a large number of discrete physical records stored in, and under the control of, different information systems. The relations between these records determine the meaning of the logical record, and also its currency and authenticity. In emerging object-oriented and hypermedia environments, these links and their rules govern whether and how the data can be viewed and what can be done with it.

Standards for structural information are underutilized and underdeveloped from an archival point of view. Standards for representing the versioning of documents in the groupware environment, for representing the links between objects in hypermedia, and for representing the logical components of textual documents which give them their distinguishing "form" have not yet been seen as critical for business operations. As a consequence little attention has been given to preserving this information in a software-independent fashion. Archivists need to press the case for why it is critical for organizations to preserve structural information across systems. At the same time they could begin to use the limited structural data interchange standards which exist, such as Standard Generalized Markup Language (SGML) which was developed initially for the publishing industry.[2]

The relationships between elements of information and physical records and objects in a database determines the meaning of the information; for example, whether the data about a person included, or could have included, a link to the record with that person's current address is an issue that could have evidential significance. In addition, the views of a database that are permitted to specific users are controlled by permission tables which are themselves data to the database. This kind of data about the database and its use is called metadata, and can currently be documented following an international standard for Information Resource Directory Systems.

ARCHIVAL STRATEGY FOR INFORMATION SYSTEMS STANDARDS

Archivists are only likely to have an impact on information systems standard development when they play an active, concerted role. They should concentrate their efforts where archival requirements depart from those of everyday business operational needs. In these areas, which are related to the archival concern for provenance,[3] they can articulate their functional requirements for standards by exploiting the potential of standardizing structural and contextual data capture in widely used information system applications. In part they must advance this agenda by critiquing existing standards based on their contextual and structural requirements. They need to illustrate to senior managers that the short-term operational requirements for transportability of standard representations of data content will not ensure retention of archival evidence essential to reconstructing the transaction or activity which is the object of the archival record.

The focus should be on those applications which are already widespread and likely to play a significant role in the changing character of work:

- office automation and electronic mail

- databases and data analysis/display

- electronic information dissemination/publication

- automatic transaction processing

In each of these areas the existing standards for data interchange do not adequately account for archival concerns but could be made to carry information required by archivists to represent structural and contextual information now associated with records in proprietary ways.

In the area of office automation, the primary concern is to capture and transmit in a non-proprietary way, the history of documents including their authorship, the source of each version, and the rules governing access and use. Presently such documents are interchanged using electronic mail facilities which have a "header" (X.500) that permits the representation of the name and electronic addresses of the sender and recipient, the time and date of transmission, and little else. Archivists should make an effort to get extensions to header standards that would require the originating system to record both structural properties of the records being sent (form notations designating parts of the document that are its content and parts that serve, for example, as a distribution list) and contextual properties (such as versioning, permissions, and views data), identification of the work process of origin, and data regarding the actions that are requested (such as replies, acknowledgments, or follow-ups requested by the sender).

With respect to databases, neither the retrieval request (query) nor the means of reporting or representing the results have been made subject to interchange standards, yet we can hardly expect to make sense of a decision based on querying a database if we do not have the question or the answer in hand in an interpretable form. Archivists should examine the standard developed for database retrieval by the U.S. library community (ANSI Z39.50) for its appropriateness for software-independent query interchange and also study methods for interchange of user-defined software display rules such as those embodied in a graphic generated by a spreadsheet or a map generated by a geographic information system.[4]

Archivists also need to exploit the abstract data structural representation capabilities of the Information Resource Directory Systems (IRDS) and other "metadata" facilities. If fully implemented, metadata systems can carry software independent representations of structure and also of such contextually significant data as permissions, views, report definitions, and calculation capabilities which affect the results of database reports.

Information dissemination and publication conveys structural information through the form of documents that cannot presently be interchanged between systems without loss. Some efforts to provide methods to standardize representation of structural features of documents (such as SGML) partially satisfy archival needs, but they do not yet represent the revisions between versions, multimedia elements in texts, and the navigation of non-linear documents. Archivists can now get involved in the definition of the Office Document Architecture and Office Document Interchange Format (ODA/ODIF) standards which are more extensive than previous efforts but will still require archival insights to ensure that they satisfy the need for software-independent representation of evidence of transactions.

Business transactions, such as the filing of a legal brief, the withdrawal of money from a bank, or ordering supplies and invoicing for them, are increasingly being conducted by electronic means. Archivists need to become involved in the representation of electronic transactions to transaction processing systems. The premium in such routine systems is on reducing the amount of information to what is the minimum that must be conveyed to successfully conclude the transaction. It may not satisfy evidential requirements. Each market niche and interchange community is developing such transactional standards on its own, often within the international frameworks for EDI (Electronic Document Interchange) but occasionally outside that framework as well.

Assertive tactics will require archivists to become involved in the standards under development for improved specifications for IRDS, X.500, SGML, and Office Document Architecture (ODA), while promoting an understanding of the need for contextual and structural standards within their institutions. Archivists in organizations using other data communication protocols (EDI, ANSI Z39.50, etc.) need to examine the extent to which these transactions convey in their standard forms the information required to locate their organizational and programmatic provenance and their place within a series of communications internal to a business process.

NOTES

[1] David Bearman and Peter Sigmund, "Explorations of Form of Material Authority Files by Dutch Archivists," *American Archivist* 50 (Spring 1987): 249-253.

[2] Although the requirement for conveying the logical structures internal to printed documents is only partially addressed by SGML, archivists could employ SGML to develop abstract, form-of-material, "fingerprints" for organizationally significant types of documents which could then be recognized by automatic parsers developed to screen for archivally significant communications. They could also develop strategies to audit, create, and break record links in database environments rather than trying to audit all modifying transactions.

[3] David Bearman, "Archival Principles and the Electronic Office" in *Information Handling in Offices and Archives*, Angelika Menne-Haritz ed. (New York: K.G. Saur, 1993): 177-193, reprinted in this volume as Chapter 5.

[4] Archivists often find it difficult to understand that the user-defined variables in software determine the output of the database. A simple example is the database report that is imported into a spreadsheet in which the cells of the spreadsheet have been predefined by the user with underlying algorithms so that a percentage increase or decrease is automatically added to the database report to represent projections for a future year. The user sees a graphic, generated out of the database but through the spreadsheet which is interpreted data. Currently the interchange capabilities for representing data content are able to send the graphic report, but will not carry the spreadsheet algorithms that produced it.

CHAPTER EIGHT

Documenting Documentation*

Taking exception to the premises underlying the principles and rules for archival description promulgated by the International Council on Archives, this chapter proposes alternative principles for documenting documentation. They have emerged from the collective activity of many archivists in the U.S. over the last decade. Documentation, which should begin close to the moment of records creation, retains contextual information about the activity that generated the records, the organizations and individuals who used the records, and the purposes to which the records were put. Information systems must be designed to retain sufficient contextual data to support archival management throughout the records' life cycles. User requirements must be considered so that a user can enter the system from knowledge of the world being documented without knowing about the world of documentation.

* Originally published in *Archivaria* 34 (Summer 1992): 33-49. An earlier version of this article, entitled "Description Standards Revisited," was presented at the Australian Society of Archivists annual meeting, Sydney, June 1991. The author wishes to thank Richard Cox, Richard Szary, Vicki Walch, and Lisa Weber for their helpful suggestions.

INTRODUCTION

An Ad Hoc Commission of the International Council on Archives proposed principles and rules for archival description in 1992.[1] Unfortunately the particular principles and rules fall short of what is needed.[2] This chapter elaborates alternative principles for documenting documentation which have been emerging from the collective activity of many U.S. archivists over the past decade but which have not been presented in one place before.

The "Statement of Principles Regarding Archival Description" (referred to as the ICA Principles throughout this text) and "Draft General International Standard Archival Description" rules (referred to throughout as ISAD(G)), circulated for comment by the ICA Ad Hoc Commission on Descriptive Standards in 1992, each consist of statements of differing degrees of generality which might be considered either principles or as rules for archival description. The ICA Principles reflect existing methods of archival description (at least in North America), while those suggested here for documenting documentation have not yet been developed, widely accepted, or even completely elaborated.

They are advanced here in part because the ICA Principles rationalize existing practice which the author believes as a practical matter that we cannot afford, which fail to provide direct access for most archives users, and which do not support the day-to-day information requirements of archivists themselves.[3] They are also advanced because of three more theoretical differences with the ICA Principles:

(1) in focusing on description rather than documentation they overlook the most salient characteristic of archival records: their status as evidence;

(2) in proposing specific content they are informed by bibliographic tradition rather than by concrete analysis of the way in which information is used in archives; and

(3) in promoting data value standardization without identifying criteria or principles to identify appropriate language
or structural links between the objects represented by such
terms, they fail to adequately recognize that the data representation rules they propose reflect only one particular,
and limiting, implementation.

The principles for documenting documentation derive directly from the relationship of documentation to historical activity. The rules for data content and data representation
which flow from them support ancillary principles which state
that the purpose of recording information (description) is to
support archives administration collections and serve the
needs of users.

Before discussing the historical background for the documenting documentation principles and examining in detail
their implications for each of these three points, let us briefly
examine some distinctions which will be central to the discussion which follows.

First, how does description differ from documentation?

Description is focused on records both as the object being
described and as the primary source of information. It seeks to
characterize archival materials by constructing a document or
collection surrogate. These surrogates, called cataloging
records, finding aids, or archival inventories, each represent a
"unit of material" or physical records. In archival description
systems, these surrogates will be the fundamental record type
or central file to which all indexes point.

Documentation is focused on activity in the records-generating institution, or activity of the creator of the records in
the case of manuscripts, as the object being documented and
as the preferred source of information. It seeks to capture data
about the relationship between the activity and the document
created or received in that activity which is necessary in order
for the document to serve as evidence. Documentation results
in the construction of systems with links between databases of
activity and databases of documentary materials (archives)

created by, for, or of an activity. In documentary information systems, both the activity and the documentary materials documentation will be physically represented in numerous files; there will be links representing relations among them but no preferred view at the "center" of the data model.

Archives are themselves documentation. Hence I speak here of documenting documentation as a process whose objective is to construct a value-added representation of archives. This is accomplished by means of strategic information capture and recording into carefully structured data and information access systems as a mechanism to satisfy identified information needs of users, including archivists. Documentation principles lead to methods and practices which involve archivists at the point, and often at the time, of records creation. In contrast, archival description, as described in the ICA Principles is "concerned with the formal process of description after the archival material has been arranged and the units or entities to be described have been determined." (1.7) I believe documentation principles will be more effective, more efficient, and provide archivists with a higher stature in their organizations than the post-accessioning description principles proposed by the ICA.

Second, how does the content of an archival description differ from that of documentation?

The data elements of archival descriptions are an amalgam of what archivists have described in the past and those attributes of documents (fields in databases) which are defined by closely allied information professionals such as librarians. The content standards for documentation, on the other hand, are dictated by the principle that the information in documentation systems must support the requirements for archives to be evidence as well as serving internal management and end-user access needs of archives.

These two critiques are independent. The ICA Principles could have been focused on description of documents rather than on documenting context, yet have justified their concrete content by reference to the value which specific descriptive data has for archival practice or in the support of access to archival materials. After all, archives are not ends in themselves but have as their purpose the preservation and retrieval of evidence of the past which has continuing value to the present. Description standards proposed by archivists might have advanced the principle that information recorded in archival descriptions should support the needs of managing such holdings.

Third, how do the data values in archival descriptions differ from those of documentation?

Although the ICA Principles say that one of their purposes is to "facilitate the retrieval and exchange of information about archival material" (1.3) and that "the structure and content representations of archival material should facilitate information retrieval" (5.1), they in fact advance a set of rules for data content and values, ISAD(G), which make sense only within a particular, if unarticulated, implementation framework. These rules dictate the construction of a specific type of output product (basically a "cataloging record"), probably intended for constructing union catalogs by international data interchange. The more general principles advanced here for documenting documentation recognize that rules for data values in documentation should derive from user needs and that the issue of control over data values is an implementation concern in a local system or an explicit service requirement of a concrete data interchange. Unlike the ISAD(G) rules, however, the principles for documenting documentation do not presume any specific information products or interchange purposes.

During the 1980s, the author and many of his colleagues, hesitantly and incompletely identified many of these distinctions without precisely locating their bearing on archival description because these implications, frankly, were not yet evident. An article on the power of provenance examined the possibility of structuring archival information systems around documentation and introduced the limitations of the concept of fonds and the reasons for preferring series-level description, but in this respect it only proposed to refocus archival description.[4] Articles on the use of archival descriptions noted that user access begins with the researchers knowledge of the context in which the activity generating records took place, but failed to connect this concretely to principles for data content or to the need to redesign archival information systems.[5] Proposals that the concrete requirements of information interchange between institutions should dictate data content suggested how different content served different requirements within and among institutions. They also advanced the principle that the content of interchanges should follow from what are now known as "service requirements," but did not extend the reasoning to information systems nor to description end products of individual archives.[6] And a preliminary report of end user "presentation language," undertaken to help define data representation for new archival information systems, did not examine how findings of such studies could or should be reflected in the capabilities of information systems.[7] An analysis of the research literature indicating the limitations of controlled vocabularies and suggesting sources of content that might be appropriate to archives did not explore the data structure of the overall documentation system that might support such access points.[8] This article will not present a comprehensive system design nor provide data to test its efficacy, but it hopes to lay out an integrated theoretical framework for documenting documentation and contrast it as necessary for its understanding with principles advanced for archival description.

DESCRIPTION OF ARCHIVES AND MANUSCRIPTS IN THE 1980S

After several decades of stability in which description meant making inventories, archival description sparked a renewed interest among North American archivists in the 1980s.

In the U.S., the current wave of professional interest in description practice grew out of an interest in building national databases of archival resources,[9] in a specific information interchange. Neither the USMARC Format for Archival and Manuscripts Control (USMARC AMC) data content standards, nor the *APPM* data value standards which are accepted by the U.S. archival community today were created in order to prescribe archival description principles. The National Information Systems Task Force (NISTF) explicitly described its efforts as descriptive (and permissive) as opposed to prescriptive or normative. It sponsored the construction of the USMARC AMC format from a data element dictionary compiled by archivists which was based on data in their existing information systems at that time[10] but NISTF never considered endorsing the data content which its working group mapped to the MARC format. Nor would it have done so both because its Chairman and Director (and probably other members) were keenly aware of the inadequacy of the existing practice which that data dictionary reflected, and because they fervently hoped that the data content standard was a process -- not a product -- and would be extended over time to reflect use requirements.

Likewise, when Steve Hensen first set out to interpret Chapter 4 of the *Anglo-American Cataloguing Rules*, 2nd edition *(AACR 2)*, he was not articulating principles but attempting to interpret rules which had been poorly applied to archives and manuscripts. As the Library of Congress manuscripts cataloger, Hensen had to use these newly adopted international rules. His publication, *Archives, Personal Papers and Manuscripts: A Cataloging Manual (APPM)*,[11] made it possible for archivists to follow *AACR 2* rules and ultimately to use the interpretation offered in creating data values in MARC AMC. In the first edition of *APPM* Hensen makes it clear that the effort did not propose description principles, even if it did show that the bibliographic description principles embodied in

AACR 2 could be "interpreted" to support a method of cataloging with which archivists could live.

Using MARC AMC and *APPM*, American archivists have been constructing a national database on the Research Libraries Information Network (RLIN) -- and to a lesser extent on OCLC, WLN, UTLAS, and other bibliographic utilities -- since 1984.[12] Building the RLIN database made them aware of how inconsistent their existing cataloging had been. Task forces within RLG, and informal working groups of the profession worked throughout the late 1980s to build the database and impose greater consistency on it.[13] But they had quite practical aims and did not attempt to define what archival description should be. A few exploratory departures from the existing content standards were attempted in order to share appraisal information and conservation advice and construct a more structured administrative history database, but these were not very successful for a variety of political and economic reasons, and possibly because they lacked adequate theoretical underpinning. In the United States, anyway, there is still no truly theoretical formulation of archival description principles that enjoys widespread adherence, in spite of the acceptance of rules for description in certain concrete application contexts.[14]

In Canada the profession has spent nearly a decade reviewing the entire area of archival description and has aimed since 1985 to build a theoretical foundation for description practice.[15] *Towards Descriptive Standards* defined archival description by reference to three of the four major functions of library description: bibliographic description, the choice of non-subject access points, and subject indexing (leaving classification aside) and the *Rules for Archival Description (RAD)* effort has accepted this framework since. Like the ICA Commission, and the majority of U.S. archivists, the reports of the *RAD* working groups assume that archival description is an activity that takes place in archives, discrete from records creation and records management, after records have been appraised, acquired, and accessioned archivists.

Throughout these deliberations over the past decade, a number of active participants have felt that all was not well, and certainly not adequate, with existing description standards and standards development efforts. Their concerns arose from at least three independent sources.

First, the MARC AMC format and library bibliographic practices did not adequately reflect the importance of information concerning the people, organizations, and functions that generated records, and the MARC Authority Format did not support appropriate recording of such contexts and relations. Since the mid-1980s, however, efforts had been proposed and undertaken to expand the concept of authority control as it was implemented in MARC-based systems, in order to accommodate a broader vision of the archival information system. This would have consisted of a number of reference files in which the records description file was not privileged.[16] Informal and formal groups also tried to develop vocabularies for indexing records based on their cultural forms rather than their physical formats.[17] A way out of the impasse seemed to be to focus archival attention on the record series, a unit having direct relations to provenancial activity, rather than the fonds or record group, whose relation to provenance was more abstract.[18] However, archival description remained a records-centered activity, and the primary representation was a "unit of material." As a result, none of these proposals truly shifted the focus to a multi-pronged documentation approach which emphasized context of creation and would produce "poly-centric" databases.

Second, archivists found MARC content definitions inadequate to support the operational information needs of the archives, which was to be expected since they were developed to support information interchange in a service defined as a union list. The U.S. National Archives (NARA) -- even though it had contributed all the data it believed in 1983 that it would want to interchange to the data dictionary which led to the MARC content designation -- rejected the use of MARC two years later because it did not contain elements of information required by NARA for interchange within its own information systems.[19] Others built extensions to MARC records to accommodate local requirements, but did not draw the conclusion that MARC AMC data content must have been designed to satisfy a certain limited, but unarticulated, interchange service requirement, or that other models of what interchange could do, and other formats for description, or an extension of the existing format, would need to be accommodated by any theoretical framework intended to support documentation. This point was made before the MARC AMC format was proposed, but archivists failed to understand then, just as the ISAD(G) standard fails to do now, that rules for content and data representation make sense in the context of the purposes of concrete exchanges or implementations, not in the abstract, and that different rules or standards for end-products may derive from the same principles.[20]

Third, archivists began to have serious doubts about the use of existing descriptions for access to archives. Analysis of cataloging products has revealed widely divergent practices.[21] Some archivists believed that not enough was known about the way in which users sought information in archives to guide in the design of archival information systems.[22] Others felt that the solution to access would be to adopt controlled vocabularies and assign them to indexed fields. After a meeting of the Committee on Archival Information Exchange of the SAA was confronted with proposals to adopt many different vocabularies for a variety of different data elements, a group of archivists who were deeply involved in standards and description efforts within the Society of American Archivists formed an ad hoc Working Group on Standards for Archival Description (WGSAD) to identify what types of standards were needed to promote better description practices. Because WGSAD recently reported on its work in two full issues of the

American Archivist,[23] I need not summarize their actions but shall again make a few observations that will be developed more fully later.

WGSAD employed a matrix of types of standards to help it conceptualize, and then identify, standards relating to archival description which could or might already exist, but whose utility was not known to archivists.[24] It discovered numerous instances of standards that might be helpful to archivists, identified areas in which standards already existed, and located some areas in which standards might potentially be developed. During the course of its deliberations, WGSAD concluded that existing standards are especially inadequate to guide practice in documenting contexts of creation. WGSAD called for additional research in three areas of greatest interest to archivists which were considered the least well-developed: (1) the documentation of the context of creation of records (recommendation 15); (2) the capture and representation of information about records and acquisitions-related activity that is required for management of archives (recommendation 13); and (3) the analysis of user requirements (recommendation 12).[25]

These three research programs were intended to establish the foundation for sound archival documentation theory, although WGSAD did not express it in those terms. Since then, considerable progress has been made in developing frameworks for documentation, archival information systems architecture and user requirement analysis, which have been identified here as the three legs on which the documenting documentation platform rests.

DOCUMENTATION VS. DESCRIPTION

Documentation of the activity which generates archival records, and to a lesser extent of that which generates manuscripts, is a fundamentally different process than description of records which are in hand. Documentation of organizational activity ought to begin long before records are transferred to archives and may take place even before any records are created -- at the time when new functions are assigned to an organization. Documentation of manuscripts begins with the identification of collecting priorities, research on people, associations, and events, which played a role in history and might have generated records.

When it acquires a function, an organization establishes procedures for activities that will accomplish it and implements information systems to support it. If we understand these activities, procedures, and information systems, it is possible to identify records which will be created and their retention requirements before they are created because their evidential value and informational content is essentially predetermined. Documenting procedures and information systems is fundamental to the management of organizations; thus documentation of organizational missions, functions, and responsibilities and the way they are assigned at various levels of structure and reporting relationships within the organization, will be undertaken by the organizations themselves in their administrative control systems. Archivists can actively intervene through regulation and guidance to ensure that the data content and values depicting activities and functions are represented in a way that will make them useful for subsequent management and retrieval of the records resulting from these activities. This information, together with systems documentation, defines the immediate information system context out of which the records were generated, in which they are stored, and from which they were retrieved during their active life.

The creators of manuscripts do not generate self-documenting information systems nor do they respond to regulation, but the contexts in which they create and use records are nevertheless documentable independent of records description. Historical subjects generate records as a consequence of the relations they maintain during their lives, and these relations exist outside the records in a manner which is useful to understanding manuscripts as evidence: by recognizing the relations which a person, informal association, or event had, we can identify the records which do and do not exist in a manuscript collection. Documentation thus sheds light on records which are not present, as well as providing independent avenues of associational references by which the remaining records can be accessed and understood.

Documentation of the link between data content and the context of the creation and use of records is essential if records (archives or manuscripts) are to have value as evidence. The importance of this link, and the need for active intervention by archivists in the contexts of record creation to ensure documentation, has become clearer as a consequence of trying to define strategies for documenting electronic records systems. In these environments it is clear that contextual documentation capabilities can be dramatically improved by having records managers actively intervene in systems design and implementation.[26] Recent reports have called for more study on how such documentation objectives can best be achieved and research is now under way.[27] But the benefits of proactive documentation of the contexts of records creation are not limited to electronic records; the National Archives of Canada revised its methods of scheduling in 1990 to ensure that such information about important records systems and contexts of records creation would be documented earlier.[28]

When documentation of the organizational, functional, and systems context of creation of records takes place close to the moment of creation, and is used by people who are intimately acquainted with the organization and its informational processes, the documentation is likely to be intellectually more valid and easier to obtain than a *post hoc* description process. It is also more likely to satisfy the needs of users who are in the first instance staff of the organization seeking documentation associated with activities and responsibilities of the organizations for which they work. Documentation of the context, independent of the records and before the records are actually

created, may be augmented at a later date by archivists analyzing the content of the records themselves and locating in
them evidence of the way that the activity was conducted.
However, as a principle, the primary source of information
about the people and organizations which generate the
records, and which have engaged in the transactions which the
records document, should be the organizations, activities, and
systems themselves.

If this documentation is created in the beginning, and the
principles for data content and representation discussed below
are followed, it will be useful for administrative control purposes such as assignment of responsibilities, establishment of
contacts, determination of records disposition and negotiation
of transfers during the pre-archival life-cycle of the records.
Both the functions of the organization and the way it established its can or should be known before any records of the
function are created. Records managers can schedule such
records based on the nature of the activity, its importance to
the organization, and the legal, fiscal, and operational need for
evidence. Documentation of functions and of information
systems can be conducted using information created by the
organization in the course of its own activity and it can be
used to ensure the transfer of records to archives and/or their
destruction at appropriate times. It ensures that data about
records which were destroyed as well as those which were
preserved will be kept, and it takes advantage of the greater .
knowledge of records and the purposes and methods of day-
to-day activity that exists closer to the events. Most importantly, archivists can actively intervene in systems that will not
generate and/or will not retain information of archival significance if they document such functions and systems at the beginning of their active lives rather than long after they have
ceased to function.

These principles apply equally, although differently, to
manuscript collections. Ultimate end-users of archives and
manuscripts are better served through the construction of full-

fledged, "context of creation" reference files, since they cannot know the characteristics of records created by an organization or a person (e.g., description), but they can know the life history of a person or the functions of an organization and seek records that document the relations and transactions which each conducted. In addition, users can know about the generic forms of material or types of cultural documents which they are seeking. In the parts of the information system devoted to recording contextual data, they can locate those organizations and functions which have particular legislated responsibilities associated with search terms relevant to their queries; identify people whose relations with each other, to events, and to organizations are of interest; and explore the forms of material which have data they require; and locate those forms within the systems documentation associated with the information systems metadata in the "context of creation" reference system.

Information systems which do not contain archival description can lead users to such records by documenting the persons and organizations which are affiliated with the contexts of records creation. In-depth study of the process by which queries to archival description systems are formulated has shown that users engage in just this sort of reasoning even if they are seeking to approach a system that does not support access by contextual documentation.[29]

In short, documentation of the three aspects of records creation contexts (activities, organizations and their functions, and information systems), together with representation of their relations, is essential to the concept of archives as evidence and is therefore a fundamental theoretical principle for documenting documentation. Documentation is a process that captures information about an activity which is relevant to locating evidence of that activity, and captures information about records that are useful to their ongoing management by the archival repository. The primary sources of information are the functions and information systems giving rise to the records. The principal activity of the archivist is the manipulation of data for reference files that create richly linked structures among attributes of the records-generating context and which point to the underlying evidence or record.

DETERMINING THE DATA CONTENT OF DOCUMENTATION

When we assert that the focus of documentation should be representation of the characteristics of human activity which result in archives, the functions which these activities are intended to carry out, and the information systems which hold the records, we have not yet provided principles for determining the content of such knowledge representations. The basis for such data content standards is again found in the difference between archives and other documentary materials, in this case a difference in their processing. When we acquire, describe, classify, and catalog library bibliographic materials, our processes do not transform them, but when we accession, transfer, arrange, weed, document, and inventory archival materials, we change their character as well as enhance their evidential and informational value. The fact of processing, exhibiting, citing, publishing, and otherwise managing records becomes significant for their meaning as records, which is not true of library materials.

The location of such principles within the matrix framework adopted by the Working Group on Standards for Archival Description is identified as data content and data values guidelines; no standards were identified in those cells. Unfortunately, WGSAD did not elect to explore these cells further in the papers it commissioned from its members. Had they, a paper on data content and data values guidelines would have stated as a principle that content and data representation requirements ought to be derived from analysis of the uses to which such systems must be put and should satisfy the day-to-day information requirements of archivists who are the primary users of archives, and of researchers using archives for their primary evidential purposes.

The Working Group had covered this ground in its meetings and reached consensus on the potential utility of a logical
data and process model of an archival information system as a
basis on which specific content rules could be constructed. A
prototype of such an data flow model was proposed by the
author in 1982 for use by NISTF in developing its data dictionary.[30] When NISTF decided to take a pragmatic approach in
using data already present in systems as a method of developing its dictionary, the process and data model was abandoned. As a consequence of discussions which began at the
WGSAD meetings, a follow-up effort to define standards for
content based on the principle that content and representation
standards follow function in the archival information system is
now nearing completion.[31]

Building on a model information systems architecture
drafted by Richard Szary, Ted Weir, and myself in 1989, fifteen
archivists involved in archival description standards efforts
received funding from the NHPRC to complete the work. The
resulting model defines the activities involved in the administration of an archives and the clusters of data (free text
"notes" or groups of data elements describing an aspect of a
particular entity and its relations) required as input to or control over each activity as well as the clusters of data produced
by each process. As such, the model defines, at the level of
data clusters rather than data elements, what the data contents
of archival description systems must be in order for them to
support each of the various activities involved in archival
administration. The data clusters are defined at a level of
granularity which does not specify representation of data elements because the model is intended as a logical model not as
a physical, or implementation, schema. The principles on
which this information architecture standard is constructed
are nevertheless quite clear about how one would derive
specific rules for actual implementations: the appropriate
content and values for the data are derived from the requirements of the archival tasks into which and out of which this

data must flow; these tasks, of course, are specific to the local application or interchange service.

The business processes reflected in the Archival Information Systems Architecture model include those involved in administering the archival repository, establishing its policies, procedures, plans, projects, and actions, as well as activities involving records description, arrangement, shelving, copying, etc. The model also includes the management of information about the creation context, including documentation of activities and of the information systems generating and storing records in organizations that transfer materials to the archives. The Information Systems Architecture working group hopes that one of the benefits of the model will be to demonstrate how information acquired about the function, activity, and/or information system in the records creating organization, such as promises of confidentiality extended to clients, can affect archival management of the evidence of these activities, influencing appraisal, transfer terms, and conditions of access and use. These kinds of relationships make it clear why the representation of data needs to serve subsequent use. By showing clearly the paths information takes and the tasks which it is intended to support, the model can assist archivists to identify how the data should be recorded when they first encounter it.

This approach to the question of what information ought to comprise an archival description does not accidentally differ from that taken by the ICA Principles. It proceeds from the radically contrary principle that the information in an archival description should be what is required by an archives (and its users), and that the way the data is represented should be dictated by the subsequent uses of the data in the system, including requirements for linking the data in the archives with data about entities in the real world contained in other information systems. Both the definition of the data requirements and the concept that this approach should be employed to define standards for archival information systems will be proposed to the Society of American Archivists Committee on

Archival Information Interchange and Standards Board in the winter of 1992-3.

The ICA Commission proposes a principle by which archivists would select data content for archival descriptions, which is that "the structure and content of representations of archival material should facilitate information retrieval" (5.1). Unfortunately, it does not help us to understand how the Commission selected the twenty-five elements of information identified in its standard or how we could apply the principle to selection of additional content. It does, however, serve as a prelude to the question of which principles should guide archivists in choosing data values in their representations.

DOCUMENTING DOCUMENTATION FOR THE USER

Even a consistent model of what contextual documentation requires, and adequate principles for determining data content standards for archival information systems, would not constitute a fully sufficient theoretical framework for principles. The documenting documentation platform rests on three legs: the third is that the language of documentation systems should provide access by users from their point of departure, and that the structure of links made by users should be explicitly represented, so that users will understand the relationship between the records and the context of creation of which they are evidence. The need to ground our principles for data representation in the perspective of the user derives from a fundamental difference between consciously authored materials (books, articles, documentary or fiction films) and archival materials which are records *of* but not *about* activity. Consciously authored materials have a subject matter imposed on them by their authors, and they are rarely appropriate as research material for other topics. Archival records on the other hand shed their light more indirectly, answering not only such factual questions as what took place and who was involved but also more subjective ones such as why participants acted as they did or how the actions were recorded. Libraries have found that subject access based on titles, tables of contents, abstracts, indexes, and similar formal subject analysis by-products of publishing can support most bibliographic research, but the perspectives brought to materials by archival researchers are both more varied and likely to differ from those of the records creators.

We know too little about what information users of archival information systems are seeking, and how they articulate their requests, to formulate, develop, or select specific vocabularies for representation of the content of archival documentation. We must therefore follow statement of the principle with a call for further study of such language. As a preliminary step, archival repositories throughout the U.S. were invited to participate in a snapshot study of what the author called "user presentation language" in the spring of 1989.[32] This was probably the first systematic, multi-institutional study of what users asked of archives ever conducted. More thorough studies by Paul Conway, completed in 1992, and others should influence archival documentation in the future.[33]

Archivists do know, however, from studies of retrieval using controlled vocabulary, that the benefits of control are not derived from the limitation of terms assigned but from the association between terms in thesauri and headings lists which effectively expand the number of routes by which one can get to the terms used in descriptions.[34] We also know that the effectiveness of controlled vocabulary depends greatly on its implementation and the availability and effectiveness of alternative implementation strategies. Rather than asserting that systems should be implemented in any particular way, we can suggest that user language be accommodated as a means of access into documentation, locating the user in appropriate reference files which employ the terms they use or synonyms of those terms, and providing for search within and among such reference files.

The principle therefore requires that archivists build structures which link the terms suggested by users concerning functions, form of material, subject content, or records creator/recipient by semantic models, to a meaningful documentation framework. One of the purposes of the rules derived from this principle will be to construct representations of archives which will no longer always require archivists to be present as intermediaries in order to translate queries into the structures by which we represent archives. One failure of the standards of description currently employed is that only those with extensive experience in archives understand how to translate a question about information content into the name of the organization or person around whom a fonds would be created. In a study conducted in the mid-1980s of the information retrieval function at the U.S. National Archives, researchers found that archivists pursued a search logic in translating users' subject-based queries into terms reflecting the provenance of records that was in principle replicable by artificial intelligence. Unfortunately their structural representations of the logical relations of the data in the agency history reference files led them to believe that human intermediaries would be required to provide testimony about each specific records-creating context in order for the retrieval to be significantly assisted by artificial intelligence, so the system was not constructed.[35] A better representation of the knowledge which they acquired from question-negotiating reference archivists would have exposed commonalties between types of semantic links that would have permitted them to represent the knowledge of reference archivists about the process rather than the content of searches. Users, they would have found, need to approach an archive from numerous perspectives other than the name of the organization or person responsible for the creation of a fonds. By modeling the relationship between subject terms in organizational histories and personal biographies, functional terms in mission statements and descriptions of activities, and knowledge about forms of material, they could have demonstrated how best to answer one of the major types of questions which they found. If the object of description at the National Archives had been the record series, as it is at many other archives, a "user interface" in which these relations among creation contexts, forms of material, and content was explicit, would have gone a long way towards enabling the user to query a system without an intermediary. A recent study of the users of the documentary heritage in the United States provides some fascinating data on the differences between the questions being asked by different researchers and the types of materials that would serve as an answer.[36] Further studies along these lines would enable us to model a variety of approaches to archives and develop representations of the documentation system that correspond to the mind set carried to the archives by its users.

The principle here is that the user should not only be able to employ terminology and perspective, which are natural, but should also be able to enter the system from knowledge of the world being documented without knowing about the world of documentation. Gaining access to the names of individuals through the names of groups with which they might have been affiliated, or events in which they might have participated, or transactions with government to which they were parties, requires that an individual's reference files (or knowledge bases) be maintained. Similarly, access by functions (e.g., licensing) or activities (e.g., public hearings) requires the maintenance of reference databases about organizations, their missions, functions, activities, and procedures. Users need to be able to enter the system through the historical context of activity, construct relations in that context, and then seek pointers down into documentation. This frees them from trying to imagine what records might have survived (documentation assists the user to establish the non-existence of records as well as their existence) or to fathom the way archivists might have described records which did survive.

Archival description, or documentation, should make sense to end users not just because the language of documentation corresponds to the terminology of end-users or because the end user is able to search in reference files in order to establish relations between entities that were involved in the creation and use of records. It also involves creating and constructing a model of the archives as an information system which users can maintain as an archetype and employ to navigate through the documentation archivists create.

Given an appropriate model of what an archives is, and how it relates to the society which it documents, the contents of archival documentation can be made accessible to everyday visitors to the reference facility along with description of the contents. This information, moreover, can be used in making judgments about archival appraisal and accessioning prior to the creation of any records by a new function, or their recording, filing, and management by the information system supporting that function.

Instead of asking users who created a document which they are seeking or what institution would have had custody over it, archivists need to be asking them what information they are seeking, so that they might go from the information they want to the forms of material in which such information is represented, and the activities that would have generated such forms or had occasion to capture such information. As Terry Cook has observed about case records, the value of such records to society lies in their ability to provide evidence of discrepancies between the "image" of the transaction promoted by the organization whose function it is, and the experience of the transaction by an individual who, in the case of governmental actions is a citizen.[37] For this we need to have information about the interaction, why it took place, how it was conducted, what information it elicited, how the organization viewed the information, how the client viewed the information, and what purposes the information would ultimately serve. The documentation of documentation, rather than the name of the creator of the fonds, is the source of the information which we use to appraise such records, and the foundation of the means by which we will ultimately retrieve them.

CONCLUSIONS

While American archivists may seem, from an outsider's perspective, to have recently arrived at a consensus about archival description and its purposes, the illusion disguises a profound confusion. When they departed from the practices of Brooks and Schellenberg in order to develop means for the construction of union catalogs of archival holdings, American archivists were not defining new principles, but inventing a simple expedient. After several years of experience with the new system, serious criticisms of it were being leveled by the very people who had first devised it. These criticisms have been growing in intensity and focus since. In the past several years, a number of efforts to move beyond the consensus on archival cataloging have been launched, including the Working Group on Standards for Archival Description, the Information Systems Architecture Standards initiative, and studies of archival users and the language they use to query reference staff and information systems. Together these initiatives are suggesting three theoretical premises for the documentation of documentation:

(1) The subject of the documentation is, first and foremost, the activity that generated the records, the organizations and individuals who used the records, and the purposes to which the records were put;

(2) The content of the documentation must support requirements for archival management of records, and the representations of data should support life-cycle management of records; and

(3) The requirements of users of archives, especially their personal methods of inquiry, should determine the data values in documentation systems and guide archivists in presenting abstract models of their systems to users.

NOTES

[1] International Council on Archives, Ad Hoc Commission on Descriptive Standards, "Statement of Principles Regarding Archival Description," First Version Revised (February 1992). Also, International Council on Archives, Ad Hoc Commission on Descriptive Standards, "Draft ISAD(G), General International Standard Archival Description" (January 1992). Both documents were published in *Archivaria* 34 (Summer 1992). Nothing in this chapter is intended to suggest that the proposed standard is not an accurate reflection of archival description principles adhered to by most archivists today or to suggest that those involved in drafting the standard have not been responsive to previous critiques of their earlier draft. The proposed standard has undergone a legitimate development and review process which is, in fact, one of the reasons it conforms so well to what archivists presently believe. These principles uphold record-centered, post-accessioning description activity centered in archives rather than an activity centered documentation and ignore the structuring requirements of data representation dictated by the purposes to which the data will be put precisely because most archivists do.

[2] Because this chapter proposes a set of principles which can be contrasted with those of the ICA, the introduction elaborates on these differences. A detailed critique of the text of the ICA Principles and ISAD(G) rules, which at the time of this writing were still in a draft form, is contained in David Bearman, "ICA Principles for Archival Description," *Archives and Museum Informatics* 6:1 (Spring 1992): 20-21.

[3] This critique of methods on purely practical, rather than philosophical, grounds is developed further in David Bearman, *Archival Methods*, Archives and Museum Informatics Technical Report #9 (Pittsburgh: Archives and Museum Informatics, 1990), 28-38. For analyses of how such systems would be structured, why they will work, and how they can raise the profile of archivists within organizations see David Bearman, *Functional Requirements for Collections Management Systems*, Archival Informatics Technical Report #3 (Pittsburgh: Archives and Museum Informatics, 1987).

[4] David Bearman and Richard Lytle, "The Power of the Principle of Provenance," *Archivaria* 21 (1985): 14-27 was originally drafted and distributed to colleagues during the life of NISTF although not published for several years because we found colleagues so hostile to its ideas.

[5] David Bearman, "'Who about What' or 'From Whence, Why and How': Intellectual Access Approaches to Archives and Their Implications for National Archival Information Systems," in *Archives, Automation and Access,* ed. Peter Baskerville and Chad Gaffield (Victoria, British Columbia: University of Victoria, 1986), 39-47.

[6] David Bearman, *Towards National Information Systems for Archives and Manuscript Repositories: The NISTF Papers* (Chicago: Society of American Archivists, 1987); also Bearman, "Buildings as Structures, as Art, and as Dwellings: Data Exchange Issues in an Architectural Information Network," in *Databases in the Humanities and Social Sciences,* vol. 4, ed. Lawrence McCrank (Medford, New Jersey: Learned Information, 1989), 41-48.

[7] David Bearman, "User Presentation Language in Archives," *Archives and Museum Informatics* 3:4 (Winter 1990): 3-7.

[8] David Bearman, "Authority Control: Issues and Prospects," *American Archivist* 52 (Summer 1989): 286-299.

[9] Kathleen D. Roe, "From Archival Gothic to MARC Modern: Building Common Data Structures," *American Archivist* 53 (Winter 1990): 56-66. Also, Bureau of Canadian Archivists, *Toward Descriptive Standards: Report and Recommendations of the Canadian Working Group on Archival Descriptive Standards* (Ottawa: Bureau of Canadian Archivists, December 1985) cites archival automation as a driver in the search for standards in Canada.

[10] David Bearman, ed., "Data Elements used in Archives, Manuscripts and Record Repository Information Systems: A Dictionary of Standard Terminology," NISTF Report (Washington, D.C.: Society of American Archivists, October 1982) reprinted in Nancy Sahli ed., *MARC for Archives and Manuscripts: The AMC Format* (Chicago: Society of American Archivists, 1985).

[11] Steven L. Hensen, *Archives, Personal Papers, and Manuscripts: A Cataloging Manual for Archival Repositories, Historical Societies, and Manuscript Libraries* (Washington, D.C.: Library of Congress, 1983).

[12] David Bearman, "Archives and Manuscript Control with Bibliographic Utilities: Challenges and Opportunities," *American Archivist* 52 (Winter 1989): 26-39.

[13] Alden Monroe and Kathleen Roe, "What's the Purpose?: Functional Access to Archival Records," in *Beyond the Book: Extending MARC for Subject Access,* ed. Toni Petersen and Pat Molholt (Boston: G.K. Hall, 1990); Marion Matters, "Authority Work for Transitional

Catalogs," in *Describing Archival Materials: The Use of the MARC AMC Format*, ed. Richard P. Smiraglia (New York: Haworth Press, 1990), 91-115 [also published as *Cataloging & Classification Quarterly* 11:3/4 (1990)]. Also see Research Libraries Group Government Records Project, "Online Record Types for Government Records," unpublished draft, July 1990.

[14] Steven L. Hensen, *Archives, Personal Papers, and Manuscripts: A Cataloging Manual for Archival Repositories, Historical Societies, and Manuscript Libraries*, 2nd ed. (Chicago: Society of American Archivists, 1989) is accepted by U.S. archivists as rules for applications involving data interchange of MARC records on national networks.

[15] Bureau of Canadian Archivists, *Toward Descriptive Standards* (Ottawa: BCA, 1992); also, Bureau of Canadian Archivists, Planning Committee on Descriptive Standards, *Rules for Archival Description* (Ottawa: Bureau of Canadian Archivists, 1990-). Not coincidentally, *Towards Descriptive Standards* envisioned an international standard congruent with the ISBD(G) which has now been produced as ISAD(G): General International Standard Archival Description with most of the same data categories identified in Appendix C of the 1985 report. (1st recommendation, p. 57).

[16] David Bearman and Richard Szary, "Beyond Authorized Headings: Authorities as Reference Files in a Multi-Disciplinary Setting," in *Authority Control Symposium*, Karen Muller ed. (Tucson, Arizona: Art Libraries of North America, 1987), 67-78; Lisa Weber, "The 'Other' MARC Formats: Authorities and Holdings, Do We Care To Be Partners in This Dance, Too?," *American Archivist* 53 (Winter 1990): 44-51; David Bearman, "Considerations in the Design of Art Scholarly Databases," *Library Trends* 37:2 (1988): 206-219.

[17] An informal working group was convened at the Smithsonian Institution in 1985 to draft a functions vocabulary. Work on a forms of material vocabulary went forward within the Research Libraries Group and the *Art and Architecture Thesaurus*, sometimes in parallel. A framework for the concept of using a form-of material as an access method appears in David Bearman and Peter Sigmond, "Explorations of Form of Material Authority Files by Dutch Archivists," *American Archivist* 50 (Spring 1987): 249-253. The AAT vocabulary was published as the "Document Types Hierarchy" in *Art and Architecture Thesaurus*, ed. Toni Petersen, (New York: Oxford University Press, 1990).

[18] Max Evans, "Authority Control: An Alternative to the Record Group Concept," *American Archivist* 49 (Summer 1986): 249-261; David Bearman, "Can MARC Accommodate Archives and Museums: Technical and Political Challenges," in *Beyond the Book: Extending MARC for Subject Access*, ed. Toni Petersen and Pat Molholt (Boston: G.K. Hall, 1990), 237-245; for a very early critique, see, Peter Scott, "The Record Group Concept: A Case for Abandonment," *American Archivist* 29 (1966): 493-504.

[19] William M. Holmes, Jr., Edie Hedlin, and Thomas E. Weir, Jr., "MARC and Life-Cycle Tracking at the National Archives: Project Final Report," *American Archivist* 49 (Fall 1986): 305-309; David Bearman, Letter to the Editor, *American Archivist* 49 (Winter 1986): 347-348; and response from Thomas Weir, *American Archivist* 50 (Spring 1987): 172-173.

[20] David Bearman, "Towards National Information Systems for Archives and Manuscript Repositories: I. Alternative Models," (August 1981), reprinted in *Towards National Information Systems for Archives and Manuscript Repositories: The NISTF Papers* (Chicago, Society of American Archivists, 1987); also David Bearman, "Archival and Bibliographic Information Networks" *Journal of Library Administration* 7:2/3 (1986): 99-110 [reprinted in *Archival and Library Administration: Divergent Traditions, Common Concerns*, ed. Lawrence McCrank (New York: Haworth Press, 1986)].

[21] Avra Michelson, "Archival Reference in the Age of Automation," *American Archivist* 50 (Spring 1987): 192-209.

[22] Lawrence Dowler, "The Role of Use in Defining Archival Practice and Principles: A Research Agenda for the Availability and Use of Records," *American Archivist* 51 (Winter/Spring 1988): 74-86, with commentaries by Jacqueline Goggin (pp. 87-90) and Anne Kenney (pp. 91-95).

[23] *American Archivist* 52 (Fall 1989); 53 (Winter 1990).

[24] Victoria Irons Walch, ed., "Report of the Working Group on Standards for Archival Description," *American Archivist* 52 (Fall 1989): 440-461; also David Bearman, "Description Standards: A Framework for Action," *American Archivist* 52 (Fall 1989): 514-519.

[25] Victoria Irons Walch, ed., "Recommendations of the Working Group on Standards for Archival Description," *American Archivist* 52 (Fall 1989): 462-477.

[26] David Bearman, "Management of Electronic Records: Issues and Guidelines," in United Nations Advisory Committee for Co-ordination of Information Systems, *Electronic Records Management Guidelines: A Manual for Policy Development and Implementation* (New York: United Nations, 1990), 17-70, 89-107, 135-189, parts of which are reprinted in this volume as Chapter 3.

[27] National Historical Publications and Records Commission, *Research Issues in Electronic Records: Report of the Working Meeting* (St. Paul: Minnesota Historical Society, 1991) defines the issues. See also: David Bearman, "Archival Principles and the Electronic Office" in *Information Handling in Offices and Archives*, Angelika Menne-Haritz ed. (New York: K.G. Saur, 1993): 177-193, reprinted in this volume as Chapter 5.; David Bearman, "Diplomatics, Weberian Bureaucracy, and the Management of Electronic Records in Europe and America," *American Archivist* 55 (Winter 1992): 168-180, reprinted in this volume as Chapter 9.

[28] National Archives of Canada, Government Records Branch, "Disposition of the Records of the Government of Canada: A Planned Approach," 3 July 1990, typescript.

[29] David Bearman, "Contexts of Creation and Dissemination as Approaches to Documents that Move and Speak," in *Documents that Move and Speak: Audiovisual Archives in the New Information Age*, proceedings of a Symposium held 30 April-3 May 1990 at the National Archives of Canada (New York: K.G. Saur, 1992), 140-149.

[30] David Bearman, "Functional Specifications of an Integrated Information Management System for Administering a Program of Active, Archival, or Manuscript Records," NISTF Report (Washington, D.C.: Society of American Archivists, August 1982). This was the precursor to the Bentley proposal.

[31] Marion Matters, "Building New Directions: The Development of the Archival Information Architecture," unpublished paper delivered at the Society of American Archivists annual conference, 1991.

[32] Bearman, "User Presentation Language in Archives."

[33] Paul Conway's studies of users conducted at the National Archives in 1990-91 have since been published as *Partners in Research: Improving Access to the Nation's Archives* (Pittsburgh: Archives and Museum Informatics, in press).

[34] Bearman, "Authority Control: Issues and Prospects."

[35] Daniel de Salvo and Jay Liebowitz, "The Application of an Expert System for Information Retrieval at the National Archives," *Telematics & Informatics* 3:1 (1986): 25-38; Avra Michelson, *Expert Systems Technology and its Implications for Archives*, NARA Technical Information Paper #9 (Washington, D.C.: National Archives, March 1991). For a critique of the de Salvo study, see David Bearman, "Expert Systems for Archives," unpublished paper delivered at the Mid Atlantic Regional Archives Conference, 8 May 1987; also, David Bearman, "Intelligent Artifices, Structures for Intellectual Control" in Bearman, *Archival Methods*, 49-58.

[36] Ann D. Gordon, *Using the Nation's Documentary Heritage: The Report of the Historical Documents Study* (Washington, D.C.: NHPRC and ACLS, 1992); see especially the multipart question #4 which is analyzed only superficially on pp. 46-48 of the report under the heading "framing research questions."

[37] Terry Cook, *The Archival Appraisal of Records Containing Personal Information: A RAMP Study with Guidelines* (Paris: Unesco General Information Programme, 1991); also review by David Bearman in *Archivaria* 34 (Summer 1992): 217-219.

SECTION V

Program Management/ Frameworks/Structures

❖

CHAPTER NINE

Diplomatics, Weberian Bureaucracy, and the Management of Electronic Records in Europe and America

❖

CHAPTER TEN

New Models for Management of Electronic Records

CHAPTER NINE

Diplomatics, Weberian Bureaucracy, and the Management of Electronic Records in Europe and America*

During the past several years, as archivists worldwide have begun to struggle with the problems of managing electronic records, two traditions of archival theory and organizational practice which remain very strong in Europe have become prominent features of the solutions being developed there. In this chapter, these theoretical influences on archival practice are explored and the way in which they are shaping European approaches to the challenges of electronic records are examined. The significance of European theory and practice for electronic records management in American is then considered.

* Originally published in the *American Archivist* 55 (Winter 1992): 168-181.

THE EUROPEAN ARCHIVAL TRADITION

During the late Middle Ages, a radical change in administrative practice swept Europe. The written documents of important transactions of the court became recognized as the "official" record and as evidence of an "act."[1] Having achieved this legitimacy, and ultimately affirmed it in the emerging court systems established to defend the legitimacy of the state, the document as a evidence immediately became subject to forgery and other fraudulent use. It became critical to the legitimacy of the established order that methods were developed to distinguish between authentic and original records and forgeries or copies. One of these methods, the science of document analysis known as diplomatics, became a central element in the training of all European archivists in the nineteenth century after the fall of the ancien regimes when the historical, rather than administrative, use of these archives became important.[2]

Also during the nineteenth century, a dramatic and thorough revolution in the organization of collective activity in society took place throughout Europe as public and private institutions took on the bureaucratic forms which still predominate in organizations today. In bureaucracies, as Max Weber revealed in his classic analysis of this quintessentially modern form of organization, the autonomy of the individual as employee is subjugated to the office, and each office, or role, is performed without respect to the personal position of either the office holder or the client.[3] This impersonal consistency is maintained by policies and procedures and by the role of written records in all formal transactions. With the progressive adoption of this form of organization in the mid-nineteenth century came the northern European tradition of the registry office with its *Aktenplan* and the respect with which southern Europe treated "original order."[4]

The twin pillars of diplomatics and the documentation practices of bureaucratic institutions, especially those with registry offices, support training and practice in European archives as the twentieth century comes to a close. However, they are being challenged by potentially radical changes in both the nature of records and the structure of organizations brought on by the so-called electronic information revolution. The response of European archivists to the electronic information revolution has been distinctively colored by their training in diplomatics and by the nature of their bureaucracies.

THE NATURE OF THE CHALLENGES POSED BY ELECTRONIC RECORDS

The electronic information revolution presents two fundamental challenges to archivists. First, it threatens to transform the relatively stable framework of bureaucratic organizations and to replace it by a type of organizational structure which is, at present, inchoate. Second, it is leading to new practices of communication and to new forms of records whose outlines are equally unclear. Each of these tendencies challenges contemporary archival practice and forces us to re-examine archival theory.

Although it is overly simplistic to assert that technology determines the shape of society, we cannot deny that technologies may have a profound impact on social structures. We need only point to the role of irrigation in the emergence of agrarian civilizations, the stirrup and gun powder in the rise and fall of the feudal system, or printing in the spread of literacy and reformation, to see how significant these effects can be. Bureaucratic structures were designed as strategies for organizational management of far-flung enterprises, and methods of organizational recordkeeping such as the registry office were especially designed to support standardized action across the distance of time and space.[5] The telephone, automobile and airplane each successively reduced the effect of distance, and communication time as isolating factors in the modern world. But the electronic information revolution is reducing these distances in a way that undermines the structure of bureaucratic organizations, a structure designed primarily to overcome the threat that time and distance posed to exerting coordinated and consistent organizational control.[6]

Bureaucratic organizations evolved to assert their authority across what were then vast distances in space and time. Through them, Chinese, and later European, governments could control remote districts and even colonies through written procedures uniformly applied. Bureaucrats were trained to follow procedures, to document their transactions on the same forms, and to submit reports to a central office for unified bookkeeping. Correspondence was managed in the same way from office to office, using common classification schemes developed to reflect organizational policy and practices for approval and recording of communications that were identical from one place in the organization to another.[7]

The advent of the telephone at the turn of the twentieth century introduced the first electronic challenge to this form of bureaucracy by providing a means for people to communicate across and beyond the organization, and at great distances in space, without leaving a documentary trail. Archivists were unable to document telephonic communication because it acquired the social protection of a private conversation even when devoted to organizational business. In response, organizations generally bar official actions from taking place solely by telephone or insist on the parallel creation of a written record. The electronic information revolution revisits the site of these battles, but it carries the seeds of a more thorough revolution in organizational behavior than was introduced by the telephone.

The electronic information revolution does not consist of the introduction of a single, free-standing piece of communications technology like the telephone, but rather of the re-creation of the organization and its activity in an electronic form which is technologically accessible twenty-four hours a day, from anywhere in the world, and without respect to the organizational role of the user. The challenge to the contemporary organization is to harness this potentially anarchistic technology for the benefit of the organization. The methods at hand are the same tools that have been used to regulate organizations forever -- organizational policy and the technology itself. The issue is whether the potential of the technology to make the organization more responsive, more flexible, more accessible, and more tactical can be unleashed without also making the organization more reactive and less strategic.

As the technologies of the electronic information revolution become widespread, administrators look forward to having direct access to information previously summarized for them by subordinates; to being able to directly discuss this information with anyone in the company or outside at any time regardless of where the person with whom they are communicating is located; and to being able to make analytic decisions (with supportive tools) and order changes in organizational behavior based on them to take effect immediately. Production managers look forward to dispersed, multi-skilled design teams responding to customer demand with new designs that can directly drive automated production facilities, creating "just in-time" inventories of new designs with dramatically reduced lead times. Workers throughout the organization see the same technologies as a means of knowing as much as their bosses know, being able to contribute usefully to decision making, and being able to respond rapidly and directly to challenges from any source.[8] They also see it as freeing them from having to be in a particular place to do their work and of freeing their clients from having to "come to the office" to have the work done for them. For each of these employees, access to information becomes a source of power that is more important than place in the hierarchy itself. These kinds of changes, long predicted by social scientists familiar with the electronic information revolution, and heralded with glee by many of the leading figures who introduced this revolution, are now being discovered empirically.[9]

The organization is, however, not without defenses. After all, it employs those who would use the technology to further such democratizing ends. But it would seem from studies to date that, both in Europe and in the United States, these technologies are having the effect of flattening organizations. It is demonstrably reducing the control exercised by central authority over transactions themselves and the recordkeeping about them.[10] Before examining these effects more closely, I will turn to the second challenge presented by the electronic information revolution.

The form of documents in any society reflects the meeting of a particular technology of recording and the generic cultural need to differentiate documents semiotically for rapid decoding. Those who know scrolls or clay tablets have no more trouble distinguishing at a glance whether they are viewing a proclamation or a record of commercial transactions than we, trained in our culture, have in distinguishing a page from a daybook from a legal brief or a utility bill. These distinctions among forms of recorded information based on their content are useful in complex societies and play a substantial role in archival theory and practice, especially in Europe.[11]

But the forms of documents are also undergoing rapid and unpredictable development at the present time as a consequence of the introduction of electronic means of communication. One obvious discontinuity is that electronic records cannot be seen except as they are re-presented under software control. To date most software has been designed to present electronic records in familiar guises so the changes are not as pronounced as they certainly will be in thirty years when a generation raised on these tools of communication invents entirely new forms rather than simply modifying the older ones that we have brought forward from the age of paper-based communications. Nevertheless, the changes in forms of records are pronounced enough to reveal three trends in the evolution of new forms of documentation that could profoundly effect archival practice.

The first is that instantaneous but asynchronous communication (it does not matter if the recipients of your communication are present when it is received, they will answer as soon as they return), has the effect within organizations of reducing the length and complexity of individual communications. Instead of writing a full report on an incident or analyzing the entire situation in detail and sending a report up the organizational hierarchy after a week or more, the pattern of communication consists of an exchange of statements and questions which do not supply any object referents or contextual clues. Indeed, it has been commented frequently that, in organizations using electronic mail communications, the written documentation is taking on the character of oral communication, especially of conversation.[12] As a consequence, the content of an electronic document is less likely to reference its context.

The second is that the speed at which underlying information upon which organizational decision making is based changes in organizations which have implemented electronic communications.[13] The premium that is placed on up-to-date information has led to greater integration between information systems, which in turn makes possible the creation of "dynamic" documents which change their content in response to the information environment in which they are (re)constructed. To date we have seen only such limited applications of this concept as the graph or spreadsheet which reconfigures itself based on the state of a remote database, but we will soon see such dynamic pointers, linked to artificial intelligence rules, redefining activities based on new policies, procedures, designs, or objectives.

The third development is the advent of the multimedia, "compound document" which again is in its infancy. To date we are seeing only linear textual documents with limited amounts of bit-mapped raster image and graphics, but capabilities to exchange non-linear "hyper-documents" and texts with voice annotation are very close to realization.[14] Within the decade we will probably see compound documents which make it possible to export manufactured goods as information (driving manufacturing facilities located near the point-of-sale) and to direct medical, environmental, or military intervention by remote devices. These kinds of documents will require us to fundamentally rethink diplomatics since they will not simply *record* the effects of actions, but *be* the effecters of action.

These three trends in patterns of communication interact and are extended by such developments as the introduction of "intelligent" systems capable of executing organizational policies without human intervention. Such systems now routinely buy and sell most of the stocks on the stock market and determine organizational responses to natural and human-made disasters. In the future, information "objects" which monitor the information environment in which they operate in order to perceive and act on changes in the information landscape will be commonplace. How archivists respond to such developments will depend on how the organizations in which they are employed deploy information technology and on how they use their training as archivists.

APPROACHES TO ELECTRONIC RECORDS MANAGEMENT

The fundamental problem in the management of electronic records is to identify the functional provenance of records (e.g., the business purpose for which they were created), so as to be able to carry out organizational retention policy. We cannot see electronic records except under software control, but the functional provenance of records may be *explicitly recorded as data* within the record by the record creator or system, *implicit in the system design* and revealed by analysis or by documentation which reveals the structural relations between data instances, or *discovered by links to the originating activity*, which is represented by the source of the records, or more exactly by knowledge of the transaction communication

path. Each of these three loci of functional provenance information (data content, data structure, and data context) provides documentation of what I have elsewhere called
"evidential historicity" and can be contributed either by individual employees, the bureaucratic system or the underlying
technology.[15]

Europeans are deploying solutions to the challenges
posed by electronic records management that differ in emphasis from those being experimented with in the United States.
In Europe, they are depending more on individual employees
and the bureaucratic system to provide functional provenance
as explicit data while in the U.S. we are relying more heavily
on technology to provide information about structure and
communications paths.[16] This impression reflects my observations at several recent meetings in Europe on electronic
records management and in the working sessions of the
United Nations ACCIS working group on electronic records
management guidelines.[17]

It has become clear to me that German-speaking Europeans generally believe employees can be instructed to classify
the business function of electronic records as they have paper-
based information. At a meeting of experts held in Marburg in
October 1991, German archivists were unanimous in their belief that traditional classification methods could be applied to
electronic records. Archivists from the province of Baden-
Württemburg and from the Bundesarchiv concurred that all
future records would be "documents," all documents would be
classified, and that classified records in any format could be
managed by registry office practices.[18] At the Macerata conference in May 1991, Christoph Graf, the national archivist of
Switzerland, also asserted that workers can and must assign
classifications to records in the electronic office.

It does logically follow that if electronic records are documents, if classifications must be assigned to documents prior
to sending them, and if the classification reflects the functional
provenance and contextual significance of the record, then

records will be associated with their correct provenance through classification by their creators. But will electronic records be documents in the sense of being software independent and having boundaries within which their data is contained? Will organizations continue to relate to the outside world through organizational structures which correlate placement of an employee in the organization to his or her function? Will classifications based on bureaucratic forms be adequate to reconstruct relations between transactions and between data in records and their information environment? And can users correctly classify transactions generating electronic documents?

At the Macerata meeting, which was influenced by Italian participation, emphasis was placed on understanding the bureaucratic pathways along which communications flow. It was assumed that certain kinds of transactions would take place in specifiable ways between communicating bureaucracies or even between departments within an organization. It was also assumed that the business source of the transactions could thereby be identified by archivists using methods of systems analysis to document such flows and characterizing the resulting transactions by the form of record they produced.[19]

In the United States, where no tradition of classifying official communications according to provenance and business purpose exists and where communication between organizations does not necessarily take place between the heads of the respective departments or units, a consensus is developing around more technological, rather than managerial, strategies. We are trying to assert archival authority into the systems acquisition and planning process in order to assure that archival requirements are embodied in acquired software. We are trying to insinuate ourselves into standards-setting efforts to incorporate certain requirements into procurement regulations. And some researchers are exploring ways to automatically mark or tag the provenance and business purpose of documents through recognition of their form and their telecommunication source (automatically generated extended headers providing business function).[20]

In part, Americans are seeking technological solutions because in our context we have reason to doubt the ability of organizational policy to constrain new technologies. In general, Europeans have greater confidence that organizational policy can adequately control the implementation of electronic systems and the way in which they are deployed.

Swedish archivists reported that the "solution" to controlling electronic records is to assure that the systems, and what they are intended for, are registered in the national metadatabase. The Deputy Archivist of Sweden has noted that under Swedish law all systems designs had to be filed with the archives and that the archives approved all potential capabilities of systems to generate records. Thus, he argues, the systems cannot be used to create unanticipated kinds of records![21] Likewise, German archivists assured their colleagues that no new technologies which threatened to transform the nature of records could be acquired by their bureaucracies unless they were previously approved by the archives. The Swedes, along with their German colleagues, were certain that policy prevented any person within the system from using software capabilities to create a kind of record for which there was no prior warrant or from deleting or changing records once they had been sent. Thus, in controlling records from databases, for example, the Swedes are content to capture the contents of the database and the regulations about what kinds of queries may be put to it. In effect they document in national, publicly available, metadatabases the diplomatic forms of records.

An unarticulated assumption of the Swedish confidence that the specific purposes of records for particular business processes can be defined up front, often in legislation, and regulated by active metadata systems, is that particular, and limited, functions in hierarchical bureaucracies are assigned to specific offices and only to those offices. Without assuming such a co-location of function and office, I proposed to the UN

ACCIS panel that the control of electronic records would need to begin identification of the business application from which the record was generated and of which it is evidence. The concept of a business application in that framework consciously had less than a one-to-one correlation with either the concept of software application or a particular office or locus within an organization. My suggestion, which is hard to carry out in practice, is that archivists intervene in software implementation so as to create a user interface layer which presents functionality to users in terms of the business processes sanctioned by the organization. This is a technological solution intended to replicate the correlation between business functions and permissible forms of documentation which the Europeans report still exists in fact in their organizations. If they are right, they are fortunate indeed; what is interesting here is that we are both forced to conclude that the correlation between the nature of the activity and the record of that activity is critical (indeed it is the essence of the concept of provenance), whether or not that activity is located in a particular organizational/bureaucratic structure.

Assuming that the full capabilities of systems will be used regardless of how they are intended to be employed, we in the U.S. are struggling with how to capture the actual transactions against databases in a machine- and software-independent format so they can be reconstructed along with the other transactions that constituted a single business activity.[22] Again the emphasis is on the automatic capture of the actual transactions from systems rather than relying on staff. When we look at metadata systems it is less as a means of documenting or regulating how systems are intended to be used than as a method of providing access to the public or building documentation libraries for use in controlling their future migration.[23]

In the United States most archivists assume that they must go with the flow as technology transforms the organization. We assume that the latest technical capabilities will be implemented and that their programmatic uses cannot be predicted, to say nothing of restricted. Assuming that guidance cannot assure that individuals in organizations label documents correctly, or even that information resides in non-dynamic "document" systems, the UN ACCIS panel report which I drafted proposes to identify those business processes whose records are archival, and to employ automatic methods for linking records to the business process which created them. The links, possibly in the form of headers, would then be exploited in the management of the data.[24]

It is extremely interesting, therefore, to examine Canadian tactics which represent a middle ground between the two strategies in part because their organizations share some of the characteristics of the traditional European bureaucracy and of the American office.[25] The IMOSA (Information Management and Office Systems Architecture) project of the National Archives of Canada, the Treasury Board (Canada's governmental regulator and oversight agency) and the Canadian Office Workplace Study Center reveals its dual policy/technology roots in its title and its co-sponsorship. Consciously two-pronged throughout, the IMOSA approach looks on the one hand towards defining the "corporate memory requirements" and emphasizing the need for guidance on the "corporate rules of the road" in the use of electronic systems, and on the other hand towards writing a specification that it hopes will become a procurement standard for office front-end and rear-end systems. The technological solution itself reveals a duality since it both shapes the interface so that users identify the activity context in which they are working when they select software functions and asks users to explicitly label corporate files based on imposition of registry office principles.

ORGANIZATIONAL CULTURE AND
RECORDS MANAGEMENT IN EUROPE
AND THE UNITED STATES

As I encountered differences in electronic records management practices in Europe and the United States, I initially attributed them to historical differences between the American and European labor market and the structure of United States and European firms. These differences between United States and European organizations have been portrayed as differences in the degree of role-formalizing and hierarchical relationships and the degree of mobility of the work force.[26]

On further examination, I still believe that the degree of career mobility of employees within and between organizations is an ecological variable that helps to explain the difference between the ways that American organizations are confronting the challenges of electronic records and the approaches taken by their European counterparts. Employees can be expected to remain in a single organization in Europe for almost twice as long as in the United States. Movements between jobs within a company are also much more frequent in the U.S. than in Europe. It seems common sense that an employee who is going to remain with the company for only a short time would be hired, oriented to the firm for a day or two, and told to get on with the job. Very few procedures would be explained and the networks of contacts with whom the individual is supposed to work in order to perform the job would include all the people with whom that employee was in contact before accepting the new post. In these organizations, methods of work are strongly influenced by the personal styles and work history of the employees who are judged by results rather than by adherence to organizational practices.

Overall the American professional employee has less than two years to learn the requirements of his or her job and the procedures of the company while Europeans have well over three. However, the trends in both Europe and the United States over the past century have been towards greater mobility and less longevity in the firm, and it would appear that they are continuing unabated. While traditional organizations are still more common in Europe today, because employees stay with the firm and even in the same job for a long time, I would expect to see procedures for records management breaking down if mobility alone was the basis for behavior. New employees in European organizations, for example, would be less likely to be oriented to the classification systems for document identification and filing used throughout the firm.

Impressionistic accounts also suggest that European organizations exercise control more hierarchically than American organizations of the same kind. Mid-level personnel in American organizations appear to enjoy substantially greater autonomy than their European counterparts, especially when it comes to requesting authority for specific actions (almost always delegated in a very general way in the United States) or reporting on actions taken (which takes place considerably less formally in the United States and involves "filing" of fewer reports). But sociological studies do not reveal systematic differences in the numbers of levels in the hierarchy of firms in the same businesses in the U.S. and abroad.

Nevertheless, when electronic information systems are introduced into American and European organizational environments, with their different traditions, they appear to exacerbate the tendencies of each organization. Distributed, results-oriented units within American organizations have embraced new technologies and used them to further reduce hierarchy and corporate procedural constraints. Technologies have been acquired in order to enhance the ability of individuals throughout the organization to do their jobs rather than in order to further corporate control or norms. European organizations have been much more hesitant to introduce these technologies, and when they do so usually develop substantial administrative controls surrounding their use. Can these differences be explained in a way that helps us to understand them and base electronic records management strategies on them?

Sociologists are finding that organizations worldwide are becoming more similar and yet the behavior of people within these organizations is retaining its cultural uniqueness.[27] Organizational culture, or how people behave in organizations, is being studied to understand differences like those between record making and recordkeeping practices of organizations in Europe and the United States. Scholars of organizational culture now seem to accept a social-psychological analysis of the differences between organizations, based largely on empirical research by Geert Hofstede.[28] This organizational culture research predicts three patterns which should be apparent in European and North American organizations, and I am impressed that they correlate closely with my observations on international contrasts between archivists in their approaches to electronic records.

Hofstede's research identifies four dimensions of organizational culture of which the degree of "power distance" and "uncertainty avoidance" are the two dimensions most relevant to my analysis. A matrix of two measures for each factor (large power distance/small power distance; strong uncertainty avoidance/weak uncertainty avoidance) yields four distinctive styles of bureaucracy. Richard Mead dubs these: *Full Bureaucracy* (characterized by wide power distance and strong need to avoid uncertainty); *Market Bureaucracy* (characterized by narrow power distance and weak uncertainty avoidance); *Workflow Bureaucracy* (characterized by narrow power distance and strong need to avoid uncertainty); and *Personnel Bureaucracy* (characterized by wide power distance and weak need to avoid uncertainty).[29]

Using Hofstede's data, France and the Mediterranean and Latin countries fall into the category of *Full Bureaucracies* where functions are tightly distinguished, communication is mainly downward, and departments will communicate with each other through their highest levels. In such organizations we would expect the fonds to reflect discrete functions and downward and outward communication to flow from the top.

The *Market Bureaucracies* include Scandinavia, the Netherlands and Anglo countries where communications are upward and downward and power is negotiated across organizational lines on the basis of personal relationships. In such organizations functions are not closely tied to place in the organization and communication flows in all directions up and down and outward from all points.

Workflow Bureaucracies include German-speaking countries and Finland where the emphasis is on regulating activity rather than relationships. In such organizations functions are closely tied to structure. Communication flows up and down and outward from many points, but only according to well-defined procedures.

Personnel Bureaucracies, not found in Europe or North America, are patriarchal authority structures with loose relations between workers at the same levels.

The pattern predicted by these studies of organizational culture is three different approaches to documentation rather than a simple Europe/America dichotomy. The location of the fracture lines is consistent with the differences in archival practices between Germanic and Romance Europe identified by Duchein.[30] In addition, it predicts that we should find commonalties between Anglo, Scandinavian, and Dutch practices. I have indeed identified some commonalties in the approach to electronic records management taken by archivists in these cultures, but some other differences between U.S. and Canadian, Dutch, or Scandinavian practice remain.

It may be that another dimension of the Hofstede analysis -- individualism -- is related to the differences between U.S. practices and those of Canadian, Scandinavian, and Dutch archivists. Archivists in these somewhat less individualistic corporate cultures show a greater faith in the effectiveness of ethical, constitutional, or legal proscriptions against the use of personal data than do American archivists. I suspect this is a factor in their greater reliance on policy rather than technology to constrain misuse of data.[31] In any case, I believe it is extremely worthwhile to explore organizational cultural differences further in order both to understand historical archival practices and to predict what might be effective records management strategies in different contexts. Because different organizational cultures are found in different companies, not just in different countries, sensitivity to corporate culture variations may help us develop electronic records management practices which will work, even if we are only interested in one nation.

CONCLUSIONS

There are two fundamental strategies that can be employed to assure the maintenance and retention of adequate documentation of organizational activity: policy and technology. In their purest forms the policy-oriented approach would define certain forms of documents and certain pathways of communication that are permissible, and dictate that employees in the organization must use the electronic information systems in these prescribed ways. The technological approach would also seek to capture certain forms of documents traveling by specified pathways but instead of requiring individuals to act in the corporate interest and to know the corporate rules, it would identify and capture such communications automatically and invisibly. Both approaches require that archivists understand which transactions are archivally important (based on analysis of organizational functions) and the forms of records they produce (based on diplomatics).

If American archivists are going to be forced by the nature of organizational culture in the U.S. to rely on technological intervention to safeguard electronic records of long-term value, they will need to use diplomatics-like principles to identify new forms of records. They will also need to use organizational analysis to model the archivally significant activities in which employees are engaged to apply rules to the segregation and disposition of records based on provenance. As a consequence, the European tradition of diplomatics should find a growing applicability both in Europe and in the United States as the character of documents change.

I believe the European tradition has a great deal to offer even the most techno-centric approach. For example, I have suggested the potential power of automatic document type analysis using intelligent parsers and SGML coupled with rule-based retention schedules linked to business functions analysis documented in metadata. To implement this kind of automatic or quasi-automatic means of archival intervention will be to extend the reach of diplomatics and refine diplomatics as a method of analysis.

Organizational analysis will also play a growing role on both sides of the Atlantic as traditional organizations are further eroded. Archivists will need to rely more on the empirical analysis of organizations as systems, rather than normative descriptions, since the functional origin of transaction and the links between dispersed agents will be of greater importance as the organizational locus of the document creator becomes less significant in less hierarchical organizations. To identify the business context of transactions for an intelligent communications gateway will require identifying activities so as to base retention decisions on functional provenance and will require us to refine methods of representing formal and informal communications within post-hierarchical organizations. Finally, no matter how different the organizational cultures in the U.S. and Europe are, the organization will still need to exert some control through policy. Identification of the policy objectives in cultures where policy functions well to control electronic records can assist those of us who live in organizations with more anarchistic cultures to identify ends that will have to be achieved by alternative means.

NOTES

[1] M.T. Clancy, *From Memory to Written Record: England, 1066-1307* (Cambridge: Harvard University Press, 1979).

[2] Luciana Duranti, "Diplomatics: New Uses for an Old Science," *Archivaria* (1988-1992), Part I, 28:7-27; Part II, 29:4-17; Part III, 30:4-20; Part IV, 31:10-25; Part V, 32:6-24; Part VI, 33:6-24.

[3] Cf. Michael Lutzker, "Max Weber and the Analysis of Modern Bureaucratic Organization: Notes Towards a Theory of Appraisal," *American Archivist* 45 (Spring 1982): 119-130.

[4] See Michel Duchein, "The History of European Archives and the Development of the European Archival Profession," *American Archivist* 55 (Winter 1992): 14-25, especially footnotes 12 through 16.

[5] Alfred D. Chandler Jr., "The Emergence of Managerial Capitalism," *Business History Review* 58 (1984): 473-503. This article compares U.S. and Europe. See also his *Strategy and Structure: Chapters in the History of Industrial Enterprise* (Cambridge: MIT Press, 1962) and his *The Visible Hand: The Managerial Revolution in American Business* (Cambridge: Harvard University Press, 1980).

[6] Harland Cleveland, "The Twilight of Hierarchy: Speculations on the Global Information Society," *Public Administration Review* 45 (1985): 185-195.

[7] JoAnne Yates, *Control through Communication: The Rise of System in American Management* (Baltimore: Johns Hopkins University, 1989).

[8] Tom Finholt, "The Erosion of Time, Geography, and Hierarchy: Sharing Information Through an Electronic Archive," in *Information Handling in Offices and Archives*, Angelika Menne-Haritz ed. (New York: K.G. Saur, 1993): 67-90. See also Shoshana Zuboff, *In the Age of the Smart Machine: The Future of Work and Power* (New York: Basic Books, 1988).

[9] J.D. Eveland and T.K. Bikson, "Evolving Electronic Communications Network: An Empirical Assessment," *Office Technology and People* 3 (1987): 103-128.

[10] United States Congress, House Committee on Government Operations, *Taking a Byte Out of History: The Archival Preservation of Federal Computer Records*, 101st Congress, 2d sess., H. Rept. 101-978.

[11] David Bearman and Peter Sigmond, "Explorations of Form of Material Authority Files by Dutch Archivists," *American Archivist* 50 (1987): 249-253.

[12] Tora Bikson, "Research on Electronic Information Environments: Prospects and Problems" Paper delivered at the NHPRC-funded Working Meeting on Research Issues in Electronic Records, Washington, D.C., 24-25 January 1991.

[13] Charles W. Steinfield, "Computer Mediated Communications in the Organization: Using Electronic Mail at XEROX," in *Case Studies in Organizational Communications*, ed. Beverly D. Sypher (New York: Guilford Press, 1990): 282-294.

[14] Ron Weissman, "Virtual Documents on the Electronic Desktop: Hypermedia, Emerging Computer Environments and the Future of Information Management," *Management of Recorded Information: Converging Disciplines*, ed. Cynthia Durance (New York: K.G. Saur, 1990): 37-58.

[15] Aspects of this synthesis of the issues involved in electronic records management, particularly the relevance of the concepts of information located in data, in structure, and in context, are contained in David Bearman, "Information Technology Standards and Archives," *Janus* (1992.2): 161-166, reprinted in this volume as Chapter 7; and Bearman, "Archival Principles and the Electronic Office" in *Information Handling in Offices and Archives*, Angelika Menne-Haritz ed. (New York: K.G. Saur, 1993): 177-193, reprinted in this volume as Chapter 5.

[16] For strategies in the U.S., see National Historical Publications and Records Commission, *Electronic Records Issues: A Report to the Commission*, Commission Reports and Papers #4 (March 1990) and *Research Issues in Electronic Records* (1991); Richard J. Cox, ed., *Archival Administration in the Electronic Information Age: An Advanced Institute for Government Archivists* (Pittsburgh: University of Pittsburgh, August 1990); New York State Archives and Records Administration, *A Strategic Plan for Managing and Preserving Electronic Records in New York State* (Albany: August 1988).

[17] For reports on the meetings in Maastricht and Marburg, see: David Bearman, "Archives and Europe Without Boundaries," *Archives and Museum Informatics* 5:3 (Fall 1991): 6, and "Impact of Information Technologies and Information Handling on Offices and Archives," *Archives and Museum Informatics* 5:3 (Fall 1991): 9-11. For the work of the United Nations ACCIS committee, see United Nations, Advisory Committee for Co-ordination of Information Systems, *Management of Electronic Records: Issues and Guidelines* (New

York: UN, 1990), parts of which are reprinted in this volume as Chapter 3.

[18] Peter Bohl, "Archival Requirements for Future Documentation in Administration," in *Information Handling in Offices and Archives*, ed. Angelika Menne-Haritz (New York: K.G. Saur, 1993): 128-137; Wulf Buchmann offered similar informal comments at the Seminar of Impact of Information Technology and Information Handling on Offices and Archives, Marburg, Germany, 17-19 October 1991. His comments are reported in Bearman, *Archives and Museum Informatics* 5:3 (Fall 1991): 9-11.

[19] For an account of the specialists' meeting on the Impact of Electronic Records on Archival Theory, University of Macerata, 13-17 May 1991, see David Bearman, "Impact of Electronic Records on Archival Theory," *Archives and Museum Informatics* 5:2 (Summer 1991): 6-8.

[20] David Bearman, "An Introduction to CALS," *Archives and Museum Informatics* 5:4 (Winter 1991). My interest in this area was sparked in 1988 by an unpublished paper entitled "Formalizing the Figural: Aspects of a Foundation for Document Manipulation" by David M. Levy, Daniel C. Brotsky, and Kenneth R. Olson of Xerox Palo Alto Research Center and renewed later that year by Andreas Dengel and Gerhard Barth, "Document Description and Analysis by Cuts," *RIAO '88 Proceedings* 2 (Cambridge: Massachusetts Institute of Technology, 1988): 940-952. Since then, several commercial software systems have combined scanning with parsing for visual clues to identify document features. See, for example, FastTag, as product of Avalanche Development Company, Boulder, Colorado.

[21] Claes Gränström, "Will Archival Theories Be Sufficient in the Future?," in *Information Handling in Offices and Archives*, ed. Angelika Menne-Haritz (New York: K.G. Saur, 1993): 159-167. See also his "Legal Problems of Access to Machine-readable Archives," *Archivum* 35 (1989). As Peter Bohl put it in "Archival Requirements for Future Documentation in Administration, "It is unrealistic to assume that government agencies will introduce processing methods which contradict legal requirements, the laws of administrative procedure, only to keep up with modern trends," an assumption that could be totally reversed and retain its validity in the United States.

[22] The World Bank has been engaged since about 1990 in a series of projects to use the models of business processes developed as part of its strategic information systems planning efforts to identify business

transactions of continuing value to the organization, and with this information to devise methods for capturing such transactions for archival retention. Reflections on this and the UN ACCIS panel debates are contained in Richard Barry, "Getting it Right: Managing Organizations in a Runaway Electronic Information Age," in *Information Handling in Offices and Archives*, ed. Angelika Menne-Haritz (New York: K.G. Saur, 1993): 27-55.

[23] Charles Robb, "IRM in Kentucky State Government, *Archives and Museum Informatics* 5:4 (Winter 1991): 2-4.

[24] I was recently informed of a similar emphasis on automatic markup by the Office of Records Management at the National Archives which is exploring the possibility of defining elements in Document Type Definitions in SGML to assure business functional source labeling of information throughout its life-cycle.

[25] "IMOSA, Information Management and Office Systems Advancement: Overview Document," November 1991; "The IMOSA Project: Phase 1 Report," Department of Communications, Canadian Workplace Automation Research Centre, Laval and National Archives of Canada, Government Records Branch, Hull, 1991; Dale Ethier Consulting Inc., "IMOSA Project: Functional Requirements -- Corporate Information Management," 5 November 1991; Treasury Board, Office Systems Standards Working Group, "Information Management in Office Systems: Issues and Directions," draft, September 1990; Communications Canada, Canadian Workplace Automation Research Centre, "Identification of Government-wide Information Management Issues and Concerns," draft, May 1991.

[26] A. Laurent, "The Cultural Diversity of Western Conceptions of Management," *International Studies of Management and Organization* 13 (Spring-Summer 1983): 75-96; and Nigel Nicholson and Michael West, *Managerial Job Change: Men and Women in Transition* (Cambridge: Cambridge University Press, 1988).

[27] John Child, "Culture, Contingency and Capitalism in Cross-National Study of Organizations," in *Research in Organizational Behavior*, vol. 3, ed. L.L. Cummings and Bill Shaw (Greenwich, Connecticut: JAI Press, 1981): 303-356.

[28] Geert Hofstede, *Culture's Consequences: International Differences in Work Related Values* (Beverly Hills, California: Sage, 1980); subsequently adopted as a framework in Nancy Adler, *International Dimensions of Organizational Behavior*, 2nd ed. (Boston: PWS Kent Publications, 1991).

[29] Richard Mead, *Cross Cultural Management Communication* (New York: John Wiley & Sons, 1990).

[30] Duchein, "The History of European Archives and the Development of the Archival Profession."

[31] Geert Hofstede, "Cultural Relativity of Organizational Practices and Theories," *Journal of International Business Studies* 24 (Fall 1983): 75. Also, in his *Culture's Consequences*, pp. 213-260, Hofstede ranks Sweden, the Netherlands, and Canada between 71 and 80 on the individualism scale, Great Britain and Australia between 81 and 90; and the U.S. alone (and on the extreme) at 91.

CHAPTER TEN

New Models for Management of Electronic Records[*]

By the end of this century, most business communication and much personal communication will be digitized and will be recorded, stored, and transmitted electronically. Archivists will have to intervene earlier in the life-cycle of records than has been necessary traditionally and participate in the design of electronic information systems. Sound information policies will utilize standards and define functional requirements that will support archival needs. Archivists must cease treating electronic records as special media and supplement their staffs with technical specialists who have the requisite knowledge of networks, data processing, and systems management. They should also exploit metadata to serve not only as a tool for control and migration of data, but also as a finding aid for access to and use of archival electronic records. Metadata will be especially useful as archival programs shift to noncustodial, evidence-focused, direct-to-client service delivery.

[*] Originally published in *Cadernos de Biblioteconomia, Arquivística, e Documentação* 2 (1992): 61-70.

The transformation of methods of communications, which began in the last century with the introduction of the telegraph and the telephone, has been accelerated and deepened in the past decade by the marriage of computing and telecommunications and the integration of all forms of information in digital representations. By the end of this century, we can anticipate that most business communication and much personal communication will be digitized and will be recorded, stored, and transmitted electronically. This will apply equally to text, image, sound, and multimedia and will be as prevalent in the home as in the office.

Archives have responded slowly to these dramatic changes and are only now formulating systematic programs to address electronic records. Some of these programs are simple extensions into the electronic realm of traditional archival practices while others reflect radical departures in philosophy, program structure, and strategy towards traditional archival functions. This article reviews the range of program variants and comments on some trends and promising innovations.

PROGRAM ORIENTATION AND PHILOSOPHY

Traditionally archives have been seen as custodial repositories for important records. They are what they collect. In this tradition most archives, including the National Archives of the United States, still assume that they will collect electronic records and equate their electronic records programs with what they have brought into their archives or will acquire in the future.[1] Some other archives, including the National Archives of Canada and Switzerland, are beginning to view electronic records also as an arena for regulating information systems of creating agencies, some of which may be authorized to control electronic archival records for extended periods of time.[2] The Australian Archives has taken the more profound step of focusing their efforts on agency data management practices and assuming that the archives will not obtain custody except as a last resort.[3]

The technical requirements of managing electronic records created in a wide variety of hardware and software systems are quite complex. While traditional repositories have responded to these challenges by enhancing the systems capabilities associated with their centralized repositories, some archives are beginning to examine the benefits of partially or completely distributed custody. Distributed custody makes sense not only because the physical location of records in electronic formats does not make much difference in their delivery to users but also because expertise in different hardware platforms is already found in different sites and is not necessarily easy to bring under one roof.

Will archives provide access to electronic records to users who visit their facilities or order tapes and disks from them as is now the case in data archives or will they support distributed access to all or some records? Clearly the same telecommunications technologies which encourage thinking about distributed custody can support access by remote users. Here the promises to archives include the potential use of archivally significant materials by archives researchers during the active and semi-active life of the records. The Australian Archives has committed itself to developing common interfaces to series of electronic records in order to support remote access. The Kentucky State Archives has made a database about state records including electronic records metadata available to public libraries throughout the state and is encouraging remote reference activity.[4]

One of the challenges of dealing with electronic records is that effective intervention must take place earlier in the life-cycle of the system than has been necessary traditionally. Many archivists feel that effective strategies will only be implemented if archivists are involved in the definition of systems requirements and the design of electronic systems and if they remain active through the acquisition and implementation of systems even before the first records are created. Traditional programs are continuing to emphasize surveying electronic records holdings, but programs such as those in New York State Archives[5] and the National Archives of Canada are intruding themselves into records management before records are created. This orientation aligns them with those responsible for administration of other citizen "Rights in Information" programs, such as privacy, security and freedom of information. In some countries, such as Sweden, the link between archival approaches to electronic records, on the one hand, and freedom of information and privacy legislation, on the other, is quite strong.[6]

While traditional archival programs were themselves reflections of national policies, they rarely regarded themselves as part of a larger information policy. Newer national information policies, such as those promulgated by the Canadian Treasury Board, explicitly recognize the relationship. As the United Nations Advisory Committee for Coordination of Information Systems (ACCIS) Panel report *Management of Electronic Records: Issues and Guidelines* made clear, policy is one of the major vehicles for realizing electronic records management and archives objectives.[7] Archives are increasingly recognizing that policy must be accompanied by action in the spheres of systems design, implementation, and standards development. The National Archives of Canada has again been a leader in pioneering the definition of archival functional requirements for office systems and promoting them as a standard for the Canadian government, but other programs, such as that of the National Archives of the U.S., have also placed an emphasis on influencing international communication, transaction, and data representation standards so that archival requirements are supported.

PROGRAM STRUCTURE

To date most electronic records programs are treated within their own archival institutions as separate functions. They may look like "special media" such as photographs, maps, or sound recordings, or they may be elevated to

"Centers for" electronic records, but generally they are not integrated with the appraisal, control, or delivery of paper records. The National Archives of Canada recently reorganized to eliminate its long-standing machine-readable archives division and to reintegrate its functions with those of the Government Records Branch. Some other archives have integrated reference servicing while preserving separation at the front end of the life cycle and in holdings management. Over the longer term, it is probably dysfunctional to separate electronic records, especially as paper records will be the "special media" of the next century.

One cause for separation at the front end is that traditional archives often single out electronic records in their legislation as a special medium rather than as a method of conducting business. In this type of authorizing legislation, electronic records or "magnetic media" have recently been appended to lists of record types including correspondence and reports, maps, publications, photographs, sound recordings, and motion pictures. Other archives are rewriting or reinterpreting their legislation to emphasize documentation of transactions in whatever form the documentation or the transaction exists.

Such redefinitions require that archives have staff skilled to manage data. Oddly, archives are still staffed almost exclusively by archivists rather than having on their staffs information systems specialists and data administrators. Instead of taking the view that archives are a function which will increasingly employ lots of specialized professionals, archives throughout the world seem determined to educate archivists in all they would need to know to become information managers.[8] Even electronic archives programs, which hire people with skills in data administration, data processing, and network management, seem to be insisting on training them as archivists rather than simply employing them as specialists in other disciplines working within archival agencies.

One consequence is that archives tend to view the primary audience for their theoretical and practical findings about electronic records as other archivists and records administrators. When the Australian Archives recently issued a videotape to explain the requirements for managing electronic records to senior administrators and sought their advice on how to run an electronic archival records programs, it was breaking new ground.[9] In the United Nations ACCIS panel report, I argued for making the case to information technology staff and program managers because the records were created as a consequence of software implemented by the one on behalf of the other.[10] The New York State Archives has encouraged its staff to become active in the New York State Forum on Information Resource Management as a way of giving archivists a broader exposure to the other information professions.

STRATEGIES FOR LIFE-CYCLE ARCHIVAL FUNCTIONS

Traditional archival practice has rarely had to formulate concrete strategies for the identification of records; after all, records were physical things which had to be handled and stored and were easy to identify when you saw them. Electronic records are not, however, physical but "virtual" things. They cannot be seen and many users do not seem to realize when they have created an electronic record or if they have disposed of one. As a consequence archivists have had to adopt explicit strategies to identify electronic records. Traditional approaches have been extended to inventorying places where such records are stored (data centers and disk drives). More innovative programs, such as that at the World Bank, have identified the business functions which could generate records of archival significance using "enterprise" or "business systems" analysis methodologies and are locating the electronic functions serving business applications with archival importance instead of looking for records themselves.[11] This places them in a more proactive stance.

Proactivity is particularly important because the character of documents is changing in the electronic world. Where archives previously were able to make many judgments about retention based on identifying the form of documentation (such as reports, diaries, memoranda of record, correspondence, telephone messages) these forms are less distinctive in electronic systems and many new forms are emerging which are closely linked to specific processes. Nowhere in the paper archives do we have documents which update their contents automatically based on the state of remote databases! Yet documents of this kind, which are intimately related to business processes of reporting and briefing, contain important archival data in the form of the models which they execute rather than in the form of their content at any particular moment. Few archives are exploring new forms of documentation and their implications for archives, because traditional archivists still think of records as outputs rather than as transactions.

Redefining the record as a transaction forces archivists to look at the types of transactions for which they must provide accountability rather than asking what kinds of records they should keep. In the electronic world, many important kinds of transactions do not typically leave a record at all. For example, searching a database in order to generate reports may be an important decision-making process, but it does not generally lead to creation of an electronic record or even assure the preservation of the particular "view" of the data or the analytical or reporting models being employed in its presentation. Some Dutch and American archivists are exploring relationships between transactions and forms of record and their implications for archival data capture, and these investigations are beginning to influence the way in which archivists view data and evidence.[12]

Traditionally there has been less difference between the record as data and its function as evidence than there is in the electronic world. In paper, the data of the record and its physical form were united in a medium which was the actual vehicle of communication and thus the carrier as well as the record of the transaction. In the electronic system, data is quite independent of the views which enable users to see it or the uses to which it is put. Saving databases does not preserve evidence, only information. Evidence resides in the conjunction of structure (as defined by software control rather than physical layout), context, and data in a transaction. Evidence is, therefore, not something which can be validated after the fact. For these reasons, archives probably need to be involved with electronic systems closer to the planning or design phase than to the system retirement date. Some archives, such as the Swiss Bundesarchiv, have put themselves in the loop to receive information about systems at the proposal stage, but most, such as the National Archives in the United States, still view record systems as passive mechanisms for holding records rather than as the forges in which they are formed. Strategies for controlling records-creating organizations are direct reflections of the view each archives takes of the archival task in an electronic era. Those who focus on "data migration" and media standards continue to see the electronic record as a physical artifact rather than a set of transient relations between data around a business function.

The physical habit of some archives means that they are continuing to employ the records schedule as a mechanism for control of electronic records in spite of evidence that records do not survive unless agency staff can identify them, recognize their importance as evidence, and have tools to assure their continued accessibility. Some archives are beginning to explore "negotiation" with agencies over outcomes rather than presuming to dictate the continued retention of records and their transfer to archives. The National Archives of both the United States and Canada have conducted such negotiations surrounding vast quantities of scientific observational data of long-term value in scientific agencies where the importance of the information was appreciated by science administrators. The National Air and Space Administration in the United States has required data management plans as part of its mission approval process for a number of years and these plans have had to address the long-term accessibility of data from the missions.[13]

While traditional archival programs focus on disposition, especially on making decisions about what to destroy, the newer emphasis on data management reflected at NASA is also found in the Australian Archives policies for electronic records. The concept of data management is one that recognizes that the value of information as evidence depends on how well it was managed during its active life. In this model, the archivist becomes something of an information auditor, examining plans for systems before their development or acquisition and testing regularly to assure that management requirements, including archival requirements, are being met in the implementation.

Like the auditor, the electronic records archivist must take the view that the business case for archiving evidence is better made with the techniques of risk management than by cost/benefit analysis. Ultimately the job of the archives is to ensure accountability; the cost of the lack of accountability is organizational legitimacy and perhaps legal liability which are more concrete that the imagined future benefits to humanity and society of keeping archives in cost/benefit equations. The archival function of appraisal thus becomes a quite new process which begins with the organization rather than the record and must consider not the "values" of the record but the risks to the organization of retaining or destroying evidence. If it is decided to keep evidence, the process must consider how to preserve not only the "record," with its data, structure, and context, but also the system (hardware/software functionality) and the view from the business application.

So called "data archives," which are actually data libraries and which reformat data to standard structures for use by re-

searchers interested in its informational content, have emphasized the physical formats in which the records should be
transferred to the repository over data interchange standards
or preserving software functionality. However, because evidential electronic archives must be concerned with structure
and context as well as data, they are increasingly trying to
identify interchange formats that assure some interoperability
and preserve some evidence. The National Archives of Canada
and of the United States are also becoming involved with ISO
(International Organization for Standardization) committees
developing standards for complete interoperability.

Some archives have decided not to effect transfer of
records at all. The Australian Archives has defined a strategy
in which the records will remain in agency custody and be migrated with current records in such a way as to preserve
maximum functionality at minimum long-term expense to the
government. Other archives have taken the view that software
documentation, including such external documentation as
films made for training and public relations purposes, can
capture functionality adequately. Most traditional archives are
still unsure of the significance of the way the system worked,
probably because their experiences to date are with systems
which do little more than store and retrieve information.

As a consequence, documentation practices in traditional
archives still focus nearly exclusively on the content of the
records and their technical characteristics. Some electronic
archives are beginning to document the contexts of the records
and the functions of the systems that created them. Documentation of the "views" of databases assigned to different offices, the analysis and reporting capabilities provided to users
of a system, the nature of the security provided for functions
and data, and the algorithms of processing routines, is captured in "metadata" systems, or Information Resource Directory Systems (IRDS) rather than card catalogs or prose finding
aids.[14] The radical departure for most archives is not so much
in documenting these new aspects of record systems as in

when archival description takes place. Electronic archives focusing on metadata will by necessity acquire documentation during the design phases and active life of systems rather than "describing" records post accessioning. Active programs of metadata management are under way at the Kentucky State Archives and in records management programs of some agencies of the U.S. government such as the Environmental Protection Agency.[15]

Metadata is a tool for control and migration of electronic information systems, but it also serves as a finding aid for access to and use of archival electronic records. Metadata can be used by remote users, across local and wide area networks, as easily as by on-site visitors to the archives. Because metadata is the tool that must be used to re-create the records in the system as evidence (e.g., the way they actually were when the system was being used actively), it is an essential intermediary to any retrieval and will be required by users, wherever they are, to document archival transactions. The terms of metadata may need to be interpreted to users, but the interpretation is less a traditional archival reference function than a technical function for information technology staff. In this respect, electronic records are revealing a fundamental strategic difference between archives in provision of reference service to electronic records. Traditional programs are trying to manage electronic records using archivists alone, while more adventuresome programs are acting through the technical staffs in the organizations which created records and through intermediaries providing network, data processing, and systems management services.

CONCLUSIONS

Electronic records are not simply a new medium for documentation. Their existence reflects the introduction into organizations of new methods of communication and the advent of dramatic changes in the way organizations conduct their business. Archives which apply traditional methods to the

management of electronic records may not yet have experienced the significance of the changes in organizational behavior, but they would do well to pay close attention to the
changes in archival program philosophy, structure, and tactics
that are evolving in archival programs which are more deeply
involved with the electronic information systems revolution.
In these tentative shifts of orientation are the seeds of the non-
custodial, evidence-focused, direct-to-client service delivery
oriented archival programs of the future.

NOTES

[1] The U.S. National Archives and Records Administration (NARA) has been increasing its investment in its Center for Electronic Records dramatically, but is still acquiring an infinitesimal proportion of the potential archival record. A recent study by the National Academy of Public Administration identified hundreds of large databases throughout the government as archival. This is many times the amount of data that has been accessioned by NARA to date. See National Academy of Public Administration, *The Archives of the Future: Archival Strategies for the Treatment of Electronic Databases*, A Report for the National Archives and Records Administration (Washington, D.C.: NAPA, 2 December 1991). Several other government reports in the past few years have criticized NARA's approach to collecting electronic records as misguided. See National Academy of Public Administration, *The Effects of Electronic Record Keeping on the Historical Record of the U.S. Government* (Washington, D.C.: NAPA, January 1989); U.S. Congress, Committee on Government Operations, *Taking a Byte out of History: The Archival Preservation of Federal Computer Records*, H. Rept. 101-978.

[2] National Archives of Canada, Automated Information Systems Division, "Conserving Valuable Information within the Health Protection Branch, A Discussion Document," 25 March 1988.

[3] *Archives and Museum Informatics* 6:2 (Summer 1992): 11-12.

[4] Charles Robb, "Information Resource Management in Kentucky State Government," *Archives and Museum Informatics* 5:4 (Winter 1991): 2-4; see also Kentucky Information Systems Commission, *Current Issues in Government Information Policy Conference Proceedings*, Louisville, Kentucky, 7-8 March 1991 (Frankfort: KISC, June 1991); Florida State Legislature, Joint Committee on Information Technology, *Remote Computer Access to Public Records in Florida* (Tallahassee: January 1985).

[5] New York State Archives and Records Administration, *A Strategic Plan for Managing and Preserving Electronic Records in New York State Government* (Albany: State Education Department, August 1988); National Association of Government Archives and Records Administrators, *A New Age: Electronic Information Systems, State Governments, and the Preservation of the Archival Record* (Lexington, Kentucky: Council of State Governments, 1991).

6 David Bearman, "Diplomatics, Weberian Bureaucracy, and the Management of Electronic Records in Europe and America," *American Archivist* 55 (Winter 1992): 168-180, reprinted in this volume as Chapter 9; Claes Gränström, "Will Archival Theories Be Sufficient in the Future?," in *Information Handling in Offices and Archives*, Angelika Menne-Haritz ed. (New York: K.G. Saur, 1993): 159-167.

7 David Bearman, "Electronic Records Management Guidelines: A Manual for Policy Development and Implementation," Chapter 2 of *Management of Electronic Records: Issues and Guidelines* (New York: United Nations, 1989), part of which is reprinted in this volume as Chapter 3.

8 A recent example of this are the curriculum guidelines developed by the SAA Committee on Automated Records and Techniques: "Learning Objectives for Archivists in Automated Records and Techniques," *American Archivist* 56 (Summer 1993): 485-490.

9 Australian Archives, videotape on electronic records management, 1992.

10 David Bearman, "Management of Electronic Records: Issues and Guidelines," in United Nations Advisory Committee for Coordination of Information Systems, *Electronic Records Management Guidelines: A Manual for Policy Development and Implementation* (New York: United Nations, 1990), 17-70, 89-107, 135-189, parts of which are reprinted in this volume as Chapter 3.

11 Richard Barry, "Getting it Right: Managing Organizations in a Runaway Electronic Age," ed. Angelika Menne-Haritz, *Information Handling in Offices and Archives* (New York: K.G. Saur, 1993): 27-55.

12 Peter Sigmond, "Form, Function and Archival Value," *Archivaria* 33 (Winter 1991-92): 141-147; David Bearman and Peter Sigmond, "Explorations of the Use of Forms of Material and Authority Files by Dutch Archivists," *American Archivist* 50 (Spring 1987): 249-253.

13 The NASA data management program was presented at a recent National Research Council ad hoc panel meeting at which the National Archives and Records Administration sought NRC help in defining the archival significance of scientific data and in identifying tactics for its long-term preservation. For an account of the meeting, see *Archives and Museum Informatics* 6:1 (Spring 1992): 14-15.

14 For an examination of the archival implications of the IRDS, see David Bearman, "Information Technology Standards and Archives," *Janus* 2 (1992): 161-166, reprinted in this volume as Chapter 7.

[15] Michael Miller, "Is the Past Prologue? Appraisal and New Technologies," in *Archival Management of Electronic Records*, Archives and Museum Informatics Technical Report #13, ed. David Bearman, (Pittsburgh: Archives and Museum Informatics, 1991): 38-49.

APPENDIX

✤

Functional Requirements for Recordkeeping

APPENDIX

Functional Requirements for Recordkeeping Systems

The document in this appendix has been developed in conjunction with a three-year project at the University of Pittsburgh to study the first three questions of the research agenda outlined in *Research Issues In Electronic Records*. The agenda was developed at a working meeting sponsored by the National Historical Publications and Records Commission (NHPRC) on 24-25 January 1991. The University of Pittsburgh project, entitled "Variables in the Satisfaction of Archival Requirements for Electronic Records Management," is also funded by NHPRC. Its three goals are (1) to identify the archival functional requirements for electronic information systems serving widespread business applications and to evaluate alternative approaches to satisfying those requirements; (2) to identify attributes in organizations, business applications, and software applications which influence the success of achieving archival control over electronic records systems, in order to assist institutional archival electronic records programs to formulate successful approaches; and (3) to suggest criteria to evaluate and indicators to measure the effectiveness of archival policies, methods, and programs in modern organizations. Principal investigators for the project are Richard J. Cox and James Williams. David Bearman has served as a consultant to the project. This is a working document which will be revised annually. Presented below is the spring 1994 version.

Recordkeeping is a critical function which is performed through the collective action of individuals and systems throughout all organizations. Recordkeeping is not the province of archivists, records managers, or systems administrators alone, but an essential role of all employees and of individuals in their private lives.

Recordkeeping systems are information systems which are distinguished by the fact that the information they contain is linked to transactions which they document. Records may be consulted for documentation of those transactions or because they contain information that is useful for some completely separate purpose, but recordkeeping systems do not just contain data to be reused; they maintain evidence over time.

Recordkeeping systems support the corporate memory of organizations by supporting business functions of the organization. All business functions require records of business transactions in order to continue their day-to-day operations, satisfy administrative and legal requirements, and maintain accountability. The following functional requirements for recordkeeping systems define a corporate requirement for any recordkeeping system, not the application requirements of archives and records management systems. Archives and records management are only one business application within the organization, just as are manufacturing, sales, service delivery or personnel management.

In designing and implementing information and recordkeeping systems, the functional requirements for any particular business applications must be considered together with various corporate functional requirements. Archives and records management systems have functional requirements specific to their business application -- such as storage management, records retention and scheduling, reference management, and access control -- which are not discussed in this document. The functional requirements presented below, on the other hand, are universal for any recordkeeping system.

They may be of special interest to archivists, records managers, security officers, freedom of information and privacy administrators, auditors, lawyers, and others with special obligations towards records, but they should be of value and relevance to program managers at all levels from corporate management to line supervisors.

Although these functional requirements were specifically developed to provide guidance for the management of electronic recordkeeping systems, they are equally applicable to manual systems. Information systems professionals should note that business functions, business processes, business transactions, and business records rather than system functions, system processes, system transactions, or system records are the consistent focus of recordkeeping.

Articulating functional requirements is the first step in effecting adequate control of recordkeeping systems. The next step is to determine an organizational strategy for satisfying the functional requirement insofar as is appropriate. Strategies might include adopting policies and procedures, designing new systems, implementing systems in a way that supports satisfying the requirement, or developing standards. Each of these four strategies may be applied separately or in combination to each separate functional requirement. The choice of strategy will depend on the degree of risk involved in failure to satisfy a requirement within the business function which the recordkeeping systems is to support, the existing systems environment including hardware, software and architecture, and the corporate culture in which the strategy must succeed.

Functional Requirements for Recordkeeping

Compliant Organization

Accountable Recordkeeping System
Responsible
Implemented
Reliable

Captured Records
Comprehensive
Identifiable
Complete
   Accurate
   Understandable
   Meaningful
Authentic

Maintained Records
Preserved
   Inviolate
   Coherent
   Auditable
Removable

Usable Records
Exportable
Accessible
   Available
   Renderable
   Evidential
Redactable

FUNCTIONAL REQUIREMENTS FOR RECORDKEEPING

Recordkeeping systems capture, maintain, and access evidence of transactions over time as required by the jurisdiction in which they are implemented and in accordance with common business practices.

Organization - Compliant

(1) Compliant: Organizations must comply with the legal and administrative requirements for recordkeeping within the jurisdictions in which they operate, and demonstrate awareness of best practices for the industry or business sector to which they belong and the business functions in which they are engaged.

(1a) External recordkeeping requirements are known.

(1a1) Laws of jurisdictions with authority over the record creating organizations are known.

(1a2) Regulatory issuances of entities with administrative authority over the record creating organizations are known.

(1a3) Best practices of recordkeeping established by professional and business organizations within the industry and business functions of the organization are known.

(1b) Records created by organizational business transactions which are governed by an external recordkeeping requirements are linked to an internal retention rule referencing the documented law, regulation, or statement of best practice.

(1c) Laws, regulations, and statements of best practice with requirements for recordkeeping are tracked so that changes to them are reflected in updated internal recordkeeping instructions.

Recordkeeping Systems - Accountable

(2) Responsible: Recordkeeping systems must have accurately documented policies, assigned responsibilities, and formal methodologies for their management.

(2a) System policies and procedures are written and changes to them are maintained and current.

(2b) A person or office is designated in writing as responsible for satisfying recordkeeping requirements in each system.

(2c) System management methods are defined for all routine tasks.

(2d) System management methods are defined for events in which the primary system fails.

(3) Implemented: Recordkeeping systems must be exclusively employed in the normal course of business.

(3a) Business transactions are conducted only through the documented recordkeeping system and its documented exception procedures.

(3b) No records can be created in the recordkeeping systems except through execution of a business transaction.

(3c) Recordkeeping systems and/or documented exception procedures can be demonstrated to have been operating at all times.

(4) Reliable: Recordkeeping systems must process information in a fashion that assures that the records they create are credible.

(4a) Identical data processes permitted by the system must produce identical outcomes regardless of the conditions under which they are executed.

(4b) Results of executing systems logic are demonstrable outside the system.

(4c) All operational failures to execute instructions are reported by the system.

(4d) In the event of system failures, processes under way are recovered and re-executed.

Records - Captured

(5) Comprehensive: Records must be created for all business transactions.

(5a) Communications in the conduct of business between two people, between a person and a store of information available to others, and between a source of information and a person, generate a record.

(5b) Data interchanged within and between computers under the control of software employed in the conduct of business creates a record when the consequence of the data processing function is to modify records subsequently employed by people in the conduct of business.

(6) Identifiable: Records must be bounded by linkage to a transaction which used all the data in the record and only that data.

(6a) There exists a discrete record, representing the sum of all communications associated with a business transaction.

(6b) All data in the record belongs to the same transaction.

(6c) Each record is uniquely identified.

(7) Complete: Records must contain the content, structure and context generated by the transaction they document.

(7a) **Accurate**: The content of records must be quality controlled at input to ensure that information in the system correctly reflects what was communicated in the transaction.

(7a1) Data capture practices and system functions ensure that source data is exactly replicated by system or corrected to reflect values established in system authority files.

(7b) **Understandable**: The relationship between elements of information content must be represented in a way that supports their intended meaning.

(7b1) Meaning conveyed by placement or appearance of data are retained or represented.

(7b2) System defined views or permissions are retained and the effects are reflected in the record are represented.

(7b3) Logical relations defined across physical records are retained or represented.

(7b4) Software functionality invoked by data values in the content of the record are supported or represented.

(7c) **Meaningful**: The contextual linkages of records must carry information necessary to correctly understand the transactions that created and used them.

(7c1) The business rules for transactions, which minimally locate the transaction within a business function, are maintained.

(7c2) A representation of the source and time of the transaction which generated a record is maintained.

(7c3) Links between records which comprised a business activity are retained.

(8) **Authentic**: An authorized records creator must have originated all records.

(8a) All records have creators which are documented.

(8b) Records creators must have been authorized to engage in the business transaction that generated the record.

(8c) A knowledge-base of persons authorized to engage in business transactions is maintained and either operates as a control over system functions such that transactions could not occur without being authorized and/or documents the authorization of the creator as part of the record.

Records - Maintained

(9) Preserved: Records must continue to reflect content, structure and context within any systems by which the record are retained over time.

(9a) **Inviolate**: Records are protected from accidental or intended damage or destruction and from any modification.

(9a1) No data within a record may be deleted, altered or lost once the transaction which generated it has occurred.

(9b) **Coherent**: The information content and structure of records must be retained in reconstructable relations.

(9b1) If records are migrated to new software environments, content, structure and context information must be linked to software functionality that preserves their executable connections or representations of their relations must enable humans to reconstruct the relations that pertained in the original software environment.

(9b2) Logical record boundaries must be preserved regardless of physical representations.

(9c) **Auditable**: Record context represents all processes in which records participated.

(9c1) All uses of records are transactions.

(9c2) Transactions which index, classify, schedule, file, view, copy, distribute, or move a record without altering it are documented by audit trails attached to the original record.

(9c3) Transactions which execute a records disposition instruction whether for retention or destruction are documented by audit trails attached to the original record.

(10) Removable: Records content and structure supporting the meaning of content must be deletable.

(10a) Authority for deletion of record content and structure exists.

(10b) Deletion transactions are documented as audit trails.

(10c) Deletion transactions remove the content and structural information of records without removing audit trails reflecting context.

Records - Usable

(11) Exportable: It must be possible to transmit records to other systems without loss of information.

(11a) Exporting protocols should be reversible or the lost functionality should be represented in a fashion that produces the same result in the target system as in the originating environment.

(12) Accessible: It must be possible to output record content, structure and context.

(12a) **Available**: Records must be retrievable.

(12a1) The system must be able to retrieve the record of any transaction at any later date.

(12b) **Renderable**: Records must display, print or be abstractly represented as they originally appeared at the time of creation and initial receipt.

(12b1) The structure of data in a record must appear to subsequent users as it appeared to the recipient of the record in the original transaction or a human meaningful representation of that original rendering should accompany the presentation of the original content.

(12c) **Evidential**: Records must reflect the context of their creation and use.

(12c1) A human meaningful representation of the contextual audit trail of a record must accompany all displays or printed output.

(13) Redactable: Records must be masked when it is necessary to deliver censored copies and the version as released must be documented in a linked transaction.

(13a) The release of redacted versions of a record is a discrete business transaction.

(13b) The fact of the release of a redacted version of a record is an auditable use of the original record and therefore results in creation of an audit trail with a link to the transaction which released the redaction.

INDEX

A

access 28 *see also* use and users
access to information 13
  see also freedom of information
  inability to provide 26
  policies governing 84-85
  retrieval standards 218
access to records 21-22, 258, 288
  see also use and users
  adversely affected 182-183
  archivists as intermediaries for 242
  corporate 203
  distributed 280
  documentation for 240
  electronic 25-26, 91-92
  organizational need for 130
  remote 30
  scientific data 286
  use of controlled vocabularies for
    241-245
  via archival description 231-232
ACCIS *see* United Nations
  Administrative Co-ordinating
  Committee on Information Systems
accountability 5, 12-32, 92-94, 149,
  180-181, 284, 286
  of employees 24-25, 188, 191-192
  of government 133
admissibility of records 20, 82, 150
agency histories 229, 242
Anglo-American Cataloguing Rules, 2nd
  ed. (*AACR* 2) 228
ANSI *see* standards
Application Level *see* Open Systems
  Interconnection
application systems 13, 94-97, 133, 178
  see also database management
  systems; electronic mail
  evidence in 150-168
  functional requirements in 186
  graphical software 161, 166-168, 218
  retention of archival records in
    217-219
  spreadsheets 163-165, 218
  word processing 159-162

*APPM see Archives, Personal Paper, and
  Manuscripts: A Cataloging Manual*
appraisal (of records) 28-29, 36, 244
  see also cost/benefit considerations;
  disposition of records
  collective 99-100, 229
  of multi-agency information systems
    137
  policies governing 83-84
  of presidential records 119, 122-123
  retention criteria 17-18
  risk management through 286
  using document analysis 272
archival description 288
  see also documentation; metadata
  Canadian 48, 52, 229-230
  definition of 48
  vs. documentation 224-225, 232-237
  finding aids 45-47
  history of 227-232
  ICA Principles 223-227, 239-240
  ISAD(G) 48, 223-227
  National Information Systems Task
    Force 7, 228, 238
  RLIN cataloging 229
  standards for 7, 48, 52, 86, 223-240,
    245-246
  USMARC formats 45, 228-231
  Working Group on Standards for
    Archival Description 7, 48,
    231-232, 237, 245
archival information systems
  architecture 46, 238-240, 244-245
archival principles and practices
  see also records managers and
  management
  adapting data management practices
    to 55, 170-171
  appraisal *see* appraisal (of records)
  changes needed in 54-55
  diplomatics 255-256, 271-272
  European 255-272
  fonds 49
  original order 15, 28, 37, 105, 147,
    150, 255

archival principles and practices, cont.
  processing 237
  provenance *see* provenance
  reference *see* access to records; users
  respect des fonds 28, 147
  traditional 28-30, 54, 279-280, 283
  variations by country 270-271
archival records *see* records
archival repositories
  functions of 239-240
  remote access to 280
  study of users in 241
archival requirements *see also*
    functional requirements
  articulation of 155-156, 158, 163, 168,
    216-219
  subordinate to administrative and
    legal requirements 132-133
*Archives, Personal Papers, and
  Manuscripts: A Cataloging Manual*
  (Steven Hensen) 52, 228-229
Archivist of the United States
  see also National Archives and
  Records Administration
  custody of Presidential records
    123-124
  failure to develop electronic records
    policies 136, 180
  statutory responsibilities 119, 177
archivists
  active intervention by 135-137, 263,
    265, 279, 280-281, 284-286
  assertion of authority by 136-141,
    263
  common concerns with other
    information specialists 2, 14,
    20-21, 47, 63, 281
  as intermediaries for users 242
  need for policy involvement by 121,
    202
  as participants in information system
    design 47-48, 80, 100, 107, 129,
    137, 155-156, 163, 233, 235, 280
  participation in standards
    development by 202, 211,
    216-219, 263

  responsibilities of 92, 105-106
  skills required by 107-108
  unique roles of 63
*Armstrong, et al. v. the Executive Office of
  the President* (Profs Case) 5, 119-141,
    177
artificial intelligence 166, 242, 260
Australia 5, 134, 279-280, 283, 286-287

B

Barry, Richard 58
bibliographic traditions 223, 228, 230
bibliographic utilities 229
Brooks, Phillip 245
business transactions *see* transactions

C

Canada *see* National Archives of
    Canada; *Rules for Archival Description
    (RAD)*
cataloging rules *see* archival description
change *see* social change
client-server architectures 42,
    55 (note 32), 201
Committee on Archival Informtion
    Exchange (CAIE) 231, 240-241
Common Command Language (CCL)
    215
communications *see also* electronic
    mail
  asynchronous 260
  changes brought by electronic
    systems 14, 81, 124-125, 162,
    256-261, 279
competancies (organizational) *see*
    functions
computer-aided design (CAD) 166-167
computer-assisted manufacturing
    (CAM) 167
computer-output microfilm (COM)
    84-85
confidentiality .20-21
  see also privacy
conservation *see* preservation

context 37
  see also evidential historicity;
    functionality; original order
  ability to capture in electronic
    systems 155-157
  in archival description 230, 232
  capturing user views 104-105, 164,
    215, 284-285
  defined 148
  in electronic mail 191, 194-195, 260
  importance of 132, 148, 214-216, 227
  and organizational boundaries 44-45
  in paper-based systems 150-157
  potential loss in electronic systems
    153-157
  preserving 102-105, 125-126, 135,
    167, 194-195
  showing organizing principles 150
controlled vocabularies 227, 230,
  241-242
conversion to hard copy 5, 84-85,
  124-126, 130, 132
Conway, Paul 241
Cook, Terry 49, 244
copies *see* conversion to hard copy;
  records
corporate culture *see* organizational
  culture
cost/benefit considerations 92,
  152-153, 156-157, 165, 171, 286
  see also risk assessment
custody *see* physical custody;
  intellectual control

D

data administration 178
data archives 286-287
data dictionaries 46, 136, 165
  see also Information Resource
    Directory Systems; metadata
  NISTF 228, 238
data integration 38
data migration *see* migration
database management systems 38,
  103-104 *see also* application
  systems

database management systems, cont.
  capturing user views of 104, 164,
    215, 284-285
  and evidential historicity 165-166
  intelligent data in 164-165
  standards for 217-218
decentralized control *see* physical
  custody
description, archival *see* archival
  description; documentation
diplomatics 255-256, 271-272
disposition of records
  see also appraisal of records; records
    scheduling;
  instructions regarding 127
  presidential 123-124
  retention criteria 17-18
  routine deletion of electronic files
    131-132
  user-designated disposition 196-197
  using document analysis 272
distributed recordkeeping *see* physical
  custody
documentatary forms
  automatic marking of 263-264, 272
    see also Standard Generalized
      Markup Language
  access using 236, 242-243
  compound 260-261
  defined 160-161
  described 39-40
  dynamic documents 194, 260
  electronic vs. paper 40
  electronic mail *see* electronic mail
  evolution of new 259-261, 284
  graphics 161
  hypermedia 161-162, 216, 260-261
  logical records 215-216
  mixed media 25-26, 84-85, 101,
    212-213
  multimedia 218, 260-261
  nonlinear records 218
  related to functions 14-15, 39-41
  virtual documents 5, 25, 38, 192-193
  vocabularies for 230, 242

documentation *see also* archival
  description
  in active systems 54-55, 199, 232-237
  by archivists and records managers
    105-106
  data content of 237-245
  defined 45, 236
  of function 53, 233, 265, 287-288 *see
    also* metadata
  importance in data migration 21, 25,
    28, 54
  manager's responsiblity for 130
  policies regarding 85-86, 224-225
  principles for documenting 223-246
Dollar, Charles 129
"Draft General International Standard
  Archival Description" (ISAD(G)) 48,
  223-227
Duchein, Michel 270

E

Eastwood, Terry 49
education and training
  of staff 107-108
  of users 19
Electronic Data Interchange (EDI) 179,
  219
electronic mail 5-6
  see also application systems
  changes in communications 14, 81,
    124-125, 162, 256-261, 279
  context in 191, 194-195, 260
  and evidential historicity 162-163,
    201
  management of 176-204
  as records 119-140
  standards for *see* X.400/X.500
    standards
Environmental Protection Agency 288
Evans, Max 49
evidence
  components of 191
  through data management 24-25
  documentation to support 234

as essential characteristic of records
  2, 5, 15-16, 35, 134, 147-149, 223,
  284-285
vs. information
  in paper-based systems 150-152
  preservation of 15-16, 35, 285
  requirements in varying applications
    150-168
  in system functionality 21
evidential historicity 6, 152-157, 262
  see also context; provenance
  application software 157-168
  in database management systems
    165-166
  defined 148
  in electronic mail systems 162-163,
    201
  in paper-based systems 152
European archival practices 255-272
Executive Office of the President *see
  Armstrong v. the Executive Office of the
  President*

F

fax communications 212-213
Federal Information Locator System
  136-137
Federal Records Act 119-122, 125-126
finding aids *see* archival description
Finland 270
FOREMOST 134, 137
forms of material *see* documentary
  forms
France 269
freedom of information
  see under laws and legal issues
functional provenance 49, 261-263, 272
functional requirements 2-4, 8, 38
  ACCIS version (1989-90) 16-22, 133
  Canadian 134, 281
  components of 57
  corporate 134
  degree to which satisfied 59, 62
  development of archival 55, 128-129,
    216-219, 281

functional requirements, cont.
  for electronic mail 177-178, 181-187
  Pittsburgh version (1993) 53-61,
    134-135
  Pittsburgh version (1994) 294-304
  purpose of 53
  serving organization-wide goals 181,
    188-189, 192, 214
  structural links 215-216
  tactics for satisfying 58
functionality 21 *see also* software
    dependency
  affecting evidential value 26-27
  capturing user views 104-105, 164,
    215, 284-285
  migration of 27-28, 89-90, 287
  policies regarding 89-90
  preservation of 26, 193-194, 287
functions (business) 178, 285
    see also provenance
  access to records via 243
  analysis of 36, 283-284
  classified by employees 261-263, 266,
    285
  documenting 53, 233, 265, 287-288
    see also metadata
  reflected in filing structures 38
  related to documentary forms 14-15,
    39-41

G

General International Standard
    Archival Description (ISAD(G)) 48,
    223-227
genre *see* documentary forms
geographic information systems (GIS)
    166-168, 215, 218
Germany 262, 264, 270
government
  accountability 133
  applications 166-167
  definition of record 93
Graf, Christoph 262
graphical software 161-168, 218

H

hardware 186
hardware dependency 26-27, 53, 89,
    101, 280 *see also* interoperability;
    software dependency
Hedstrom, Margaret 8, 137
Hofstede, Geert 269-271
hypermedia *see* documentary forms

I

IBM Profs System 119-140
ICA *see* International Council on
    Archives
IEEE *see* X.400/X.500 standards
IMOSA (Information Management and
    Office Systems Architecture) 134,
    266
implementation
  critical success factors 188-189
  as tactic for managing electronic
    records 23, 109-113, 178, 184
Information Resource Directory
    Systems (IRDSs) 28, 46, 52, 72,
    85-86, 106, 165, 215-216, 218-219, 287
    see also data dictionaries
information systems architecture,
    archival 46, 238-240, 244-245
information systems *see also*
    recordkeeping systems; systems
    in archival repositories 244-245
    see also archival information
    systems architecture
  defined 36
  design of 22-23, 27-28, 178, 183-184
  effects on organizations 73-76
  inaccurate mental models of 191-192
  intelligent systems 261
  procurement standards for 266
information technology standards
    210-219
intellectual control (of records) 19-20
    see also documentation
  metadata as a mechanism for 28, 30,
    50-53, 62-63, 106, 165, 169, 264-265,
    280, 288

intellectual control (of records), cont.
   policies governing 84-85
intelligent systems 261
interchange standards *see also*
   USMARC Format for Archival and
   Manuscripts Control
   and application software 157-168
   archival reliance on 213-216, 287
International Council on Archives. Ad
   Hoc Commission on Descriptive
   Standards 223-227, 239-240
International Organization for
   Standardization (ISO) 287
International Standard Archival
   Description, General (ISAD(G))
   48, 223-227
interoperability 6, 21 26, 167 *see also*
   entries beginning Open Systems
IRDS *see* Information Resource
   Directory System (IRDS)
ISO 9000 185
Italy 263

K

Kentucky State Archives 280, 288

L

laws and legal issues
   admissibility of records in court 20,
      82, 150
   authenticity 101
   definition of records 93, 282
   electronic records as evidence 20, 24,
      81-82, 150
   external recordkeeping requirements
      185
   Federal Records Act 119-122, 125-126
   Federal Rules of Evidence 181
   freedom of information 20-21, 119,
      122, 130, 134, 138, 140
      see also access to information
   Paperwork Reduction Act 137
   Presidential Records Act 119-122,
      139-140
   privacy 13-14, 20-21, 81, 134, 187, 281

libraries and librarians 139, 218, 223,
   225, 228
Library of Congress 228
life cycle of records 97-98, 245, 282-289
logical records *see* documentary forms
Lytle, Richard 171

M

Maastricht (Germany) 7
Macerata (Italy) 134, 262-263
Manual of Archival Description (MAD) 52
manuscript collections 41, 233-236
Marburg (Germany) 134, 262
MARC AMC *see* USMARC Format for
   Archival and Manuscripts Control
Martin, Kate 139
McDonald, John 137
Mead, Richard 269
Menne-Haritz, Angelika 49
metadata *see also* data dictionaries;
   documentation
   archival applications of 178, 215-216,
      218, 264, 287-288
   data, content, and context require-
      ments 7, 19, 197-198, 202-203
   Federal Information Locator 136
   Information Resource Directory
      Systems (IRDSs) 28, 46, 52, 72,
      85-86, 106, 165, 215-216, 218-219,
      287
   as mechanism for intellectual control
      28, 30, 50-53, 62-63, 106, 165, 169,
      264-265, 280, 288
   in Sweden 264
microforms 20, 82, 84-85, 150
migration 54 *see also* functionality;
   interchange standards
   of archival records 20-21, 168-170
   of data 19, 74-75, 87-89, 285
   of functionality 27-28, 89-90, 287
   maintaining integrity during 25, 87,
      157-158
   policies regarding 89-90
mixed media *see* documentary forms
Monash University (Melbourne,
   Australia) 5

Morrison, Alan   139
multimedia *see* documentary forms

N

National Air and Space Administration
   286
National Archives and Records
   Administration (U.S.)   129, 139, 285
   see also Archivist of the U.S.
   file management guidelines   38
   participation in standards
      development by   281, 287
   use of MARC format   230-231
   user studies in   241-243
National Archives of Canada   6, 134,
   137, 234, 266, 279, 281-282, 285, 287
National Association of Government
   Archives and Records
   Administrators   136-137
National Historical Publications and
   Records Commission   134, 171, 238
National Information Systems Task
   Force   7, 228, 238
National Institute of Science and
   Technology   136-137, 161, 178
National Security Archive   119, 139
National Security Council   119, 121, 123
Netherlands   270
New York State Archives   137, 281, 283
noncustodial archives *see* physical
   custody
nonlinear records *see* documentary
   forms
nonrecord materials   40   *see also*
   personal records; records
   defining   77-78, 93-95
   determining status   120
   segregation from records   133

O

object-oriented environments   42, 166,
   193, 201, 216
obsolescence   74, 86, 101
   see also hardware dependency;
   migration; software dependency
OCLC   229

office applications *see* application
   systems
Office Document Architecture/
   Office Document Interchange
   Format (ODA/ODIF)   219
Office of Management and Budget   129
Office Systems Working Group
   (Treasury Board of Canada)   134
Open Systems Environment (OSE)   6,
   58, 178, 186, 197
   Application Platform Interface layer
      186, 193, 197-198
   layers in   198
Open Systems Interconnection (OSI)
   90, 201, 210
optical character recognition   84-85
organizational accountability
   see accountability
organizational culture   6, 8
   see also social change
   changes in   17, 73, 171, 179-180,
      268-272
   choice of tactics affected by   187
   promoting use of information
      technology   108-109, 112-113
   shift from hierarchical to group de-
      cision making   103, 258-260, 272
organizations
   accountability in   5, 12-32, 92-94
   assigning responsibilities within   19,
      78-80, 106-108, 130-131, 200-201
   bureaucracies   255-257
   controlling technology in   264-265
   corporate memory   202, 266
   documentation by   233-237
   effects of automation on   73-76,
      211-213, 256-261
   European vs. American   267-271
   functions in   243   *see also* functions
      (business)
   hierarchies in   268-270
   implementing an electronic records
      program in   109-113
   line managers in   63, 108, 113, 130
original order *see under* archival
   principles and practices

P

paper copies of electronic records 5, 84-85, 124-126, 130, 132 *see also* conversion; copying
paper record systems 140-141, 150-157, 168-171, 194-195
Paperwork Reduction Act 137
personal records 40-41, 94, 122, 124-125, 127, 130, 190, 233-236, 257
Perth (Australia) 134
Petersen, Trudy 139-140
physical custody 19-20, 137
  decentralized control 28-30, 87, 280-281, 287
  distributed recordkeeping 41-42
  noncustodial archives 8
  policies regarding 86-88
policy 4, 22, 76-113, 178, 183
preservation (of media) 30, 86, 285
  data on RLIN 229
  policies regarding 88-89, 202-203
President of the United States 119-140, 177, 179-180
Presidential Records Act 119-122, 139-140
printouts *see* paper copies of electronic records
privacy 13-14, 20-21, 81, 134, 187, 281
Profs Case *see Armstrong, et al. v. the Executive Office of the President*
provenance 28, 171 *see also* context; evidential historicity; functions
  and business functions 43-44, 59, 61, 147, 163, 219, 261-263, 265
  capturing 147, 215, 226-227, 265
  of electronic mail 163, 215
  functional provenance 49, 261-263, 272
  in geographic information systems 167
  providing access through 227, 242
publishing applications 217-219 *see also* Standard Generalized Markup Language

R

record series 48-49, 230, 243
recordkeeping systems 34-70
  see also information systems
  boundaries in 44-45
  and business functions 40-41, 146-171, 195-196
  definition of 35
  distributed 41-42
  descriptive metadata models of 50-53
  electronic mail 126-127
  functional requirements for *see* functional requirements
  guidelines for users of 131-133
  as organic wholes 44-45
  paper vs. electronic 140-141, 150-157, 168-171, 194-195
  as subset of information systems 182
records *see also* access to records; nonrecord materials
  authority to define 140-141
  classified 127
  convenience copies of 130
  copies of 102-103, 255
  defined 77-78, 93-94, 120, 122, 131, 133, 188-191, 282
  as evidence 2, 5, 15-16, 35, 134, 147-149, 223, 284-285
  evidential vs. informational value 36
  federal 119-140
  filing rules for 134
  identification by creators 127-130, 134, 225, 234-235
  laws governing *see* Federal Records Act; Presidential Records Act
  life cycle 97-98, 245, 282-289
  personal 40-41, 94, 122, 124-125
  paper copies of electronic records 5, 84-85, 124-126, 130, 132
  presidential 119-141
  segregation from nonrecord material 133
  structure of 148
  users and uses of archival 63

records managers and management
see also records scheduling
and archivists 138
control of application systems 97
duties of 92, 105-106
of electronic information systems
129-133
implementing an electronic records
program 109-113
skills required by 107-108
records scheduling 8 *see also*
disposition of records; retention
criteria
built into electronic systems 17-18,
100-101
documentation and 234
life cycle 97-98, 245, 282-289
policies governing 82-83, 125-126
systems management 97
via data management 285-286
reference *see* access to records; users
research 171, 232
Research Libraries Information
Network (RLIN) 229
respect des fonds *see under* archival
principles and practices
retention criteria 17-18
see also records scheduling
retrieval standards 218-219
risk assessment 18-19, 24, 185 *see also*
cost/benefit considerations
risk management 13-14, 23-24, 286
Rules for Archival Description (RAD) 48,
52, 229-230

S

Scandinavia 270
scheduling *see* records scheduling
Schellenburg, Theodore 245
scientific data 285-286
Scott, Peter 49
security 14, 20-21, 90, 134, 159
social changes *see also* organizational
culture
adjusting to change 80-81

brought on by automation 14, 73,
179-180, 256-261
electronic democracy 139
Society of American Archivists 139,
231 *see also* Committee on Archival
Information Exchange; National
Information Systems Task Force
software applications *see* application
systems
software dependency 6, 21, 26-27, 42,
53, 75, 86, 89, 101, 181-183, 201, 218,
259 *see also* functionality;
hardware dependency; migration
spreadsheets *see* application systems
Standard Generalized Markup
Language (SGML) 198, 216, 218, 272
standards 6-7, 170 *see also* archival
description standards; information
technology standards; interchange
standards
in archival applications 237-240
archivists participation in developing
202, 263, 281, 287
for electronic mail 162-163, 214-215,
217-219 *see also* X.400/X.500
standards
for graphical software 167-168
for hypermedia 161
for information technology 210-219
ISO 9000 185
as tactic for managing electronic
records 23, 178
Z39.50 218-219
"Statement of Principles Regarding
Archival Description" (ICA)
223-227, 239-240
Structued Query Language (SQL) 215
Sweden 264
Switzerland 262, 279, 285
system functionality *see* functionality
system implementation
critical success factors 188-189
as tactics for managing electronic
records 23, 109-113, 178, 184
systems
defined 36

systems, cont.
  management of 97-101
systems analysis 263
systems, information *see* information
  systems
systems, recordkeeping *see*
  recordkeeping systems
Szary, Richard 238

T

technical standards *see* standards
telephone communication 95-96, 130,
  256-257, 279
thesauri *see* controlled vocabularies
Towards Descriptive Standards 229
TP/REM *see* Technical Panel on
  Electronic Records Management
  under United Nations Administrative Coordinating Committee on
  Information Systems (ACCIS)
transactions (business) 37, 244
  as basic unit of documentation 4, 284
  creation of records documenting 17,
    24-25, 41
  defined 35
  in defining a record 94, 133, 135, 147,
    199
  standards for 219

U

United Nations Administrative Co-
  ordinating Committee on
  Information Systems (ACCIS)
  16-22, 133, 136, 262, 265-266
  *Management of Electronic Records:
    Issues and Guidelines* 72-113
    (Chapter 3), 183, 189, 199, 281; 283
  Technical Panel on Electronic Records
    Management (TP/REM) 4-5
University of Pittsburgh 3, 5, 8, 55-57,
  59, 134-135, 202
U.S. Congress 122-123
U.S. District Court 5, 119-140, 177 *see
  also Armstrong, et al.* v. *the Executive
  Office of the President*

U.S. National Archives and Records
  Administration *see* National
  Archives and Records
  Administration (U.S.)
user views *see under* context
use and users *see also* access;
  functionality
  approaches employed by 243-245
  education of 19
  needs of 240-245
  studies of 241-243, 245
  terminology used by 243-245
USMARC Format for Archival and
  Manuscripts Control (USMARC
  AMC) 45, 228-231
USMARC Format for Authority Data
  230

V

version control 152-153, 159-160
video standards 213
virtual documents *see* documentary
  forms
vital records 14
voice mail 213

W

Weber, Max 255
Weir, Ted 238
White House *see* President of the
  United States
word processing *see* application
  systems
Working Group on Standards for
  Archival Description 7, 48, 231-232,
  237, 245
World Bank 283

X

X.400/X.500 standards 162, 201-202,
  214-215, 217-219

Z

Z39.50 218-219